ANALYTICAL TRANSPORT PLANNING

Analytical
Transport Planning

ROBERT LANE
Chief Traffic and Communications Engineer
London Borough of Camden
TIMOTHY J. POWELL
Senior Economist, Freeman, Fox, Wilbur Smith
and Associates
PAUL PRESTWOOD SMITH
Senior Planner, W. S. Atkins and Partners

A HALSTED PRESS BOOK

JOHN WILEY & SONS
New York

Published in the U.S.A. by Halsted Press,
a Division of John Wiley & Sons, Inc., New York

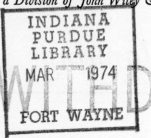
Library of Congress Cataloging in Publication Data

Lane, Robert.
  Analytical transport planning.

  Bibliography: p.
    1. Transportation. 2. Traffic engineering.
3. Cities and towns—Planning—1945–
I. Powell, Timothy J., joint author. II. Smith,
Paul Prestwood, joint author. III. Title.

HE151.L27 1973   388.4   72–11852
ISBN 0–470–51440–X

Printed in Great Britain by
The Anchor Press Ltd,
and bound by Wm Brendon & Son Ltd,
both of Tiptree, Essex

Contents

Appendixes

Foreword

Transport planning is only a part of the planning of cities and regions, but it is an important part. Nearly all we do depends on some form of transport. The planning of all land uses, employment, education and shopping must therefore be related to transport facilities, although transport planning should not be allowed to dictate land-use planning. The problems of efficient transportation are always likely to conflict with environmental planning, and the needs of the environment should often take precedence.

Analytical transport planning is a relatively new science which has developed in an attempt to predict travel patterns in different areas with different transport systems. Since it tries to apply general mathematical relationships to the travel behaviour of individuals whose particular travel patterns obey no fixed mathematical rule, it cannot claim to be an exact science. Nevertheless the techniques can when correctly applied form a sound basis for the quantitative assessment of alternative courses of action and the evaluation of particular transport proposals.

In the following pages we try not only to explain the conventional method of analytical transport planning, but also to show its limitations, and on occasion to suggest how some of these limitations can be overcome. Attitudes to transport studies tend towards two extremes. At one extreme is the belief that all problems can be solved by mathematics; at the other the belief that models are at best a poor substitute for common sense. Both these extremes should be avoided. Analytical transport planning does not provide all the answers, but when it is properly applied and sensibly interpreted it provides insight into the consequences of alternative courses of action. We hope that this book may help to further understanding of analytical transport planning.

August 1971

Glossary

All words in this glossary are italicised at their first mention in the text.

Accessibility. A term frequently used in a general sense to mean the degree of access to a particular place in terms of distance, time or cost. Specifically, the term also implies the number of opportunities available, for a given amount of *travel cost.*

Area speed/flow relationship. The relationship, calibrated from survey data, expressing the capacity of a network in an area or zone in terms of the speed and flow of traffic in that area.

Assignment. The process whereby trips surveyed or forecast from an origin zone to a destination zone are assigned (allocated) to definite routes, based on factors known to influence route selection.

Calibration. A process, usually mathematical, whereby survey information is used to establish or fix a relationship between two or more variables. See also *Model building.*

Category analysis. A means of analysing survey data by dividing the information into specified categories and establishing one relationship which is applied to all the elements within the category. Often used in transport planning to analyse trip generation and attraction.

CBD. The Central Business District of a town or city. Often referred to in the UK as the Central Area.

Centroid connector. An imaginary link connecting the zone centroid to the network. In the case of a road network, such a link would represent the access or local roads.

Cordon. An imaginary line which completely encloses a given area (e.g. a central business district) and at which traffic counts and interviews may be taken for control purposes.

Correlation coefficient. A statistical term used to quantify the degree with which one variable relates to another. It takes a value between 0 and 1, and the closer the coefficient is to 1 the more the two variables are said to be correlated.

Cost-benefit analysis. An analysis of the costs and benefits associated with two or more alternative courses of action. The costs and benefits are usually related in the form of a cost-benefit ratio or rate of return.

Demand. The amount of travel which would arise at a given cost of travel.

Design year. The future year for which alternative transport plans are to be tested and evaluated. Design years are usually ten and twenty years hence.

Elasticity of demand. The ratio of the percentage change in travel to the percentage change in travel costs.

Enumeration district. A small area, used by census authorities as the unit area for which each enumerator was responsible for gathering information. Wherever possible, traffic zones should be composed of groups of entire enumeration districts.

Environmental evaluation. The part of the evaluation process concerned with assessment of environmental effects such as noise, visual intrusion, etc. Generally, these factors are not quantified in monetary terms at present.

External cordon. An imaginary line which completely encloses a study area and at which volume counts and interviews may be taken for control purposes.

External trips. A trip which has both ends outside of the study area.

Generated traffic. Traffic, usually measured in vehicle-kilometres, which is directly caused by the introduction of a new travel facility.

Generation. A term defined as the home end of a home-based trip; the origin of a non-home-based trip. See also *Trip generation* and *Trip attraction.*

Generation and attraction rates. The trip rate of a person, household or other unit expressed as a trip generation rate or trip attraction rate.

Gravity model. A commonly used trip distribution model based on Newton's second law of gravity.

Grossing-up. The process of multiplying the sample data by factors to represent the universe from which the sample was drawn.

Growth factor. A method of trip distribution whereby the growth in interzonal trips is predicted using a simple factor.

Home-based trip. Trips which have one end at the home of the person making the trip.

Interactance model. A refined distribution model based on the gravity model.

Internal rate of return. The discount rate at which the benefits when discounted at a fixed rate per annum are exactly equal to the costs when similarly discounted.

Interzonal trips. Trips which have an origin in one internal zone and a destination in another.

Intrazonal trips. Trips which have both origin and destination in an internal zone.

Journey speed. The speed of traffic including running speeds and intersection delay.

Level of service. A qualitative measure of the effect of a number of factors on travel flow, which include speed and travel time, safety, comfort and convenience.

Link. An element in a network which connects two nodes.

Matrix. An arrangement of values in the form of a table. In transport planning, the values often arranged are intrazonal and interzonal trips in the form of a *trip matrix*.

Modal opportunity group. A group of people who have similar opportunities as a consequence of the modes available to them.

Modal split. The proportions of trips using various modes of travel.

Mode availability. A term which defines the mode or modes available to a potential traveller at a particular time.

Model building. A mathematical process used to formulate relationships between two or more variables. See also *Calibration*.

Multiple regression analysis. A standard statistical technique for establishing a unique relationship between one dependent variable and two or more independent variables.

Network. A road, rail, bus or other transport system; an arrangement of links which represent a transport system.

Node. A numbered point which defines the end of a link in a network. In a road network each node generally represents either a road intersection or a zone centroid.

Non-home-based trips. A trip which has neither end at the home of the person making the trip.

Operational evaluation. The part of the evaluation process concerned with the assessment of the assigned volumes and the operational ability of the network being tested.

Opportunity model. A distribution model based primarily on the number of opportunities available at given distances, times or costs from an origin zone.

Planning parameters. Statistics concerning population, employment, car-ownership, business and retail centres, schools and school attendance, land-use densities and other data.

Road pricing. The means of charging for road space for vehicles both when they are moving and when they are stationary.

Running speed. The speed of traffic between intersections, excluding intersection delay.

Screenline. An imaginary line drawn across part of a study area. The total number of movements of any particular type observed crossing the screenline is compared with the estimated present-day volumes obtained from the traffic model, and the comparison used to assess the ability of the traffic model to forecast the present-day patterns of movement.

Speed/flow relationships. A quantitative means of expressing the capacity of a road by relating speed of traffic to the volume of traffic.

Testing. The use of the *transport model* for assessing the effect of alternative transport plans.

Traffic management. The use of traffic regulations and orders and traffic devices to control road users in order to obtain the most efficient use of the existing road system for the benefit of the community as a whole.

Traffic restraint. A quantitative term which indicates an imposed reduction in traffic volumes.

Traffic zones. A basic unit for travel analysis, drawn up on the basis of the transport systems, major barriers to traffic flow and land-use characteristics.

Transport model. The series of models including the trip end model, distribution model, modal split and assignment model.

Trip attraction. The non-home end of a home-based trip; the destination end of a non-home-based trip. See also *Generation.*

Trip distribution. The mathematical process of distributing trip ends to produce a trip matrix.

Trip ends. The origin or destination of a trip.

Trip generation. Often used as a general term to describe the trip-end forecasting models of generation and attraction.

Trip matrix. See *Matrix.*

Updating surveys. A survey to check the validity of forecasts made with the transport model. An updating survey should usually be carried out in a design year.

Welfare economics. The application of economic principles to the study of whether a proposed change leads to an overall increase in well-being.

Zone. See *Traffic zone.*

Zone centroid. A point which represents a traffic zone for the purposes of traffic analysis.

CHAPTER I

Introduction: the quantitative transport planning process

1. THE NEED FOR TRANSPORT PLANNING

The state of the roads has been a favourite topic of conversation from earliest times, and the coming of the railway generated its own controversy between the proponents of progress and of preservation. The debate continues today. The problems of inadequate public transport, of road congestion and of the need to preserve the environment from the ravages of the road builder provide an indispensable source of news for all local newspapers, thus creating the public interest which in turn supports the advertisements for second-hand cars and new property development.

In fact the necessity for transport planning is largely self-evident. Throughout the day and night people are engaged in a variety of activities, which include work, shopping and recreation, and in order to take part in these activities they frequently want to, or have to, travel some distance. Many of these activities are also dependent on the transport of manufactured goods and raw materials to and from point of sale or point of production. The need for transport, moreover, is reflected in a huge expenditure. Over 15% of the UK National Income is now devoted to transport, either in new investment projects, or in the operating costs of vehicles, particularly the private car.

The growth in private car-ownership since the war has increased the need for transport planning particularly within the major towns and conurbations. People are concerned at the growth of road congestion but at the same time they may be equally or more concerned with the threat to the environment posed by new road construction. This problem is likely to increase with time. Improving technology, leading to higher real income and a shorter working week, means that an ever larger proportion of disposable income can and will be devoted to activities involving travel. At the same time there is growing interest in the preservation of amenity and environment, and a growing ability to afford the costs that may be incurred by such policies. These problems are particularly acute in the urban areas and throughout the world the main urban areas are growing fast as a result of migration into the cities from the rural areas.

If there is little doubt about the need for transportation planning, there is much more doubt about its success. In this book we concentrate on the quantitative techniques available to the transportation planner. Many of these techniques are still relatively new, and their strengths and limitations are not always well understood. The reader who expects to find a universal solution to all transportation planning problems will be disappointed. We hope, however, to provide some insight into what can be achieved by the use of these techniques of transportation planning, so as to help the planner and administrator decide which decisions and policies can be aided by the use of some form of *transport model*, and which decisions are best decided with the aid of less formal analysis.

2. A BRIEF OUTLINE OF THE TRANSPORTATION PLANNING PROCESS

There is a common basic approach which can be applied to all forms of transportation planning, whether planning for a specific new transport facility, such as a new airport, road or rail improvement scheme, or planning a national, regional or local transport policy. In all cases the approach may be summarised by three distinct phases: a survey, analysis and *model building* phase; a forecasting phase; and an evaluation phase.

The survey, analysis and model building stage answers two important questions. First, what is the existing travel demand, and secondly, how is this demand satisfied on the existing transport facilities? To answer these questions, a survey and analysis is made of the existing travel demand, and the relationship between the present demand and the existing urban environment is examined. This examination enables models to be built of these relationships which can then be used in the forecasting phase.

The forecasting stage uses the relationships established in the analysis and model building stage to make estimates of the future travel demand. As such it requires the planner to provide a plan for *testing*. Information is needed on the population, and on transport facilities proposed within an area, so that the results that would follow from such a plan can be forecast. It is worth stressing that to date the techniques of land use and transportation planning can, for a given set of policies and conditions, only distinguish between one situation and another specified situation. They are not designed directly to select optimum policies or optimise transport systems. It is up to the intuitive ingenuity of the planner to select those policies and arrangements of transport facilities he thinks most suitable, and to test and then modify these so as to determine a preferred plan or policy.

The evaluation stage assesses the results of the two previous phases to see whether they satisfy defined social, economic and operational objectives. Because more than one set of policies and transport investments may meet these objectives to a greater or lesser extent, it is common practice to test a series of differing assumptions in the course of producing a preferred plan.

The three phases of the transportation planning process, survey analysis and model building, forecasting and evaluation, are discussed in detail in subsequent chapters. In the rest of this chapter we introduce some of the main elements in this process to serve as a framework for later, more detailed discussion. The sequence of operations normally followed as part of the transport planning process is shown as a flow chart in Figure I.1.

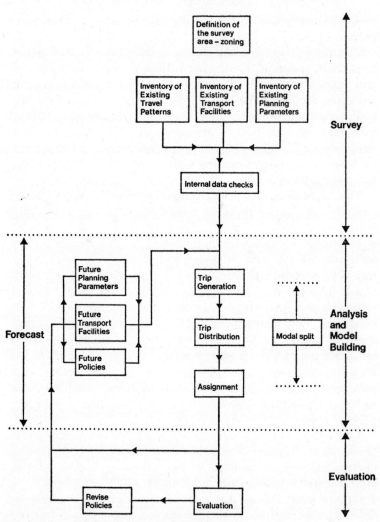

FIGURE I.1 Transport planning process.

2. (i) *The survey phase* (zoning, surveys, network building)

The first element in Figure I.1 is the definition of the area to be studied in detail. Large-scale studies such as the London Traffic Survey[1] have described travel over a whole conurbation and as such have been concerned with the traffic expected to use the more important strategic transport facilities such as motorways, major through routes, rail and underground services. Smaller-scale studies, such as those being carried out by the London Boroughs,[2] can describe travel in considerably more detail.

The main objective of a transport model is to predict the number of trips that will take place by the different available modes of transport, to predict the origins and destinations of these trips, and to decide the route which will be chosen between origin and destination. To describe the origins and destinations of these journeys the study area is divided into a number of *traffic zones*. The size of these zones depends upon the amount of detail required, the smaller the size of the zones, the greater the potential accuracy of the model, but the cost of the model also rises appreciably as the number of zones increases. The rest of the country outside the study area is also divided up into zones, though of a much larger size. In general, the further away a district is from the study area, the less will be the effect in travel terms that it will have upon the study area.

The inventory of existing travel patterns consists essentially of collecting information on the origins and destinations of journeys. There are several ways by which the travel patterns may be established. For the smaller studies, use can be made of registration number plate surveys, or roadside interviews, or pre-paid postcards. The larger urban studies employ the method of household interviews allowing more information to be collected more cheaply and more easily. The household interview, however, only collects information on survey area residents, and so mainly on internal journeys.

In the larger studies the household interviews are supplemented by roadside and public transport interviews at selected points (*screenlines*) which are then used to check and adjust the proposed transport model. Further surveys may also be required to collect information on trips entering or leaving the study area, on commercial vehicle trips and possibly also on taxi trips.

Separate inventories are usually prepared for the road and public transport systems. Detailed information is collected on the facilities making up each network, and plan drawings (often known as *networks*) are prepared of the major transport systems in a form suitable for coding as input to the traffic model. The amount of work involved in the preparation of these inventories varies from study to study, but in the more detailed studies a large amount of information has to be obtained. For roads, this includes data on daily and hourly traffic volumes, average vehicle occupancies, the proportions of light and heavy commercial vehicles in the traffic, and probably some information on *speed/flow relationships*. Public transport networks can be more complicated and sometimes require data on several other travel parameters, such as fare paid, walking time, waiting time, frequency of service, and walking and waiting time at interchange stations.

A planning or land-use inventory is necessary, since it provides information which can be used in the investigation of the relationships between land use and journey behaviour. For each traffic district or zone, information is collected on the type and intensity of land use, usually measured in terms of floor area together with population and employment statistics. Wherever possible the information on population includes details of the distribution of household incomes, as this is an important determinant of *trip generation*.

2. (ii) *Analysis and model building*

The data collected in the surveys contains a large amount of information on journey behaviour. Analysis of this mass of data can be of great use in the design of existing facilities, such as large-scale traffic management schemes or the routing and scheduling of the bus system. More importantly, however, it provides an understanding of the relationship between travel behaviour and the urban environment. For example it has been found from past studies that the vast majority of work trips take place in the morning and evening peak, that most journeys begin and end at home and that offices and shops attract more journeys per unit of area than industrial or commercial land use. By an understanding of travel behaviour, relationships between these travel characteristics and the urban environment can be established and synthesised quantitatively, using modelling techniques.

The building of models is a most challenging part of transportation planning and is the key to forecasting future travel demands. Because this is a most important phase of the transportation planning process, a large section of this book will be devoted to a detailed description and discussion of the main component parts of the transport model. A brief outline of the model procedure is given below.

The transport model is conventionally divided into three main stages. These are (1) the decision to make a journey, or trip generation, (2) selection of a suitable destination, or *trip distribution*, and (3) the actual making of the journey on an appropriate transport facility by a particular route, known as *assignment*. These three stages are generally treated separately although in the real world the stages are all interlinked and trip generation is not entirely independent of trip distribution and assignment. The other important feature in the transport model, *modal split*, namely the choice of private or public transport, is effected by all of these stages.

Trip generation is an examination of the relationship between the number of trips made and certain quantifiable parameters. Early studies were confined to a numerical description of origins and destinations by zone. Better understanding of the relationships between generation and planning parameters came about with increasing stratification of journeys, for example, disaggregation by journey purpose. Other parameters which determine trip generation have been found to include household income, car-ownership, intensity of land use and distance of the origin from the central area.

The next stage in the transport model is trip distribution, or an analysis of the trips between zones. The trip patterns between all zones for the base or survey year, together with network information, is used to establish relationships between these journeys, their geographical origins and destinations and the transport facilities they will use. In the very early models, simple growth factor or analogy methods were used. These models used data on the base-year trip patterns but took no account of other effects on the demand for travel. However, it was noted at a very early stage in model development that the number of trips from one zone to another was dependent upon some function of the distance between the two zones. Growth factor models were thus eventually replaced by synthetic models of trip interchange. The term synthetic is used because although the existing trip pattern is used to calibrate the model, the surveyed trip origins and destinations are not used directly in the model. Instead a relationship is developed which determines the number of trips between two zones as a function of their size and distance apart. The most widely used model is the *gravity model*, although many other forms of model have been used.

Trip assignment is the process by which the route a traveller will take between two zones is determined. It is commonly assumed that the route that can be assigned to a trip between two zones can be determined from the network as the minimum time or minimum cost route between the two zones. Sophisticated computer programs have been developed to calculate these minimum time or minimum cost routings. More recently multi-path assignment techniques have been introduced which assign a percentage of the trips between two zones to all the available alternative routes.

The transport model has one further stage, in that the individual chooses a particular mode of travel. Modal split, as it is called, has been integrated in the transport model at various stages between trip generation and assignment. There have been, basically, two approaches; those at the trip generation stage and those at the assignment stage. When related at the trip generation stage, a disadvantage is that the modal split takes no account of route characteristics. The other approach has been to effect modal split at the assignment stage. Data collected at the survey stage is used to establish the proportions of people making public transport trips, using for example as criteria the ratios of travel times or travel costs. This method has the disadvantage of neglecting the effects of choice of mode on the distribution of journeys. The appropriate place of modal split in the transport model is discussed in more detail in subsequent chapters.

When a completed transport model has been assembled, various internal data consistency checks are carried out. Actual counts of vehicles across various natural barriers or screenlines are checked with the volumes from the synthetic model. Any discrepancies are corrected at this stage by adjusting the mathematical relationships postulated in the various stages of the transport model. After satisfactory *calibration* the model is ready to be used to forecast future travel demands.

2. (iii) *The forecasting phase*

In order to make forecasts of future travel demands, it is first necessary to obtain as much information as possible for the *design year*, concerning all the factors found in the analysis and model building phase to affect travel behaviour. It is here that transportation planning interfaces with other fields of the urban planning process. In particular, forecasts are required of the planning parameters, population, employment and income distribution, and these parameters themselves require sub-models to develop appropriate forecasts. Assumptions also have to be made of available finance for investment, desired *levels of service*, and what environmental standards may be possible.

One of the most important planning forecasts is population distribution. The Registrar General[3] makes forecasts which show national and regional trends but do not indicate growth in the detail required for planning in urban areas. Area-wide population forecasts can be made based on past trends using census data, or by building population models based on esti-mates of birth, death and migration rates, but in order to determine the zonal distribution of population, it is also neces-sary to know the expected future distribution of residential land use.

The other main feature affecting the distribution of future travel throughout the survey area is the location and nature of the future employment expected in the area. Changes in indus-trial and commercial employment are very difficult to estimate and may be the subject of a separate economic study. Future income and expenditure patterns also have to be considered as any changes in personal wealth will have a marked effect on trip generation patterns. In particular the future level of car-ownership is very dependent on the expected rate of economic growth. The sub-models which deal with the forecasting of population, employment, income growth and car-ownership will be discussed in Chapter IV.

The forecasting phase of the transportation planning process requires one further input and that is a description of the future transport systems that are to be investigated. Future coded net-work inventories similar to those for the base year have to be prepared. The various forms of transportation systems that could be incorporated into a town or city transport plan are discussed briefly in Chapter IV. It is, however, worth mentioning that, because planning is a slow continuous process, much of the future land-use distribution and future transport networks for, say, the next twenty years, are already well established. For example, important urban motorway routes are often safeguarded for some ten to twenty years.

2. (iv) *Evaluation*

On completion of the traffic forecasting process the results must be examined and evaluated. The evaluation can be considered in four stages. First there is the numerical evaluation. At all stages of the forecasting process it is necessary to check the output to ensure against computational or coding errors. Assuming the model is judged to be mathematically correct, the next stage is to assess the apparent accuracy of the resultant forecasts. This is an essential prerequisite to all subsequent evaluation, since the interpretation of the results of a transport model depend on the circumstances in which the model has been applied. Provided one is satisfied that the results of the transport model adequately predict the movement pattern that would result from the transportation system, it is possible to move on to the next stages in the evaluation process, namely operational and economic evaluation.

Operational evaluation is carried out to check if a proposed network adequately satisfies the forecast travel patterns. In the initial tests this is very rarely the case. Either networks have to be modified or new policies tested: for example, acceptance of traffic restraint in certain areas together with lower operating standards and a poorer level of service.

In economic terms the best network may be defined as that network which for a given budget constraint yields maximum benefit to the community by minimising the cost of travel. Since vehicle-kilometres are not a commodity which are directly bought and sold, the price mechanism cannot be used as an investment criterion. In consequence, *cost-benefit*[4] studies have been used as a technique to guide investment. Costs include the capital outlay for improvements and new facilities, together with land costs and maintenance costs. Benefits are measured by savings in operating costs, journey time savings and a reduction in the number and severity of accidents.

3. Limitations of the Transportation Planning Process

The transportation planning process has been briefly introduced in this chapter, and different aspects will be discussed in more detail in the subsequent chapters. It is, however, essential for the reader to realise from the outset that transportation planning is not an exact science. There are two distinct problems which limit the accuracy of the transportation forecasting process. The first is cost. The transport model is a very cumbersome exercise in repetitive mathematics, which has been made possible only by the development of the electronic computer. However, it is still not a cheap process and in many instances a decrease in potential accuracy has to be accepted to save excessive expenditure on computation. But even if computational expense were ignored it would still not be possible to develop a perfect transport model, owing to the impossibility of mathematically reflecting the many varied factors, conscious and subconscious, which influence the individual's travel decisions. The best that can be hoped for from any transport model is that it will adequately represent the demand for travel on the more important elements of the transportation system being studied. In each case the form of transport model and the level of detail at which a network is represented must be related to the potential decisions that are to be made. The model is essentially an aid to decision-making rather than an answer in itself. The apparent results of a transport model are normally of little use without someone trained to interpret these results.

CHAPTER II

Surveys, zoning and network building

1. DESIGN OF SURVEYS

In order to plan, it is essential to have information. All transportation planning is thus dependent on surveys. These surveys may take many different forms. The earliest studies in traffic engineering were concerned with the flows expected to use individual and unrelated projects. As such the information required was obtained from measurements of the speeds[1] and flow[2] of traffic along individual roads, perhaps supplemented by simple origin and destination surveys.[3] Later, when comprehensive urban transportation plans were developed, it was found necessary to carry out rather more extensive surveys designed to give a more all-embracing knowledge of travel[4] on a conurbational or regional scale.

As the transportation planning procedures have become better established, the survey requirements for transportation planning have become more standardised, and the home interview survey in particular has come to be the accepted source of information on which much transport planning is based.

But before any surveys or data collection can be started it is important that the purpose of and the area for which a study is being conducted must be clearly defined. There is a tendency in all work of this nature to collect a large amount of information, on the grounds that it ought to be useful. In many of the earlier transportation studies much of the information initially collected was later found to be inappropriate to the form of analysis finally adopted. But the natural desire to begin something 'positive' by collecting data at the earliest possible stage of a study should be resisted. Data collection is an expensive and time-consuming process, and it is almost certain that more studies have suffered from an over-emphasis on data collection relative to problem analysis than from any one other of the many pitfalls that surround the transportation planning process.

Transport planning can be carried out at several different levels (i.e. national, regional, conurbation or local). But, whatever the position in this hierarchy of planning, it is nearly always the case that considerable quantities of data are required, and great care is needed in designing the survey stage of a study to ensure that the results are statistically significant. There is a danger of not collecting enough data to calibrate models with reasonable levels of significance, but there is also the possibility that too much data is collected. This is both a waste of resources and a hindrance to an understanding of the problem. It should be remembered that the survey stage is not an end in itself but rather a means towards an end—an end which is crucially dependent on good data collected at the survey stage.

2. Definition of study area

In an ideal situation, transportation planning would be initiated at a national level. Control totals for long-distance trips could then be passed on first to regional studies and subsequently to conurbational and local studies. This need not be a totally one-way process. In practice, there would of necessity be a two-way conversation between each level in the hierarchy, with information and policies continually adjusted to meet the needs of both national and local planning. Developments of this nature are already taking place in some regions and conurbations. In London, strategic planning is the responsibility of the Greater London Council while the more detailed planning is the responsibility of the individual boroughs. The Greater London Council carry out transport planning using a conurbation-wide model.

The results from this model are then used as part of the input for separate borough models.

An early necessity in any study is to define the area which is to be studied in detail. The boundary of the study area is known as the *external cordon*. In a conurbation study the boundary should be drawn in such a way that all major parts of the developed area and those parts which are likely to be developed within the planned period of the study, are included. Neighbourhoods adjacent to the main area may also be incorporated into an extended study area if they rely on the major centre for employment or shopping. The most important factor to be considered when locating external cordon lines is that they should be selected so that they are compatible with previous or projected studies of the region.

The first task after the definition of the external cordon line is to subdivide the internal area of the study into small units usually referred to as zones (Figure II.1). This is done both so that the origins and destinations of travel can be closely defined geographically and so that the many factors associated with trip-making, such as population, employment, etc., can be spatially quantified. The external area is also broken down into zones. These external zones will become larger the further they are from the study boundary because the influence of other areas on the traffic pattern in the study area decreases with distance from the study area (Figure II.2).

The zoning arrangements should be related to the hierarchy of planning, for example, the larger zones of a regional study falling within a conurbation would be subdivided for a conurbation study and further subdivided in a detailed local study.

To simulate travel with a high degree of accuracy it would obviously be desirable to have very small zones. However, the disadvantages would be that larger-scale surveys would be required and larger and more expensive computers would have to be used at the model building stage. There is usually therefore a practical limit to the number of zones which is determined by the amount of money available and the size of computer to be used. With the further development of computers the second factor may become less important.

An initial requirement of a zone is that it should ideally

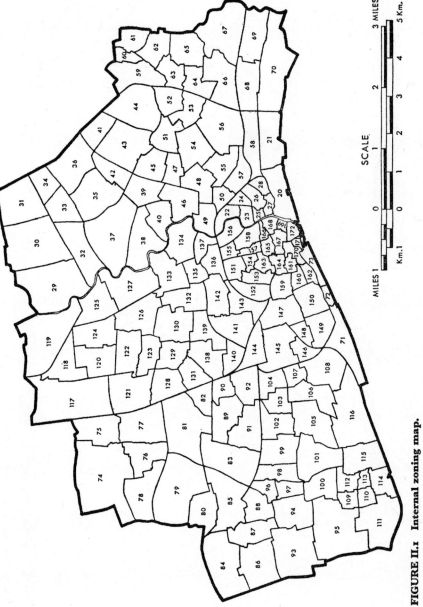

FIGURE II.1 Internal zoning map.

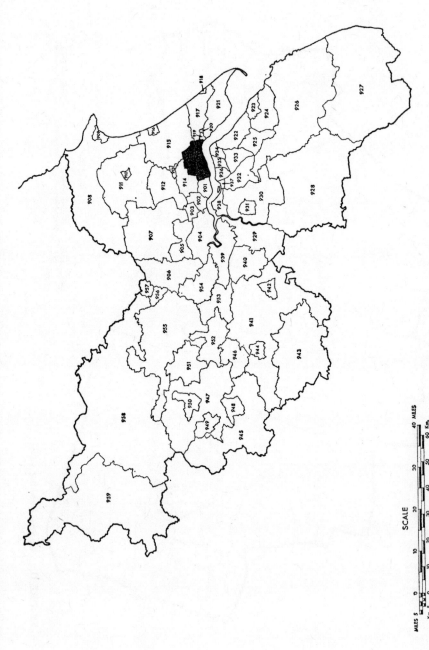

SCALE

FIGURE II.2 External zoning map.

contain a homogeneous activity. Activities are, of course, closely related to type of land use. An approximation therefore to homogeneity of activity is the existence of one type of land use. This is, of course, often difficult or even impossible to find in an existing situation. A compromise has usually to be determined so that most zones have a predominance of one land use. The largest area of land in a city is devoted to residential development and special attention must be paid to the zoning of these areas. Households of a similar type, and therefore ones with a similar traffic generation rate, should preferably be grouped together in a zone. The other land uses should be treated in a similar manner, e.g. various types of industry and commerce should be divided into separate zones. At times it may be worth while using *sub-zones* or *pseudo-zones* to identify particular areas of attraction for travel analysis such as large office complexes or shopping centres.

The size and, therefore, number of zones required to synthesise travel in a particular area is obviously related to the type of study being undertaken (i.e. regional, conurbational or local). A general consideration is that the size of zone should not be so small that the data collected is statistically unreliable. At the other extreme, zones should not be so large as to produce a poor synthesis of travel. In the more recent studies for small and medium-sized urban areas, residential zones have had populations between 1,000 and 3,000[5] and in the larger conurbational studies between 5,000 and 10,000.[6]

The *zone boundaries* must also be considered in conjunction with the transport network configurations. The designation of networks should therefore be carried out at the same time as the zoning. If possible, the zone boundaries should form watersheds of trip generation to the transport network. For example, a zone may completely enclose one bus stop or one railway station. This point will be discussed later in this chapter in relation to *zone centroid* connections to the transport network. The location of road and rail routes may often mean that a compromise from an otherwise ideal zoning arrangement has to be found. The zone boundaries should also, if at all possible, attempt to anticipate expected changes in land use and in the transport network. It is, of course, the purpose of transportation planning to determine the future transport network; however,

B

much will already be known at this stage about proposals
for the future networks.

The use of information from the Registrar General's Census
of Population[7] (particularly data derived from the more recent
development of the census, first introduced in 1966) is invaluable in transportation planning. Traffic zone boundaries should,
therefore, be compatible with census *enumeration district* boundaries. Because enumeration districts are very small there is
usually little difficulty in accomplishing this.

Having divided the study area up into zones, usually on
1:2500 Ordnance Survey maps, they should then be discussed
with the local planning authorities. This is necessary to ensure
that proper account is taken of future changes in land use anti-
cipated by the various planning authorities. If the area under
examination is to expand considerably over the planned period,
then it may be convenient to have finer zones in some areas in
the future plan. However, compatibility of zone boundaries
should still be maintained.

At this stage, 'screenlines' should be defined on the zoning
map and should coincide if possible with zone boundaries
(Figure II.3). The purpose of screenlines is to check on data
collected in the interview and cordon surveys. They should be
located in such a way that the survey area is split into approximately equal areas and so that only a few main routes are inter-
cepted. For this last reason natural barriers to communication,
such as rivers and railways, are often suitable for the location of
a screenline.

3. INTERVIEW SURVEYS

3. (i) *Home interview surveys*

Home interview surveys are designed for two main purposes.
They are intended first to collect statistical information on
travel by residents of the study area, and secondly to provide
an insight into the general characteristics of households in the
study area so that in the model building phase relationships
can be established between household characteristics and trip
generation.

The travel behaviour of individuals tends to be repetitive

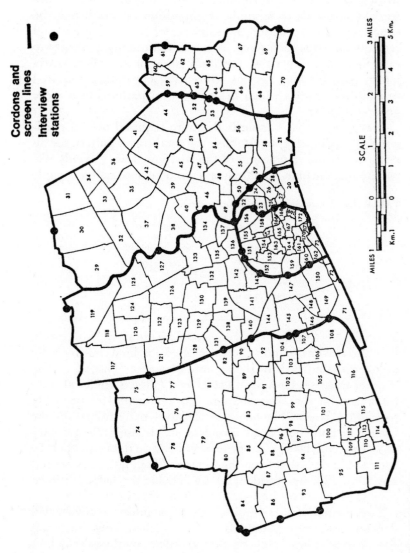

Cordons and screen lines ——

Interview stations ●

SCALE

FIGURE II.3 Screenline map.

and occurs according to relatively fixed patterns. These patterns may be common to large groups. For example, most people at work have to make a given number of work trips per day or per week, households of a similar composition or status may be expected to make about the same number of shopping and recreational trips each week. It is thus not usually necessary to interview all residents of the study area, or to collect travel information for long periods. Only sufficient data is required to calibrate models which describe travel patterns in a more general manner.

A representative sample is therefore required over a particular period of time, to establish the total travel pattern for all residents. If the population of the study area were evenly distributed by income, social class, etc., a representative sample

TABLE II.1   Home interview sample sizes.

Population of area	Sample size
Under 50,000	1 in 5 households
50,000–150,000	1 in 8 ,,
150,000–300,000	1 in 10 ,,
300,000–500,000	1 in 15 ,,
500,000–1,000,000	1 in 20 ,,
Over 1,000,000	1 in 25 ,,

of the journeys made in an area would be obtained by ensuring that the persons or households selected for interviewing were evenly distributed throughout the survey area. This, of course, is never the case. However, a sufficiently large sample taken at random from the households in any one zone still probably provides a reasonable measure of travel patterns within the zone. The household is a convenient unit to use as the primary unit from which trips are generated because data can then be compatible with that from the Census of Population. However, not all people are resident in households so that additional surveys may be required for hotels and other institutions.

The amount of data required in a home interview survey will depend on the type of models used in the forecasting stage and the degree of accuracy of the complete synthesis which is required. Experience in the USA has led the Bureau of Public Roads[8] (BPR) to recommend the sample sizes shown in Table II.1.

Current practice in United Kingdom studies has been to follow the BPR standards. It is possible that for most future studies these sample sizes may be unnecessarily large as the purpose of future surveys may be to adjust, for the particular study area, relationships which have previously been derived from earlier nation-wide interview studies.[9]

In the United Kingdom the basic information from which the sample may be drawn is either

(a) the Register of Electors,[10] which includes a list of addresses and occupants who are qualified electors; or

(b) the Valuation List of all separately rated units, compiled by the Inland Revenue and held by local authorities.

Unfortunately neither of these records lists households as defined by the census, and allowance has to be made for this in the sampling procedure.

The disadvantages of using the Register of Electors are that they do not include addresses at which all residents are under eighteen years of age, or otherwise not eligible for voting. The Register is compiled annually and is not continuously updated. The methods of updating also vary between electoral registration districts. It is possible to adjust the lists to provide a list of addresses rather than a list of electors but errors will still occur owing to the updating methods used.

The disadvantages of using the Valuation Lists are that rateable units such as shops and offices are mixed up with dwellings and that several local authorities' lists may occur within the study area. However, these problems can be overcome and the Valuation Lists usually form the better basis for sampling.

Having compiled a complete list of households within the study area, every 'nth' household is selected as a place at which home interviews are to be made. The value of 'n' is obtained from the table of sample sizes quoted above. Considerable care should be taken in compiling the list of households and selecting the sample to ensure that an unbiased sample results.

There are two ways in which home interview studies have in

the past been carried out; the full interview technique[11] and the home questionnaire technique.

When the full interview procedure is adopted an explanatory letter is sent to the selected address a few days before the proposed interview so that the householder is aware of the nature and objectives of the study. The interviewer makes contact with as many members of the household as possible in one or two visits, and records all the information. No data is in this case recorded by the householder. In a recent study the time quoted per household was one hour which makes the survey expensive but a very accurate set of data should result. A disadvantage is that interviewers may cause the interviewee to give inaccurate data due to prompting.

If the home questionnaire procedure is adopted then again an explanatory letter is sent out in advance, but this time the interviewer collects only the household information himself and leaves forms for the residents of the household to complete in respect of travel information for the following day. A day or so later the interviewer returns to collect the forms and checks them for completeness. About eighteen households per day were completed in a recent survey[12] using this method.

The full interview procedure is probably best suited to large urban areas where travel patterns do not vary markedly from one weekday to another and interviewing can then proceed continuously from Tuesday to Saturday over a long period. Travel information is usually collected for the previous twenty-four-hour period because it is considered that people cannot remember what trips were made over a longer period. Indeed even twenty-four hours may tax the memory of those who have made several trips. As well as determining average weekday patterns it may be desirable to investigate week-end travel patterns. In smaller urban areas where travel varies considerably from one weekday to another it may be more appropriate to use the home questionnaire procedure. With this method of interviewing travel information can easily be collected for the most typical day of the week. There are problems in identifying a typical day but continuous traffic counts on selected streets should indicate which would be the appropriate day for study.

The accuracy required of the home interview surveys is obviously of a very high order and to obtain such standards a procedure manual[13] has been developed for use by the interviewers. The manual gives an insight into why the surveys are being made and gives a full description of such items as trip purpose, mode of travel and land use. Definitions of all the terms used are given and examples of the type of question likely to be encountered, together with the appropriate reply are included. In addition, precise instructions on the way in which the interview is to be conducted are given, to ensure that all the data is collected in a uniform manner.

The survey form is usually divided into two sections to cover the trip data and household information separately. A form which is used in a full interview survey is shown in Figures II.4 and II.5. Great care is needed in the design of questions in these forms to ensure that the questions are easily understood and are not ambiguous. Space should also be provided on the forms for coding the data.

Figure II.5 each journey or trip is separately listed, the definition of a journey being 'the one-way travel from one point to another for a particular purpose'. In general, stops are regarded as the end of one trip and the beginning of another, unless the stops are made for relatively casual purposes which do not determine the route or mode of travel, e.g. a stop by a person on his way to work to buy a newspaper or cigarettes would not be mentioned.

3. (ii) *Commercial vehicle surveys*

Information on trips made within the study area by commercial vehicles is best obtained from the vehicle operators who are normally willing to instruct their drivers to keep a log of the trips they make during a specified day. If a land-use survey has been completed for the survey area this may be used to determine the addresses from which commercial vehicles might operate. These addresses are then contacted and the drivers of a stratified sample of the vehicles operated from each depot are asked to record their movements.

Another way of obtaining the sampling base is to use local vehicle excise records. In this case the sampling unit becomes the vehicle itself rather than the vehicle operator. Because of the smaller number of commercial vehicles and the difference

LONDON TRAFFIC SURVEY – 1962
HOUSEHOLD INTERVIEW REPORT   PART I — HOUSEHOLD INFORMATION

Page Number _____ of _____

Card Number ...
Serial Number ...
Sampling District ...
Zone Number ...
Report Classification ...
L.T.E. Sample ...   1–17

ADMINISTRATIVE RECORD

Interviewer's Name _____

A. Interview address _____
B. Name of owner of sample vehicle _____
C. Vehicle registration mark _____ Vehicle make _____

D. Does any person living at this address have regular use of a car? _____ Sample owner? _____
E. Day of travel (yesterday) _____ Date of travel _____
F. How many persons live in this household? _____
G. How many persons living in this household are employed? _____
H. How many cars are owned? _____ Company or Government cars available yesterday _____
I. Is there off-street parking space available here for these cars? _____
J. How many motorcycles are owned? _____ How many other vehicles are owned? _____
K. Relative income level of total household _____
L. Total number of journeys by mode   18–33

CALLS

1. Date _____ Time _____
2. Date _____ Time _____
3. Date _____ Time _____
4. Date _____ Time _____

Telephone No. _____

REPORT CLASSIFICATION

SUPERVISOR'S COMMENTS

OTHER COMMENTS

Report Completed _____
Office Check _____
Field Check _____
Approved for Coding _____
Coding Approved _____

London Traffic Survey
Freeman, Fox & Partners
118, Westminster Bridge Road,
London, S.E.1. Tel.: WAT 2512.

PERSON INFORMATION (for persons 5 years of age or over)

M Person Identi-fication	N Jrny's Made Yes / No	N Inter-viewed Yes / No	O Sex and Age	P Main Mode of Travel to Work or School	Q Occupation—Employment Status	Q Place of Work or School (Address)	R Industrial Classification	No. Journeys by Mode Group (Office use only) C.D. / P.T. / Total
Person No. 34			50					40
			45					44
								72
34			50					40
			45					44
								72

FIGURE II.4 Home interview survey form—household information.

in trip pattern followed by different commercial vehicle operators a relatively larger sample size may be required for the
commercial vehicle than the household interview study. A
typical commercial vehicle survey form is shown in Figure II.6.

In the centre of large urban areas there may often be a significant amount of taxicab movements so that a taxicab survey
may occasionally be required. Such surveys are, however,
particularly difficult to carry out accurately because of the
large number of short-distance movements that the taxicab
driver has to be asked to record.

3. (iii) *Grossing-up factors*

In the home interview, commercial vehicle and taxicab surveys,
a sample of the travel will have been recorded. The recorded
journeys must therefore be adjusted by using *grossing-up factors*
to represent total travel.

The grossing-up factor for a home interview sample for each
zone can be calculated using the following formula:

$$\text{Grossing-up factor} = \frac{z - \dfrac{z}{s}\left(d + \dfrac{d}{n} - n\right)}{s - d - n}$$

where for each zone

$z =$ the total number of addresses which were subjected
to the sample procedure (i.e. those which had a
chance of being selected);

$s =$ the number of addresses selected as samples;

$d =$ the number of sample addresses which turned out to
be ineligible;

and $n =$ the number of addresses where there was no
response.

Similar grossing-up factors should be used to derive the total
number of commercial vehicle and taxi trips in the study area.

4. CORDON AND SCREENLINE SURVEYS

In large-scale transportation studies it is customary to divide
the survey area into a series of major areas known as sectors.

FIGURE II.5 Home interview survey form—journey information.

Card Number ☐

S	T	U	V
Person No.	Journey No.	Origin of Journey (Address and Land Use)	Destination of Journey (Address and Land Use)
		Address	Address
18		Land Use	Land Use
		Address	Address
46		Land Use	Land Use
		Address	Address
18		Land Use	Land Use
		Address	Address
46		Land Use	Land Use
		Address	Address
18		Land Use	Land Use
		Address	Address
46		Land Use	Land Use

W	X		Y	Z	Public Transport Journeys			Special Notes
Purpose of Journey	Time of Journey		Mode of Travel	Persons in Car	Bus Route	Ticket Type	Cost of Journey	
	Start	End						
0. Work 0. 1. Employer's Business 1. 2. Personal Business 2. 3. Entertainment 3. 4. Sport 4. 5. Social 5. 6. Shopping (conv.) 6. 7. Shopping (goods) 7. 8. School 8. 9. Home 9. X. Serve Passenger X. Y. Change Travel Mode Y.	A.M. P.M.	A.M. P.M.	0. Car Driver 1. Car Passenger 2. Cycle Driver 3. Cycle Passenger 4. Public Transport Bus 5. L.T.E. Rail 6. British Railways 7. Taxi Passenger 8. Coach 9. Goods Vehicle Passenger and Other	1 2 3 4 5 6 7 8 9	0 1 2 3	0 1 2 3 4 5 6 7 8 9 X	45
0. Work 0. 1. Employer's Business 1. 2. Personal Business 2. 3. Entertainment 3. 4. Sport 4. 5. Social 5. 6. Shopping (conv.) 6. 7. Shopping (goods) 7. 8. School 8. 9. Home 9. X. Serve Passenger X. Y. Change Travel Mode Y.	A.M. P.M.	A.M. P.M.	0. Car Driver 1. Car Passenger 2. Cycle Driver 3. Cycle Passenger 4. Public Transport Bus 5. L.T.E. Rail 6. British Railways 7. Taxi Passenger 8. Coach 9. Goods Vehicle Passenger and Other	1 2 3 4 5 6 7 8 9	0 1 2 3	0 1 2 3 4 5 6 7 8 9 X	73
0. Work 0. 1. Employer's Business 1. 2. Personal Business 2. 3. Entertainment 3. 4. Sport 4. 5. Social 5. 6. Shopping (conv.) 6. 7. Shopping (goods) 7. 8. School 8. 9. Home 9. X. Serve Passenger X. Y. Change Travel Mode Y.	A.M. P.M.	A.M. P.M.	0. Car Driver 1. Car Passenger 2. Cycle Driver 3. Cycle Passenger 4. Public Transport Bus 5. L.T.E. Rail 6. British Railways 7. Taxi Passenger 8. Coach 9. Goods Vehicle Passenger and Other	1 2 3 4 5 6 7 8 9	0 1 2 3	0 1 2 3 4 5 6 7 8 9 X	45
0. Work 0. 1. Employer's Business 1. 2. Personal Business 2. 3. Entertainment 3. 4. Sport 4. 5. Social 5. 6. Shopping (conv.) 6. 7. Shopping (goods) 7. 8. School 8. 9. Home 9. X. Serve Passenger X. Y. Change Travel Mode Y.	A.M. P.M.	A.M. P.M.	0. Car Driver 1. Car Passenger 2. Cycle Driver 3. Cycle Passenger 4. Public Transport Bus 5. L.T.E. Rail 6. British Railways 7. Taxi Passenger 8. Coach 9. Goods Vehicle Passenger and Other	1 2 3 4 5 6 7 8 9	0 1 2 3	0 1 2 3 4 5 6 7 8 9 X	73
0. Work 0. 1. Employer's Business 1. 2. Personal Business 2. 3. Entertainment 3. 4. Sport 4. 5. Social 5. 6. Shopping (conv.) 6. 7. Shopping (goods) 7. 8. School 8. 9. Home 9. X. Serve Passenger X. Y. Change Travel Mode Y.	A.M. P.M.	A.M. P.M.	0. Car Driver 1. Car Passenger 2. Cycle Driver 3. Cycle Passenger 4. Public Transport Bus 5. L.T.E. Rail 6. British Railways 7. Taxi Passenger 8. Coach 9. Goods Vehicle Passenger and Other	1 2 3 4 5 6 7 8 9	0 1 2 3	0 1 2 3 4 5 6 7 8 9 X	45
0. Work 0. 1. Employer's Business 1. 2. Personal Business 2. 3. Entertainment 3. 4. Sport 4. 5. Social 5. 6. Shopping (conv.) 6. 7. Shopping (goods) 7. 8. School 8. 9. Home 9. X. Serve Passenger X. Y. Change Travel Mode Y.	A.M. P.M.	A.M. P.M.	0. Car Driver 1. Car Passenger 2. Cycle Driver 3. Cycle Passenger 4. Public Transport Bus 5. L.T.E. Rail 6. British Railways 7. Taxi Passenger 8. Coach 9. Goods Vehicle Passenger and Other	1 2 3 4 5 6 7 8 9	0 1 2 3	0 1 2 3 4 5 6 7 8 9 X	73

Form HI - 1.

EMPLOYMENT & GOODS VEHICLE SURVEY

Firm/Owner:__ __ __ __ __

Address:__ __ __ __ __ __

__ __ __ __ __ __ __

__ __ __ __ __ __ __

__ __ __ __ __ __ __

Person Interviewed:__ __ __ __

Telephone No: __ __ __ __ __

VISIT	TIME	DATE	Int's Name:
1			Comments:__ __ __ __ __
2			__ __ __ __ __ __
3			__ __ __ __ __ __
4			__ __ __ __ __ __
5			__ __ __ __ __ __
6			

Page__ __of__ __

Serial No. | 3

Zone No.

PART 1.   BUSINESS   INFORMATION

A Nature of business __ __ __ __ __ __ __ __ __ __ __

B Total number of staff   male__ __ __

                                  female__ __ __

C Number of vehicles operating from address

   Cars/estate cars   Parked on premises__   Parked elsewhere__ __

   Light goods   Parked on premises__   Parked elsewhere__ __

   Heavy goods   Parked on premises__   Parked elsewhere__ __

D Day of travel__   Date of travel __ __ __ __

E Total number of trips made on day of travel__ __

F Type and number of vehicles interviewed

   Vehicle No.   1.__ __ 2.__ __ 3.__ __ 4.__ __ 5.__ __ 6.__ __ 7.__ __ 8.__ __ 9.__ __ 10.__ __

   Vehicle Reg. No.   __ __, __ __, __ __, __ __, __ __, __ __, __ __, __ __, __ __, __ __

PART 2. VEHICLE TRIP INFORMATION

G	H	I	J	K	L	
VEHICLE	VEHICLE	TRIP	ORIGIN	DESTINATION	TIME OF TRIP	
TYPE	NUMBER	NUMBER	ADDRESS	ADDRESS	START	FINISH
					AM	AM
			__ __ __ __ __	__ __ __ __ __		
			__ __ __ __ __	__ __ __ __ __		
			__ __ __ __ __	__ __ __ __ __	PM	PM
			__ __ __ __ __	__ __ __ __ __		
			Nature of business__ __	Nature of business __ __		
			S.I.C. ZONE	S.I.C. ZONE		
					AM	AM
			__ __ __ __ __	__ __ __ __ __		
			__ __ __ __ __	__ __ __ __ __		
			__ __ __ __ __	__ __ __ __ __	PM	PM
			__ __ __ __ __	__ __ __ __ __		
			Nature of business__ __	Nature of business __ __		
			S.I.C. ZONE	S.I.C. ZONE		

EG6

FIGURE II.6   Commercial vehicle survey form.

These sectors are usually bounded by screenlines or *cordons* (see Figure II.3). A sample of all traffic crossing these screenlines is interviewed to provide further information on trip patterns throughout the study area. The screenlines and cordons are usually designed to follow some natural barrier to movement such as a river or a major railway line, thus reducing to a minimum the number of places at which traffic can cross the screenlines.

The cordon and screenline surveys are used partly to check the results of the home interview and commercial vehicle surveys. The grossed-up trips found from these surveys are assigned to the base-year network and the assigned traffic flows across the screenlines and cordons are compared with the observed flows found from the cordon and screenline surveys. If these sources do not agree it is customary to adjust the inter-view information to allow for the discrepancy. If the trips across all screenlines appear too low then the trip rates obtained from the household interview may be adjusted upwards to allow for the tendency with all household interviewing for some trips to be under-recorded.

The screenline interview information is also used to provide more detailed information on the sector-to-sector trip move-ment pattern. If too much reliance were placed on an area-wide transport model, particular sector-to-sector movements might be substantially in error. To prevent this the predicted sector-to-sector movements are compared with the observed move-ments found in the screenline interview surveys and where necessary the information obtained from these surveys is used to adjust the *trip attraction* and *generation* equations or the trip distribution functions for particular areas, thus obtaining a more realistic representation of traffic survey movements throughout the area. This process is described in Chapter III when the calibration of the distribution model is discussed. The information obtained from the external cordon survey is essen-tial as a measure of trips to and through the survey area by people not resident there.

External cordon surveys of private road-traffic are usually carried out in one of two ways: either by roadside interview[14] or by issuing a pre-paid postcard.[15] Whichever method is used, roadside interview stations should be established at all points where major routes cross the external cordon line. If a few minor roads intersect the cordon line, they may be excluded from the survey provided that the remaining roads account for a very high proportion of the traffic crossing the cordon.

Often roadside interviews are carried out for less than the full twenty-four-hour period used in the home interview surveys. This does not matter provided there is not an unusually large volume of traffic during the night and that vehicle counts are made for the remainder of the day to give twenty-four-hour control totals. The survey work at the interview station should preferably be carried out over several days to reduce the possibility of bias due to abnormal conditions on particular days.

The data obtained from a roadside interview must be compatible with the data collected in the home interview survey. This causes some difficulty because the questionnaire must be kept as short as possible in order not to delay motorists unnecessarily. An example of a roadside interview form is shown in Figure II.7.

Unless the road is very lightly trafficked, a sampling procedure should be adopted. A sample as low as 10% may be sufficiently accurate on the most heavily trafficked routes. Because the roadside interviewers can only carry out a limited number of interviews in any one hour, the proportion of trips interviewed tends to vary throughout the day. A separate enumerator, therefore, should count all traffic passing the interview site so that control totals can be established. Particular care then has to be taken to ensure that the sampled interviews are correctly grossed-up to reflect the variation in the percentage of traffic interviewed throughout the day.

If the alternative method of issuing pre-paid postcards is adopted, then again vehicles are stopped at the cordon station, but instead of interviewing the driver, a brief explanation of the survey is given and a pre-paid postcard questionnaire handed to the driver to complete later. The method is simple and causes less inconvenience to motorists, but usually results in a very poor response rate so that the reliability of the data is often unknown.

In large cities interview surveys may also be required on public transport facilities. In particular it may be necessary to

INTERVIEWER	....		CHECKED	....
STATION NUMBER	....	1 2	CODED	....
HOUR BEGINNING	....	3 4	CODING CHECK	....

LIGHT AND HEAVY GOODS VEHICLES ONLY

VEH. TYPE	NO. IN VEH.	ORIGIN ADDRESS	DESTINATION ADDRESS	DESTINATION LAND USE	GARAGE ADDRESS	EXIT ROUTE	T.M. (TYPE GOODS)
1. Light Goods 2. Heavy Goods		Town and County .... Exact address	Town and County .... Exact address	1. Farms, Mines, Factories 2. Construction 3. Utilities 4. Transport, Communications 5. Shops 6. Wholesale Warehouses 7. Other Services 8. Residences	1. Origin 2. Destination Elsewhere:- (Town and County)		
5 6		7	10	13	14	15	17
1. Light Goods 2. Heavy Goods		Town and County .... Exact address	Town and County .... Exact address	1. Farms, Mines, Factories 2. Construction 3. Utilities 4. Transport, Communications 5. Shops 6. Wholesale Warehouses 7. Other Services 8. Residences	1. Origin 2. Destination Elsewhere:- (Town and County)		
18 19		20	23	26	27	28	30

CARS, TAXIS AND MOTOR CYCLES ONLY

VEH. TYPE	NO. IN VEH.	ORIGIN ADDRESS	DESTINATION ADDRESS	TRIP PURPOSE	GARAGE ADDRESS	EXIT ROUTE	T.M.
3. Car 4. Taxi 5. M/C		Town and County .... Exact address	Town and County .... Exact address	1. Work 2. Employer's business 3. Personal business 4. Shopping 5. Social/recreation 6. Education 7. Serve passenger 8. Other (specify)	1. Origin 2. Destination Elsewhere:- (Town and County)		
31 32		33	36	39	40	41	43
3. Car 4. Taxi 5. M/C		Town and County .... Exact address	Town and County .... Exact address	1. Work 2. Employer's business 3. Personal business 4. Shopping 5. Social/recreation 6. Education 7. Serve passenger 8. Other (specify)	1. Origin 2. Destination Elsewhere:- (Town and County)		
44 45		46	49	52	53	54	56
3. Car 4. Taxi 5. M/C		Town and County .... Exact address	Town and County .... Exact address	1. Work 2. Employer's business 3. Personal business 4. Shopping 5. Social/recreation 6. Education 7. Serve passenger 8. Other (specify)	1. Origin 2. Destination Elsewhere:- (Town and County)		
57 58		59	62	65	66	67	69

FIGURE II.7   Roadside interview form.

obtain information on public transport trips by people not resident in the survey area. In the largest urban areas, trips by bus and rail will be of interest but in medium-sized cities only bus travel is likely to be worth investigating.

An external cordon rail survey[16] may be carried out by issuing

Please complete and drop this card in one of the special collection boxes provided at stations, or post. No stamp is required.	LONDON TRAFFIC SURVEY Sponsored by the London County Council and the Ministry of Transport.	For office use 1963 Serial No. № 113292 Classification Day................Date........... Route..........	

Station **MAIDSTONE WEST**

Please provide the following details regarding the particular journey you were making when you received this card whether or not you consider the journey typical.

A. WHERE DO YOU NORMALLY LIVE? Town..........   No.
     Please give the address. County..........   20

B. HOW DID YOU TRAVEL TO THE STATION AT WHICH YOU RECEIVED THIS CARD?
    Please tick only ONE of the boxes.
  ☐ ₁By car now parked at or near station.
  ☐ ₂By car driven away (or taxi).   ☐ ₃By motor-cycle.
  ☐ ₄By walking or cycling.   ☐ ₅By bus.

C. WHAT WAS THE SCHEDULED TIME OF DEPARTURE OF YOUR TRAIN?..........

D. AT WHICH STATION WILL YOU LEAVE BRITISH RAILWAYS?..........

E. WHAT IS YOUR MAIN METHOD OF TRAVEL FROM BRITISH RAILWAYS TO YOUR FINAL DESTINATION?
  Please tick only ONE of the boxes.
  ☐ ₁By Underground.   ☐ ₂By bus.
  ☐ ₃By car or motor-cycle.   ☐ ₄By taxi.
  ☐ ₅By walking or cycling   Time

F. WHERE IS YOUR FINAL DESTINATION? No. & Street..........
    Please give the full address. Town or district..........

G. WHAT IS THE MAIN PURPOSE OF YOUR JOURNEY? Please tick only ONE of the boxes.
  ☐ ₁To or from work.   ☐ ₂To or from school or college.
  ☐ ₃Business other than to or from work.
  ☐ ₄Shopping.   ☐ ₅Entertainment, sport, social.
  ☐ ₆Other personal affairs.

H. WHAT KIND OF TICKET DO YOU HOLD? Please tick boxes for class and type.
  Class { ☐ First. ☐ Second. } Type { ☐ Weekly season. ☐ Cheap day return (reduced fare). ☐ Other season. ☐ Other (full fare). }

I. HOW MANY CARS DOES YOUR HOUSEHOLD HAVE AVAILABLE FOR PERSONAL USE?
  Please tick the appropriate box.   ☐ ₁None.   ☐ ₂One.   ☐ ₃Two or more.   42

- - - - - - - - - - PLEASE DETACH BEFORE POSTING - - - - - - - - - -

LONDON TRAFFIC SURVEY, 118, Westminster Bridge Road, S.E.1.

As you may already know, the London County Council and the Ministry of Transport are jointly sponsoring the London Traffic Survey—a comprehensive survey of travel in Greater London. The purpose of the Survey is to provide facts needed to plan the future road and rail system in the London area.

Information on travel in London by all forms of transport is being collected and has already been collected on journeys made by car and motor-cycle. To complete the survey, we need information on journeys made in the London area by rail, and to obtain this, your assistance is required.

You have been given a postcard with this notice, and we would be grateful if you would answer the questions on it about the journey being made when you received it. When it is completed, would you please place it in one of the collecting boxes provided at stations or drop it in a post box.

You are asked to do this, even if you are not making a journey to London, since we need information about the journeys made by all passengers who receive cards.

Only by carrying out a survey of this kind can we know your needs and plan the improvements required to cater for them. Your co-operation will help us to do just that.

FIGURE II.8 Rail survey questionnaire.

questionnaires at stations outside the survey area to all passengers travelling in the direction of that area. The questionnaire can either be pre-paid for posting back to the survey centre or simply collected at the end of the trip at the stations inside the survey area. Because the average traveller is unable or unwilling to understand extensive questionnaires, the number of questions should be kept to a minimum. A typical questionnaire is shown in Figure II.8. When the response rate for such a survey is less than about 70% it is probably necessary to carry out checks for geographical bias on the returned questionnaire. An alternative procedure to the postal questionnaire study is to interview passengers on the train. A bus passenger external cordon survey can be organised in a similar manner to that used for rail passengers, although it is rather more difficult to use a postal questionnaire. It is thus normal practice to interview passengers.

Public transport surveys are usually also required at the internal screenlines. It is, however, more difficult to interview bus passengers crossing the screenlines because the average distance travelled by the passenger is much shorter than at the

TABLE II.2 Traffic volume comparisons—secondary screenlines and cordons.

Name of screenline or cordon	Summarised interview data* (Col. 1)	Volume census data (Col. 2)	Per cent. Col. 1 × 100 Col. 2 (Col. 3)
Central Area Cordon	970,000	1,097,000	88·4
LCC Cordon	1,122,000	1,166,000	96·2
River Lea screenline	339,000	341,000	99·2
Kent–Surrey screenline	57,000	60,000	95·0

* Excludes bus traffic, internal journeys by non-residents of survey area and intrazonal journeys.

external cordon. A useful check on bus travel may, however, be made by estimating the approximate number of passengers in buses as they cross the screenline.

The total volume of travel by each mode crossing a screenline is used to check the accuracy of each of the cordon and home interview surveys. Table II.2 shows such a comparison. Acceptable limits on the accuracy of data have been suggested by the Bureau of Public Roads[17] and these would appear to be sensible standards for general adoption since more accurate data can only be obtained at very great expense.

The interviews carried out at the external cordon often concern non-residents of the survey area. Particularly in the larger conurbations these people are likely to make further trips, *non-home-based trips*, within the survey area. The household interviews will not, of course, record these trips and this has led to serious underestimates of trips, particularly in central areas.

If it is at all possible, information should also be gathered on these journeys, possibly by interviewing a selection of travellers at the external cordon as they leave the study area.

5. INVENTORY OF TRANSPORT FACILITIES

Information on traffic volumes and composition for all parts of the networks will be required as a check on other survey data for use in the transport model. Volumes over the day vary considerably, indeed variations may well occur between days and most certainly between a weekday and the week-end. Travel information in the home interview surveys may have been collected over a relatively short period of time at one period of the year. A more general knowledge of volumes over a longer period of time may be required to check whether the survey data is representative of travel over the whole year. If the survey data is not found to be representative of the longer period then this can be recognised and taken account of in the subsequent stages of the planning process.

Automatic recording counters[18] may be used for this work. These counters record the total flow of traffic past a point in a street (both directions included in a two-way street) in quarter- or one-hourly intervals either by printing on to a paper tape or punching on to special tape for computer analysis. Recording counters do not, of course, classify vehicles into various classes, and in places a separate survey may be required for this purpose. It may also be necessary to use observers to count information on turning movements at intersections as these cannot usually be measured with automatic counts.

Although the measurement of volumes using public transport is more difficult, the data required on public transport networks is similar in nature. Data is required on passenger volumes for each section of each service in the public transport network. Very often the operator may be able to estimate passenger volumes on individual parts of the public transport network from his own records.

Travel times on each of the links of the network are needed for the determination of zone-to-zone travel times. Because travel times vary from hour to hour, it would be desirable to measure them for each hour of the day. This is naturally an impossible task and therefore measurements are frequently made to represent average peak-hour and average off-peak conditions.

Road travel time may be measured by use of a technique known as the moving observer method[19] whereby observers in cars moving in the traffic stream record times for each link and intersection delays for the whole network. If, due to traffic congestion, it is difficult to measure peak period travel times then it may be possible to estimate these using a speed/flow relationship derived from off-peak surveys. The lengths and widths of roads in the network will also be required when this method of obtaining travel times is to be used, because these are factors incorporated in the relationship between the volume of traffic on a link and the speed at which that traffic can travel.

The travel times on public transport systems are again difficult to measure, although more information may be available from the operator, particularly for fixed-track systems. Usually data from an operator would be checked by observers travelling on the buses and trains and noting the travel times involved. A difficulty peculiar to public transport is the measurement of walking and waiting times. These often form a substantial proportion of total trip time.

6. NETWORK DESCRIPTION FOR COMPUTER ANALYSIS

The transport networks within a study area have been described in such a way that a variety of analyses can be performed. The main purposes for which these network descriptions are used are: first, to compute zone-to-zone travel time or cost for use in calibrating the traffic demand or distribution model; secondly, to obtain information on the relative time or cost of travel by alternative modes so that a modal split analysis can be carried out, and thirdly, to assign to the most appropriate routes the elements of the matrix of demands for movement.

The transport system is defined by a series of *links* and *nodes*. A link is defined as a length of a road or rail network which has no major intersections. The links are bounded by nodes which are defined as the point at which a link terminates. Usually the nodes represent a junction at the intersection of two roads or bus routes. The BPR method[20] identifies a link for computer analysis by reference to the nodes at either end which are numbered, and a travel time is associated with movement along the whole length of the link. Figure II.9 illustrates a network description using the BPR techniques.

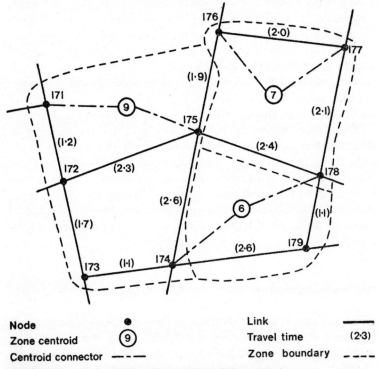

Node	●	Link	▬
Zone centroid	⑨	Travel time	(2·3)
Centroid connector	— · —	Zone boundary	— — — —

FIGURE II.9 Network description using BPR method.

An alternative method[21] considers trips between the centres of adjacent links, and travel times are allocated to sections of network between the mid points of these adjacent links. This method of identifying road networks is little used, partly because the resultant method of computer analysis is more complex. The method does, however, have the advantage that it may be easier to include delays at intersections, particularly delays due to turning movements.

With both systems zone *centroids* have to be identified and numbered. A zone centroid is assumed to represent the point of origin or destination of all trips generated by or attracted to that zone. It should thus be located at the centre of gravity of all trips from that zone. The centroid is then connected to the coded network at selected nodes. These links between the centroid and the nodes of the network are termed *centroid*

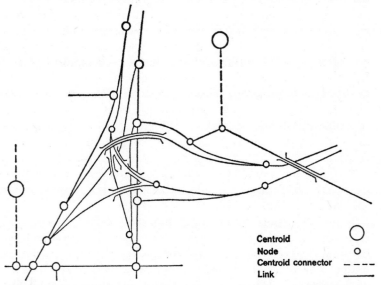

Centroid	◯
Node	○
Centroid connector	_ _ _ _
Link	————

FIGURE II.10 Intersection description for analysis of turning movements.

connectors. A travel time should be given to each centroid connector to reflect the average time required for trips beginning or ending in that zone to reach the node in question. The precise specification of these centroid connector links requires much care, attention, and practical experience as their travel time allocation and geographical description can have considerable influence on the choice of route assumed to and from that zone.

At times, traffic engineers may wish to know the precise turning movements expected at certain intersections. This can easily be done by detailed coding of individual junctions but consideration of all intersections would very substantially increase the number of links in the network. (In general, computational costs increase as the square of the number of links in the network.) One method of identifying the turning movements at a larger intersection is shown in Figure II.10.

The type of roads to be included in the designated networks will depend upon the level within the hierarchy of planning at which the study is being conducted. The type of study being undertaken will also govern the total number of links required, although the computer to be used at the model building stage may prove an overriding factor. The roads selected for designation in a regional study should represent the strategic network for the area. This would probably include all motorways and trunk roads and most of the more important class I and II roads. The study of an urban area within the region would include all of these links plus all other routes which carry a significant volume of traffic. When planning at an even more detailed level it is necessary to include quite minor roads.

Initially, it is usually better to include too many rather than too few links in a coded network, because it is a simple matter to delete some links at a later stage.

Public transport differs fundamentally from private road transport since the fixed services following given routes limit freedom of choice of route and time when the journey can be made. The methods of route description which are used in connection with road networks must therefore be modified before they can be applied to public transport networks.

In the procedures developed by Freeman, Fox, Wilbur Smith and Associates,[22] links and nodes are defined in the 'conventional' manner, but the network is built up by the description of individual public transport services, each service being described by the nodes it passes through, the time or speed between nodes, and the frequency of operation.

7. PLANNING PARAMETER INVENTORY

Information on the present pattern of activities, where are the shops, schools, factories and houses, is an essential input to the transport model. It is thus necessary to prepare a *planning parameter* inventory including the resident and employed population and numbers of full- and part-time students in each zone. Local planning authorities in this country are continually involved in the collection and processing of such land-use data; sometimes in connection with the preparation of statutory development plans and at other times in connection with particular planning proposals or small area studies. Local authorities have a statutory obligation to carry out a survey of their area and this is being accepted more and more as a process of continuous review of the pattern of land use. Much of this data can be useful in transportation planning. Other sources of data include the Registrar General's Census of Population, the Department of Employment and Productivity's[23] employment exchange records and the Department of Economic Affairs' Family Expenditure Surveys.[24] Two further censuses may also be of some value for forecasting. These are the Census of Production,[25] which gives details on industry every few years, showing how the population earns its living, and the Census of Distribution[26] which gives information on how the population spends its income.

The census of population is made in this country every ten years in the second year of each decade. Information is collected for every household and is quite extensive. The 1961 census included counts of the population subdivided into males and females, marital status and age-groups. Other information includes the place of work, size of household, nature of occupation and classification of employment.

To keep the data confidential, they are aggregated to give information only at the enumeration district or larger zonal scale. Enumeration district boundaries are principally determined by street blocks, but most unusual shapes are sometimes found. These boundaries may be modified from one census to another. This makes the data somewhat difficult to use in the base-year appraisal. A 10% sample of the population was included in an additional census in 1966.[27] Enumeration district boundaries were redrawn and additional information was collected on car-ownership and the journey to work. This latter information has been particularly useful for transport planning. The 1971 census was taken on the same basis as before using enumeration districts as collecting units, but the results will be tabulated by 1 kilometre and 100 metre grid squares (depending on the nature of the area and the availability of OS maps) as well as the normal EDs and this should make the information far more useful in transport studies. The 100-metre grids will have the advantage of being fixed from one census to the next but being large in size they do not offer all the flexibility required of an integrated information system.

Much of the data from the national census such as population and age structure can be used as a check on the accuracy of the home interview survey as well as for input to the forecasting models. Employment statistics are usually obtained from the Department of Employment and Productivity's records which are compiled in two series; ERI and ERII. The latter is produced by sampling the insurance cards of insured workers who for each Employment Exchange Area are allocated to one of twenty-four groups under the Standard Industrial Classification. This source has two main objections for use in transport planning. First, all workers do not have insurance cards, and secondly, employment exchange areas often cut across administrative boundaries and rarely coincide with units for which other data is available. The ERI series is known as the Employer's Register. Planning authorities only recently obtained access to this source which consists of a card index of firms referenced by type of work, address, number of employees and other information intended primarily for the benefit of the Employment Exchange Manager. These records provide very useful data on employment but unfortunately any firm employing fewer than five people, as well as the self-employed, the part-time workers and public employees are excluded. These data have to be adjusted both for the unreported employment and to conform to the zonal boundaries required for transportation planning. Usually this adjustment can be successfully applied using local knowledge of the employment structure in any particular area, but in certain areas it is necessary to carry out a fresh survey of employment to be used as input to the transport model. Mention should also be made of the proposed annual Census of Employment, to be carried out by the Department of Employment, which was the subject of a successful trial in 1970 and which will, in future years, give a 100% coverage of all employed persons (including self-employed) by sex and type of employment by standard industrial classification at place of employment. The sample frame is obtained from Inland Revenue lists of employed persons and the return of information is mandatory on all concerned. The principal short-coming is that the Department of Employment have at present (1971) no plans for the publication of information below regional or employment exchange level.

Data on the number of students at schools and colleges in each zone can usually be obtained without much difficulty from the local education authorities.

Retail shopping centres are principal points of attraction in urban areas and require detailed examination. The measure of attraction could be simply the number of shops, but other para-meters such as floor space or retail sales are more useful. The sample Census of Distribution (1966) gives this information for shopping centres but not for smaller retail areas. The 1971 Census of Distribution will provide floor space and turnover by units of 100-metre grids provided that the number of shops in each category exceeds the minimum number required to ensure confidentiality of the information.

Preparation of the planning parameter inventory is a most important part of the survey phase and can be both time-consuming and expensive. Much of the data can of course be used for planning in other fields and as such the inventory provides a valuable insight into many problems. The work must be carefully programmed so that the data are available at the correct time for use in calibrating the sub-models of the trans-port model.

8. CONSISTENCY CHECKS

A major part of the survey phase of a transport study is con-cerned with the processing of original data to secure information in a usable form. The result of this work is a number of tabula-tions from which base-year characteristics may be assessed. The survey data can be further reduced from tabulations to charts, histograms, maps, etc., and standard computer programs[28, 29] are available.

It is essential to check the accuracy of all the surveys and this can be done by carrying out internal consistency checks. Comparison may be made of the population, household structure, employment and car-ownership values for each zone derived from the home interview survey and the planning parameter inventory. The information collected from screenline interviews is used to check and 'calibrate' the information obtained from other sources.

The most common consistency checks are:

(a) reported trips against observed trips, total across the screenlines;

(b) reported trips across the external cordon with observations of the movement of residents across the cordon;

(c) trips to work as reported by the home interview of residents plus trips reported by non-residents crossing the external cordon compared with known or surveyed employment figures within the study area;

(d) trips to school reported by home interview against known school places.

9. UPDATING SURVEYS

Transportation planning should be a continuous process and therefore periodic monitoring of the transport model over time must be allowed for when the study commences. *Updating surveys* are required to check the accuracy of forecasting of each of the sub-models of generation, distribution, assignment and modal split, discussed in the next chapter. Unfortunately, very large updating surveys would be required to do this adequately for each model over the whole area. *Generation rates* are probably the most easily checked from small samples in just a few of the originally designated zones. The general form of the distribution function may also be checked using these same data as also may the modal split model. The assignment model cannot easily be verified from these surveys but volume counts on sampled links may provide sufficient comparison.

Few studies in this country or the USA have accomplished

adequate appraisal of forecasts made with the transport model, but such an exercise is to be undertaken in London in 1971–2 (ten years after the original survey).

10. ORGANISATION AND PROGRAMMING OF SURVEY STAGE

It is essential to have a well-formulated organisation for both the collection and processing of data. It is also essential to have the inventories implemented according to a scheduled programme so that the data from various sources is available at the correct time.

A flow chart covering the survey stage should be prepared to provide a basis for critical path planning. An estimate of time required for each item of work must be made. Estimates are also needed of manpower requirements so that proper provision can be made for the training of survey staff before work is begun. A typical organisation and programming flow chart for the survey, analysis and forecasting stages of a large transportation study is shown in Figure II.11.

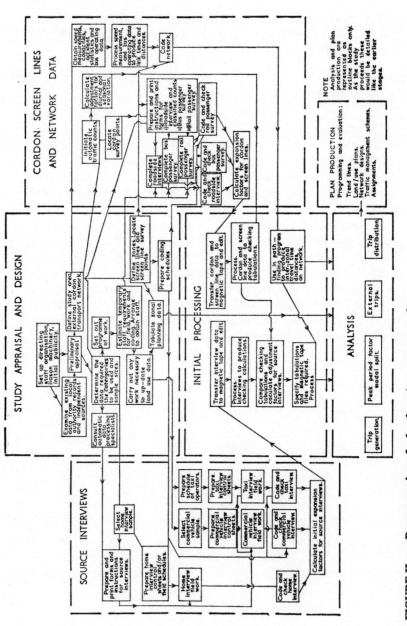

FIGURE II.11 Programming of a land use/transport study.

STUDY APPRAISAL AND DESIGN

Set up directing staff organisation, liaison machinery, initial publicity.

Examine existing data from local authority records and sources.

Preliminary appraisal.

Define study area, external cordon and transport network.

Consult automatic data processing specialists.

Determine the data required, the categories to be used and sample sizes.

Set out programme of work.

Estimate temporary staff requirements for fieldwork and coding. Arrange to obtain staff.

Carry out any work necessary to up-date land use data.

Tabulate zonal planning data.

Define zones. Locate screen lines and survey points.

Prepare coding schedules.

CORDON, SCREEN LINES AND NETWORK DATA

Obtain speed measurements, capacities, coefficients and bus operating data.

Process speed measurement, and bus operating data to produce link times and distances.

Code network.

Initiate automatic traffic counts.

Calculate adjustment factors for seasonal variation.

Locate survey points.

Prepare and print instructions and forms for
a) Roadside interview and classified counts.
b) Bus passenger survey.
c) Rail passenger survey.

Complete roadside interviews.

Complete bus passenger survey.

Complete rail passenger survey.

Code and check roadside interviews.

Code and check bus passenger survey.

Code and check rail passenger survey.

Calculate expansion factors for cordon and screen lines.

INITIAL PROCESSING

Transfer cordon and screen line data to magnetic tape and edit.

Process. Correct screen line data to produce checking tabulations.

Use in path-finding program to produce inter-zonal travel time distances on network.

Transfer interview data to magnetic tape and edit.

Process, initiate data checking calculations.

Compare checking tabulations and calculate adjustment factors. Process source interviews.

Specify tabulations and magnetic tape files required. Process.

SOURCE INTERVIEWS

Prepare and print forms and instructions for source interviews.

Select home interview sample.

Prepare home interview control sheets and/or field schedules.

Home interview field work.

Code and check home interviews.

Prepare schedule of taxi operators.

Prepare taxi interview control sheets.

Taxi interview field work.

Code and check taxi interviews.

Select commercial vehicle sample.

Prepare commercial vehicle interview control sheets.

Commercial vehicle interview field work.

Code and check commercial vehicle interviews.

Calculate initial expansion factors for source interviews.

ANALYSIS

Trip generation.

Peak period factor modal split.

External trips.

Trip distribution.

NOTE

Analysis and plan production are represented as outline blocks only. As the study proceeds these would be detailed like the earlier stages.

PLAN PRODUCTION

Programming and evaluation:
Trend lines.
Land use plans.
Network designs.
Traffic management schemes.
Assignments.

CHAPTER III

The transport model

1. INTRODUCTION: THE NATURE OF MODELS

Model building is a very important part of the transportation planning process. The accuracy of the traffic forecasting model dictates the use that can be made of the transportation planning process and the scope for evaluation. The detail and scale of any surveys also reflect the accuracy expected from the forecasting model.

Because model building is an essential element of the transportation planning process, it is useful to outline some general points about models. The term model[1] is used to describe both simple mathematical relationships, such as a 'trip generation model' which might describe trip-making behaviour, and complementary linked systems of relationships, such as the transportation planning process. A complex model such as the transport model comprises a number of sub-models, such as the trip generation model.

As an example of a simple model, the transportation planner may observe the situation in an urban area in which journeys are made. He may define certain variables which he might expect to describe the situation he is observing, such as the total number of journeys and the population of the area. Furthermore, he may intuitively suggest that the number of trips made is directly proportional to the number of people in the area. If T_i is the number of trips and P_i the population in this area, then the relationship may be modelled by the equation:

$$T_i = gP_i$$

This type of model is useful in three ways. First, it is a form of communication between one observer and another, in that before this event of trip generation can be properly understood, certain measurable facts, or parameters, have to be chosen, namely numbers of trips T, numbers of people P and a constant g. Secondly, it scales down the situation to manageable proportions, that is, this simple equation represents many people, vehicles and movement. Thirdly, most importantly, it may be able to help illuminate some particular problems. For example, in this form the model may be used not only to describe the number of trips made by a particular population but also to calculate the new number of trips made by a new population. To do this the observer may measure population P_i and the number of trips T_i and by division establish g. Knowing a new population P_k, a forecast can be made of the trips that would be made, T_k, using the model and making the assumption that the value of the constant g, measured in the one case, may be applied to the other case. Relationships of this kind are most useful because they can answer questions involving change and it is the changing situation that planners are most able to influence by choosing appropriate policies.

The parameters used in model building should be readily available statistics, and should be carefully chosen to represent typical homogeneous or 'average' groups of people, land use, etc. The choice of parameter is therefore critical, since it will define what measurements are required and so the size, scope and detail of the survey required to obtain the information. For example the model above has grouped the whole of the population P together. On closer examination, better forecasts might be achieved using two more homogeneous groups of people, those with cars and those not having cars. However, total population is a readily available statistic; a breakdown into car- and non-car-owners might require special surveys.

Change frequently involves time. It is particularly important, therefore, that the causal relationships used for forecasting purposes should distinguish between parameters which are invariant with time and those which are not. The invariant in the above equation has been assumed to be the constant g, the trip rate per person, and establishment of a value for g could be called calibration of the model. It is, however, by no means certain that the value of g will remain constant over time.

Because models can be used to predict future events and scale down the size of the problem, they are of particular value in the repeated testing of new policies. Various different transport facilities, varying environmental conditions, can all be tested by repeated use of the model.

Models are in general not as simple as the example used above. The full transport model is much more complex. The transport model attempts to describe the travel patterns of large numbers of people, using a series of linked sub-models, and can be considered a description of the decision-making process the average person might be expected to use when he considers making a journey. For example, someone wishing to take part in a particular activity may consider all the opportunities nearby where he may take part in that activity. In general, a person consciously or subconsciously weighs up the benefits and disbenefits of taking part in that activity, including the travel involved, making sure that he derives an overall benefit to himself. In this way, he chooses whether to take part or not. He first decides to make a journey (trip generation), he selects a destination (trip distribution) and then makes a journey (assignment and modal split). In practice, of course, no one individual conforms to such a simple model. However, as a group, people appear to behave in this way, and therefore the model may be interpreted as describing the behavioural pattern of a group of individuals. Generation, distribution, modal split and assignment can all be considered as linked sub-models together making up the transport model.

Research and experience have now formalised not only the transport model but also the whole of the transportation planning process, and flow charts of the process as shown in Chapter I have become familiar. This chapter will now discuss the formulation and detail of the transport model under the sub-model headings, outlined above, of generation, distribution, modal split and assignment.

2. TRIP GENERATION

2. (i) *Introduction*

The trip generation stage of the transport model describes the reasons why trips are made and determines the places where trips start and finish. These *trip ends* are then used as input to the later stages of the transport model.

Trips are usually made by people taking part in particular activities, such as work, shopping or visiting friends. Three types of journey may result.

1. Journeys within the same building;
2. Pedestrian movement between buildings;
3. Journeys which require the use of some form of vehicular transport.

It has been general practice in transportation planning to consider only trips that involve the use of a mechanised means of transport, and for the rest of this chapter the word *trip* will refer only to such mechanised journeys.

2. (ii) *Trip generation and attraction (definition)*

Before discussing the factors which most influence trip generation, some commonly used terms must be defined. First, a journey or a trip will have two trip ends, an origin and a destination. At both ends there will be an associated purpose, for example 'from home-origin' 'to work-destination'. Trip ends in this form were used in many of the early studies. Later, as transportation planning technology developed, it was found necessary to introduce new definitions.[2] It was observed that trips could be classified into two types, *home-based* and *non-home-based*, the former being defined as having one end of the trip at the home of the person making the trip (the end may be either the origin or the destination of the trip), and the latter having neither end at the home of the person making the trip. It was also found convenient to split trip ends into two classes: ends from which trips radiated, known as 'trip generations' (e.g. a trip starting from home) and ends to which trips were attracted

known as 'trip attractions'. A 'trip generation' was therefore
defined as the home end of a home-based trip, or the origin of
a non-home-based trip, while a trip 'attraction' was defined as
the non-home end of a home-based trip or the destination of a
non-home-based trip.

The following simple examples may help to explain this
terminology of trip generation models. A trip from home to
place of work is a home-based trip, like the return journey
from work to home. In this example both trips were considered
as having been 'generated' at home and 'attracted' to place of
work thus making two work-purpose trip end generations in the
home zone and two work-purpose trip end attractions in the
work zone. An example of a non-home-based trip is a trip
from work to the shops. In these cases the origin of the trip is
considered the point of 'trip generation' and the destination the
point of trip attraction.

2. (iii) *Trip purpose*

The concept of trip 'purpose' is important to all elements of the
transport model, different trip purposes are associated not only
with different trip generation rates but also with different trip

TABLE III.1 **Trip purpose classification** (% by purpose).

	GB	London*
Work	39	39
School	9	6
Firms' business		3
Personal business ⎫	19	16
Shopping ⎭		8
Entertainment, sport	9	6
Social or recreational	15	7
Other	9	15

* Car-owning households only.

Sources: National Travel Survey, 1964.
London County Council, London Traffic Survey, Volume I, 1964.

distribution and modal split characteristics. A typical classification of trip purpose is given in Table III.1 which shows the
percentage of trips in each trip purpose found in two particular
studies.

C

2. (iv) *Use of households as the statistical unit*

It has become customary in most transportation studies to consider trip generation as being related to the characteristics of complete households rather than being directly related to individual members of a household. The main reason for this is that it is much easier to collect information and derive a usable statistical sampling basis for households than for individuals. It has also been shown that trip generation can be related to certain household characteristics (particularly household income and use of a car).

2. (v) *Factors affecting trip generation and attraction rates*

Table III.2 lists some of the factors found to influence household trip generation. A most important factor affecting the trip rate of a household is the number of cars that the household owns. The private car will open up many more opportunities than

TABLE III.2 Independent variables found significant in work trip generation and attraction equations.

Generation equations	Attraction equations
Income	Employment—either
Car-ownership	disaggregated into manual
Residential density	and non-manual or by SIC
Distance from centre	Floorspace
Rateable value	Accessibility to work force
Household size	

public transport, particularly for non-work trips and non-central area trips, and for this reason it can be expected that a car-owning household will generate more trips than a non-car-owning household. The number of cars owned by a household is, of course, related to the income of the household.[3]

The number of trips from a household is also related to its size and composition. For example, a household with two grown-up children at work will generate more work trips than if those children were still at school. For this reason certain of the more recent studies[4] have used a trip generation model which makes some allowance for the structure of the household.

In particular the number of employed residents in the household is considered an important factor determining trip generation rates.

Another factor found[5] to be important as an explanation of trip generation rates is the density at which people live. This is a more difficult factor to explain because it is cross correlated with a number of other explanatory variables, such as distance from the town centre, accessibility to public transport and average household income. All other things being equal, we might expect trip rates to increase with residential density, as high-density situations produce more potentially accessible opportunities. In practice this tendency appears to be more than counterbalanced by the effects of the cross correlation with other factors, especially the inverse relationship often found between residential density and household income. Another factor tending to reduce trip generation rates in high-density zones is the increased likelihood of making walking trips which are generally excluded from trip generation equations.

We have so far been concerned with the home end (or 'generation' end) of home-based trips, but it is also necessary to locate the attraction end of home-based trips, and also the number of non-home-based trips.[6] The attractions are usually forecast by simply relating trip ends to such parameters as floorspace and number of employees. This part of trip end forecasting has in fact been studied in much less detail than trip generations. The factors generally considered most important in determining trip generation rates are listed in Table III.2.

In total the number of non-home-based trips usually represents a small proportion of all trips (although in the central areas they may form a much more significant proportion) and disaggregation by trip purpose is usually unnecessary. Again it is usual to relate the number of non-home-based trip ends directly to the planning parameters of a zone such as retail floor space, employees in employment, and zonal population.

In the survey chapter we referred to the possibility of special surveys for residents of the survey area who do not live in households, for example, people who live in hotels. These can at times be very important in determining the number of non-home-based trips. For example it was found in the London

Traffic Survey that there was a serious under-reporting of trips on the Central London underground. This could be attributed largely to non-home-based trips, many of which were made by people resident in hotels and institutions.

A final category of trip for which a trip generation forecast is required is the commercial vehicle movement. We might expect to treat the generation and attraction of these trips as person trips are treated, but instead of having categories of trip purposes having categories of commodity. This has been done in several studies but clearly leads to considerable increase in computation and expense.[7] The most usual method is to relate commercial vehicle trip ends directly to zonal information on employment and population. Commercial vehicle trip generation is a poorly understood element in the transportation planning process and more research might be useful.

2. (vi) *Balancing attractions and generations*

The total number of attractions in the study area for any trip purpose should by definition be equal to the total number of generations. But since attractions and generations are calculated separately they may not be initially identical. In these circumstances it is normal practice to adjust the initially forecast zonal attractions upwards or downwards by a constant factor so that in total the final forecast attractions match the forecast generations.

2. (vii) *Analytical methods for forecasting trip ends: simple expansion or growth factors*

Early studies in traffic engineering[8] relied upon past rates of growth for forecasting future travel, although it was soon realised that these simple techniques did not reflect the underlying causes of travel and could not therefore predict future travel very accurately. For short-term forecasting in rural areas, these methods may still be of some value. Indeed they are often used to forecast external–internal and through trips. In fast-changing urban areas, a more complex model is obviously required which may include several explanatory variables.

2. (viii) *Regression analysis*

Multiple regression analysis techniques[9] are often used to calibrate a model when more than two variables are being considered. The problem then is to derive an estimated relationship between the dependent variable, the number of trip generations for a particular purpose in a given zone, and a number of independent variables. The variation in the number of trips generated in that zone is then explained by the influence of the independent variables.

The general form of a multiple regression equation is:

$$Y_p = a_1 + a_2 x_2 + a_3 x_3 + \ldots + a_k x_k + U$$

where Y = number of trips for specified purpose p

$a_1 \ldots a_k$ parameters fixing a unique linear function

$x_1 \ldots x_k$ zonal planning input factors (the independent variables)

U is a disturbance term.

The principle of regression analysis is that the coefficients (i.e. $a_1 \ldots a_k$) of the equation should be so calculated that deviation of individual observations for each zone, from the estimated line, when squared and summed should be as small as possible and is known as the 'principle of least squares'. The goodness of fit of a regression equation is measured by the *correlation coefficient*. Standard statistical formulae[10] can be developed to calculate correlation coefficients and in general the square of the correlation coefficient measures the percentage of the variations in the dependent variable that can be explained by changes in the independent variables.

When making preliminary investigations into the relationship between trip-making and the urban environment, it is useful to compute correlation coefficients between trip-making and separate independent variables. The result of a typical computation for trip generation is shown in Table III.3. From this matrix some appreciation of the pattern of linear relationships between pairs of variables may be obtained.

It can be seen that for all types of trip the dependent variable is highly correlated with the number of cars owned per person as would be expected. Rateable value of the household, being

TABLE III.3 **Matrix of linear correlation coefficients for numbers of trips generated per person by motor vehicle and various independent variables.**

Dependent variable/Independent variable	All home-based trips	Home-based work trips	Home-based business trips	Home-based shopping trips	Home-based social and recreational trips
Number of cars owned per person	0·86	0·71	0·79	0·71	0·37
Rateable value per household	0·80	0·73	0·75	0·61	0·34
Residential density	−0·59	−0·76	−0·52	−0·52	−0·15
Travel time to town centre	0·49	0·68	0·39	0·34	−0·03
Average household size	0·17	0·41	0·02	0·02	−0·03
Proportion of population of school age	0·30	0·50	0·16	0·21	−0·01
Proportion of persons employed	−0·30	−0·54	−0·32	−0·22	−0·18

Source: Road Research Laboratory, Studies of Travel in Gloucester, Northampton and Reading, RRL Report, LR 141, 1968.

a pseudo-measure of income, has a strong positive effect on the number of trips generated. A negative correlation with residential density is also significant. The travel time by car to the town centre appears in this study to affect the trip rate for most types of trip.

The main purpose of examining the simple *matrix* of correlation coefficients is to find evidence of a number of strong and plausible linear relationships which individually are capable of explaining a large part of the variation in the travel variables. The independent variables which individually make a strong contribution can then be combined and included in a multiple regression analysis. A difficulty arises in this simple treatment when two independent variables are closely related to a dependent variable, and are themselves highly correlated. It is then possible that they do not both need to be used to explain the variation in the dependent variable. Whether one or other of the independent variables can be dropped or whether they both jointly contribute in influencing the dependent variable can be decided by a stepwise multiple regression technique[11] involving the calculation of several multiple correlation coefficients.

A number of general criteria[12] for evaluating trip generation models can then be applied to the results of the regression analysis. First, the model should have *accuracy*. A model is considered to be more likely to give correct forecasts of future traffic if it can recreate the existing volume of travel correctly. Next, the model should have validity. Each equation should express a reasonable relationship, preferably a direct causal relationship, between dependent and independent variables. The third criterion put forward is simplicity. An equation should be simple both in the logic of the relationship it expresses and in the statistical concepts it employs. Another criterion is sharpness, i.e. an equation is said to be sharp if it is sensitive to the effect of alternative explanatory variables and to changes throughout the whole numerical range of independent variables. The final criterion is that of constancy (the extent to which the regression coefficients will remain constant through time), and it is the most critical if the model is to be used for forecasting. The crucial question is, will the relationships established today hold in the future?

The choice of dependent variables will be influenced by the

position of the modal split process in the transport model. In the early transportation studies modal choice was computed at the trip generation stage, that is to say, the dependent variables were of the form home-based trips to work by car, home-based trips to work by bus, etc., thus incorporating modal choice into the trip generation equation. In more recent studies modal

TABLE III.4 Work purpose trip generation equations from several studies.

Study area	Equation	R^2
London (1970)	$Y^* = 1 \cdot 153 LF + 0 \cdot 017C - 0 \cdot 0004 LF \cdot I$	—
Northampton (1968)	$Y = 2 \cdot 483 LF + 210 \cdot 1$	0·953
Thurrock (1969)	$Y = 0 \cdot 91 I + 0 \cdot 77 H - 33 \cdot 7$	—
Cardiff	$Y = 0 \cdot 097 P - 351 H + 0 \cdot 773 LF + 0 \cdot 504 C - 43 \cdot 6$	—
Toronto (1964)	$Y = 0 \cdot 135 P + 0 \cdot 145 DU - 0 \cdot 253 C$	0·91

* Generations from car-owning households only,

where Y = Trip generations for work by all modes
P = Population of generating zone
DU = Dwelling units in zone
C = Cars owned in zone
LF = Number of employed residents in zone
I = Income in zone
H = Households in zone

Sources: Greater London Council, Research Memorandum.
Road Research Laboratory, Studies in Travel in Gloucester, Northampton, and Reading, RRL Report, LR 141, 1968.
Essex County Council, The application of regression analysis to the construction of a trip end model, 1969.
Buchanan, Colin and Partners in association with W. S. Atkins, Cardiff Development and Transportation Study, Main Study Report, Supplementary Technical Volume No. 5.
Metropolitan Toronto and Region Transportation Study, 1964.

split has often been included after trip distribution. In these cases trip generation equations are more general including trips by all modes of travel.

A list of some independent variables found significant in trip generation and attraction equations was given in Table III.2, but it should be emphasised that not all of these variables have been found significant in any one study.

In Table III.4 the regression equations, together with the multiple correlation coefficients obtained in a number of studies are quoted. The fact that so many different equations have been derived is somewhat disturbing, because it is not only coefficients that are different from one study to another but also the variables. It is impossible to account for all these variations and hence to recommend one particular set of equations to the reader. Inevitably some differences occur from the adoption of different definitions. For example, one of the more obvious reasons why different equations have been computed is the definition of a trip. Most studies concern themselves only with mechanised vehicle trips. Clearly, high-density situations where more trips are made by walking may have lower trip rates and so use different variables to low-density areas. One further complication has been the split between internal and external trips which are usually forecast separately. Zones closer to the external boundary will have fewer internal trips and more external trips than zones nearer the centre of the study area.

If *multiple regression analysis* is to be used to calibrate trip generation equations, then all of the independent variables found significant in previous studies should at first be included. Variables which are found to be contributing little explanation in the variation of the dependent variable can then be excluded and the resulting equations considered appropriate to the study area.

Equations for trip attractions may also be developed by using multiple regression analysis and some typical equations are included in Table III.5. A pattern of plausible relationships is usually evident and in some cases such a strong relationship is shown with one independent variable that this single variable is sufficient to explain the variation in the number of trips attracted to zones.

2. (ix) *Category analysis*

One of the great disadvantages with regression techniques is that the coefficients are established by way of a cross-sectional study, i.e. the data, and therefore the relationships, are established at a particular time. These coefficients are then assumed to remain constant over the period for which a forecast is made. It is also necessary to assume that a smooth function applies to each relationship, whereas for certain variables such as household size a 'stepped' function may at times be more applicable.

TABLE III.5 Work purpose trip attraction equations from several studies.

Study area	Equation	R^2
London (1970)	$Y = 2 \cdot 424 E_R + 0 \cdot 851 (M - E_S) + 2 \cdot 020 (W - E_S)$ $+ 0 \cdot 524 (N - E_S) + 1 \cdot 450 E_S + 0 \cdot 820$	—
Northampton (1968)	$Y = 2 \cdot 820 E + 9 \cdot 716 E_{PB} - 1 \cdot 970 E_{HS} + 3 \cdot 2$	0·989
Thurrock (1968)	$Y = 0 \cdot 88 E + 0 \cdot 90 E_R + 133 \cdot 0$	—
Toronto (1964)	$Y = 0 \cdot 013 P + 0 \cdot 349 M + 0 \cdot 158 E_R + 0 \cdot 107 E_S$ $+ 0 \cdot 436 N$	0·93

where
Y = Trip attractions for work by all modes
E = Total employment in attracting zone
E_R = Retail employment
E_{PB} = Employment in public buildings
E_{HS} = Employment in health services
P = Population
M = Manufacturing employment
E_S = Service employment
N = Other employment
W = Wholesaling employment

Sources: As for Table III.4.

In marked contrast to the multiple regression method a recent approach developed by Wootton and Pick[13] assumes that only three factors are of any real importance in affecting the amount of travel a household generates. The method is further based on the assumption that a number of ranges within each variable can be established in such a way that all households can be described by a limited number of categories of household. A trip rate is then assumed for each category of household.

Analysis has shown that the three variables which together give the greatest explanation of trip generation are car-ownership, household structure and income. In the case of car-ownership, Oi and Shuldiner[14] attempted to determine the relationship between the number of trips generated by a household and the number of cars the household owned. It was found that families owning one car generated 2·2 more trips than a non-car-owning household. However, the addition of a second and third car only produced approximately one more trip per household. Wootton and Pick's assumption of three ranges of car-ownership of none, one, or more than one therefore appears to be sufficient.

In multiple regression analysis the effect of the variable

household size and structure was unimportant because data
was used on a zonal basis and the variation in average household size from one zone to another would be quite small.
However, if trip generation is to be computed with the household as the basic unit, then clearly we must examine how both
the size and structure of a household influences the amount of
travel generated. Oi and Shuldiner considered only the size of
household, whereas Wootton and Pick have in addition considered the number of resident employed persons. The results
of Oi and Shuldiner's study are shown in Table III.6. As we

**TABLE III.6 Mean number of total trips per household classified by
household size.**

Number of persons per household	Average household size	Number of trips per household
1 and 2	1·76	4·00
3	3·00	6·93
4	4·00	7·91
5 or more	5·83	9·55
Total	3·38	6·64

Source: Oi W. Y. and P. W. Shuldiner, *An analysis of urban travel demands*, Northwestern University Press, 1962.

would expect, the mean number of trips per household increases
proportionately less as the household size is increased. Oi and
Shuldiner then went a stage further to isolate the effect of
household size from the other effects of income, car-ownership
and distance from the *CBD* and concluded that household size
had an independent influence on the number of trips generated.
Wootton and Pick, when defining their categories of household
size, also considered the number of employed residents to be
important. They defined six categories of household structure,
ranging from the smallest with no employed residents and one
non-employed adult to the largest with two or more employed
residents and two or more non-employed adults.

The importance of income on consumer demands for all
commodities is well known, and the influence of income on
travel demand is no exception. Early studies did not include
income as an independent variable in trip generation analysis
because it was believed the variables car-ownership and
distance from the CBD (both of which are found to have high

correlation with income) entirely explained the influence of income. Again Oi and Shuldiner attempted to isolate the influence of income, and although the sample was very small, it did appear that income exerts some particular influence on trip generation rates when the other independent variables are kept constant. Wootton and Pick selected six categories of income, which, together with three categories of car-ownership and six categories of household structure defined a total of one hundred and eight household classifications. With the use of data from two studies in England, a trip rate for different trip purposes was then associated with each household classification. Good agreement was found when each household classification trip rate from the two studies was compared.

It is possible to apply the results of Wootton and Pick's study in any urban area direct from the 1966 sample census data without a further large-scale home interview. The following information[15] from the census is required for each zone.

1. Number of people
2. Number of households
3. Number employed
4. Number of cars
5. School attendance.

Standard relationships are then assumed to give the number of households falling into each household category. The trip rates by household category found from previous home-interview studies are accepted, usually subject to a small sample household study to check that the trip rates by category in the area being considered are similar to those found in earlier studies. This can lead to considerable savings in both the collection and processing of home interview data. It is, however, necessary from time to time to carry out a larger home interview study, preferably on a national basis, to form a basis of trip rate information for local studies.

Category analysis has two other advantages over regression equations. The computational process is much simpler than that required for multiple regression analysis. The forecasts should also be more accurate in that they assume the trips generated by individual households increase in a stepwise fashion as they own more cars or an additional resident becomes

employed. The trip rates for these individuals are then aggregated to obtain zonal travel predictions. Clearly this is a closer
simulation of household travel behaviour than predicting travel
on the basis of zonal average household characteristics.

A form of category analysis can also be used for trip attraction
analysis when information such as employment by standard
industrial classification, possibly categorised by size of establishment, is required.

2. (x) *Mode availability*

Perhaps one of the greatest deficiencies in trip generation studies
to date has been the way in which the availability of alternative
modes of transport has been treated. Clearly a person can only
make a trip by car, even in a car-owning household, if the
car is available to him at the time he wishes to make the
trip.

Some studies[16] have attempted to overcome this problem by
making separate trip generation analyses for car-owning and
non-car-owning households, but this does not provide a true
picture of mode availability. A further improvement could be
made in trip generation models by disaggregating the trip
generation dependent variables into categories of *modal opportunity groups*. The groupings might be as follows:

1. Individuals who have only public transport available
2. Individuals who have public and private transport
   available
3. Individuals who have only private transport available.

There is no reason why this factor should not be included in
either multiple regression equations or category analysis. It
would, however, be necessary to devise a more detailed household interview questionnaire to provide the basic information
on mode availability to different members of the household at
different times of the day and for different trip purposes. If,
however, the two factors of trip purpose (with, say, six categories) and model opportunity group (with three categories)
are incorporated with the three previously discussed variables
influencing the trip rate, a total of about 400 classifications

would result. With this large number of classifications a problem arises of obtaining enough data to compute a reliable figure for each cell. Even in the London Traffic Survey where interviews took place in 50,000 households, it is apparent that difficulties would arise when an attempt was made to associate a trip rate with each cell. This problem can, however, be solved in any one particular element by appropriate statistical techniques designed to smooth out random variations.

2. (xi) *Transport accessibility*

All trip generation and attraction rates are measured at a given instant of time and in so doing we are bound to be measuring, either explicitly or implicitly, the effect of *accessibility*. Clearly the number of trips made by each mode is affected by the availability and level of service offered by each of the competing modes, and these factors can be considered in a modal split model. But the total number of trips by all modes from any zone will also be influenced by the ease of travel to and from that zone, and this total may be reduced by factors such as road congestion.

One of the main difficulties with both category and regression analysis is that it is assumed that the observed trip rate for a household is a measure of the total demand for travel by the residents of that household. In fact the observed trip pattern also reflects supply factors such as the level of service provided by various modes. It is quite clear that zonal accessibility is therefore a most important factor as yet not adequately incorporated into trip generation models. This is discussed in more detail in the later sections on congestion and the transport model.

3. TRIP DISTRIBUTION

3. (i) *Introduction*

Trip distribution is a part of the transport model that has received much research attention, particularly in the early transportation studies. Indeed, many observations on patterns of travel were made by sociologists and economists well before transportation studies on a large scale were attempted. For example, Reilly,[17] in his study of the relative attractions of moderately sized American towns as shopping centres, came to the conclusion that attractive power could be measured by the town's population divided by the square of the distance from the area from which the trip was made. Losch,[18] a German economist, thought that distance raised to the power of 1·6 gave a better measure than the power of 2. The trip distribution models which are now used, though more sophisticated, owe their origins to some of this early research.[19]

Before discussing the various distribution models available, it is useful to review the function of trip distribution in the context of the transport model. The previous section of this chapter has looked at trip generation and the development of models relating trip ends to planning parameters. The outcome of the trip generation stage was the production of trip ends by purpose and perhaps by mode. It is the function of trip distribution to calculate the number of trips between one zone and another, given the previously determined numbers of trip ends in each zone together with further information on the transport facilities available between these zones. For example, given that in zone i, g_i trip ends are generated and that in zone j, a_j trip ends are attracted, it is the purpose of the trip distribution model to determine the number of trips (t_{ij}) which would go from zone i to zone j. That is, the trip distribution model calculates the proportion of the trip ends generated in zone i which would travel between i and j and so take up a certain proportion of the available attractions in zone j.

In early studies, the number of zones was kept comparatively small, to permit manual computation. Present-day studies using computers can use many more zones representing a considerable number of different possible trips. For example, an area containing n zones would have n^2 possible zone-to-zone movements. These movements can be most easily described in the form of a matrix of trips where the sums of individual rows and columns of trips are the total numbers of origins g_i at zone i and destinations a_j in zone j. For an area containing n zones, a *trip matrix* would look as follows:

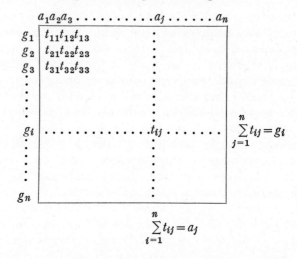

The outcome of the trip distribution stage is therefore the production of various trip matrices, where each cell in the matrix represents the trips between two zones.

There are certain underlying principles common to all distribution models. These principles are that travel between any two points will rise with an increase in demand for travel from the first point, or with an increase in the opportunities derived from travel to the second, and will decrease as the difficulty of reaching that point increases. Stated more formally, the number of trips from an origin zone i to a destination zone j (t_{ij}) is directly proportional to the generation of trips in zone i (g_i) and to the attraction of the destination for such trips (a_j). Further, t_{ij} is inversely proportional to some function of the travel resistance between the two zones $f(c_{ij})$. Written as a mathematical expression:

$$t_{i-j} = g_i \times a_j \times f(c_{ij}) \times k$$

where t_{i-j} = number of one-way trips from origin zone i to destination zone j

g_i = number of trips generated in zone i

a_j = some measure of the attraction of zone j

$f(c_{ij})$ = some measure of the resistance of travel from zone i to j

k = constant

There are two basic methods of trip distribution from which all other methods have been developed; these are growth factor methods and synthetic models.

3. (ii) *Growth factor methods*

The early traffic engineering studies relied upon large-scale origin and destination studies in an attempt to give estimates of all observed interzonal movements. This information was usually collected using roadside survey techniques. Household interview techniques were later used, but required large sample sizes in order to obtain reliable data of all zone-to-zone movements. The base-year information was used for immediate design purposes and growth factors were used to estimate future flows. *Growth factor* models simply grossed up observed base-year interzonal flows to give future design-year flows.

Stated more formally:

$$t^f_{i-j} = t^o_{i-j} \times E$$

where t^f_{i-j} = future design-year flows from zone i to zone j
t^o_{i-j} = observed flows from zone i to zone j
E = expansion factor

Although growth factor techniques are not now generally used in urban transportation planning, they are still used in certain special circumstances, for example, the treatment of external trips. A brief discussion of growth factor methods also helps outline points of general interest in all distribution models.

Growth factor models can be divided into four types of model, uniform factor, average factor, Fratar and Detroit methods. The uniform factor method was the earliest and simplest method of projecting travel patterns and computes a single growth factor for the entire urban area. The expansion factor E was calculated by dividing the total number of projected trip ends by the existing trip ends. All existing interzonal flows were then multiplied by this factor to give estimates of future interzonal flows.

$$t^f_{i-j} = t^o_{i-j} \times E$$

where t^f_{i-j} = traffic flows in the future zone i to zone j
t^o_{i-j} = traffic flows in the base-year zone i to zone j
E = expansion factor

This method can lead to gross error when significant changes take place in the distribution of population, commerce and industry. Trips between already intensively developed zones are underestimated while the predicted flows associated with the less intensively developed zones are too low. For example, waste land in the base year would generate very few trips. Such areas, when developed, would generate many more trips. Use of the base-year flows and a common growth factor would give a very poor forecast of future trips from such areas. For this reason the uniform factor method is now rarely, if ever, used.

In the average factor method, existing interzonal flows t^o_{i-j} are multiplied by a growth factor based on growth factors calculated separately for both ends of the trip. The most obvious estimate of this growth factor is the average growth associated with both origin and destination zone. The zonal growth factors are again calculated using projected trip ends. Future trips are therefore given by the following formula:

$$t^f_{i-j} = t^o_{i-j}\tfrac{1}{2}(E_i + E_j) \qquad E_i = \frac{O^f_i}{O^o_i} \qquad E_j = \frac{D^f_j}{D^o_j}$$

where O^f_i = future origins zone i
$\quad O^o_i$ = base-year origins zone i
$\quad D^f_j$ = future destinations zone j
$\quad D^o_j$ = base-year destinations zone j

After all interzonal flows have been calculated, that is, the whole trip matrix completed, the sums of the trips from zones i will probably not agree with the projected trip ends in zone i, nor will the sums of trips to zone j agree with projected trip ends in zone j. That is:

$$\sum_{j=1}^{n} t^f_{i-j} \text{ will not equal } O^f_i$$

$$\sum_{i=1}^{n} t^f_{i-j} \text{ will not equal } D^f_j$$

To overcome this discrepancy, an iterative process, based on revised interzonal growth factors, must be used. That is, new values of t_{ij} must be calculated from:

$$tf'_{i-j} = tf_{i-j} \times E'_{i-j}$$

$$E'_{i-j} = \frac{1}{2} \left\{ \frac{Of_i}{\sum\limits_{j=1}^{n} tf_{i-j}} + \frac{Df_j}{\sum\limits_{i=1}^{n} tf_{i-j}} \right\}$$

Iteration is usually continued until balance to within a given limit, say plus or minus 1%, is achieved. That is:

$$\frac{Of_i}{\sum\limits_{j=1}^{n} tf_{i-j}} = 1 \pm 1\%$$

$$\frac{Df_j}{\sum\limits_{i=1}^{n} tf_{i-j}} = 1 \pm 1\%$$

Iteration, or the balancing of sums of rows and columns of the trip matrix with observed or projected trip ends, is a procedure common to all distribution models and can be regarded as an entirely arbitrary process; different trip matrices can be produced, depending upon what balancing procedure is adopted. For example, in certain cases slightly different trip matrices can result, depending upon the order of the iteration techniques. Although the difference is not great, balancing of trip ends is not a behavioural technique in that it can obviously represent some function of personal trip-making. It is simply a technique to make the trip matrix fit observed information on trip ends.

Use of iteration was first introduced in traffic forecasting by T. J. Fratar[20] in a method of trip distribution called the Fratar expansion method which overcomes some of the disadvantages of the uniform factor and average factor methods. In the Fratar method, it is first assumed that any trip movement (t_{i-j}) from zone i will increase in proportion with the increase in trip ends at i, namely by $\frac{Of_i}{O^o_i}$. Next it is assumed that the distribution of future trips from i will be proportional to the base-year distribution t_{i-j}, modified by the growth factor of the zone to which these trips are attracted. This multiplication of growth factors by the base-year flow would give a total number of future trips out of zone i greatly in excess of the actual forecast number of trip origins. Therefore the trip interchange has to be normalised by the ratio of the sum of all base-year trips from zone i $\left(\sum\limits_{k=i}^{n} t^o{}_{i-k} \right)$ to the sum of each trip from zone i ($t^o{}_{i-k}$) multiplied by its own growth factor $\dfrac{D^f{}_k}{D^o{}_k}$, namely $\sum\limits_{k=i}^{n} t_{ik}\dfrac{D^f{}_k}{D^o{}_k}$. The formula then becomes:

$$tf_{i-j} = t^o{}_{i-j} \times \frac{O^f{}_i}{O^o{}_i} \times \frac{D^f{}_j}{D^o{}_j} \times \frac{\sum\limits_{k=i}^{n} t^o{}_{i-k}}{\sum\limits_{k=i}^{n} t^o{}_{i-k}\dfrac{D^f{}_k}{D^o{}_k}}$$

The following simple examples will illustrate the method. Consider an origin zone with twelve trips numbering 2, 4 and 6, to three destinations, j, k, l. Assume that the growth in trips from i is twice that of the base year, namely twenty-four trips, and that the growth factors of j,k and l are 3, 3 and 5 respectively, then the future flows from i to j,k and l are as follows:

$$tf_{i-j} = 2 \times 2 \times 3 \times \frac{12}{2 \times 3 + 4 \times 3 + 6 \times 5} = 3$$

$$tf_{i-k} = 4 \times 2 \times 3 \times \frac{12}{48} = 6$$

$$tf_{i-l} = 6 \times 2 \times 5 \times \frac{12}{48} = 15$$

If it is assumed that the number of trips from i to j equals those from j to i, then the equation becomes:

$$tf_{ij} = t^o{}_{ij} \times \frac{tf_i}{t^o{}_i} \times \frac{tf_j}{t^o{}_j} \times \left(\frac{L_i + L_j}{2} \right)$$

where $L_i = \dfrac{\sum\limits_{k=i}^{n} t^o{}_{ik}}{\sum\limits_{k=i}^{n} t^o{}_{ik} \times \dfrac{D^f{}_k}{D^o{}_k}}$

L_i can be considered the reciprocal of the average attracting force of all other zones on zone i and as such has been called the location factor. The form of this equation can be seen to conform more nearly to the propositions made at the beginning of this section on distribution models. That is to say, future travel tf_{ij} is proportional to the growth in generation $\dfrac{tf_i}{t^o_i}$ proportional to the growth in attraction $\dfrac{tf_j}{t^o_j}$ and inversely proportional to travel resistance; travel resistance in this case being interpreted as $\frac{1}{2}(L_i + L_j) \times t^o_{ij}$, which is a direct function of the base-year movement. As such the function cannot be used for forecasting when it is necessary to take into account changes in travel resistance brought about by changes to the transport networks.

The Detroit method[21] is a simplification of the Fratar method, and consequently reduces computer operations. Again, this method assumes that the number of trips from zone i will increase proportionally with $\dfrac{tf_i}{t^o_i}$ and will be attracted to zone j in proportion to $\dfrac{tf_j}{t^o_j}$ but modified by an overall growth factor for the area. Hence the equation may be written, again assuming $t_{i-j} = t_{j-i}$:

$$tf_{ij} = t^o_{ij} \times \frac{tf_i}{t^o_i} \times \frac{tf_j}{t^o_j} \times \frac{T^o}{T^f}$$

where $T^o =$ total base-year trip ends
$T^f =$ total design-year trip ends

In the use of growth factor methods it was common practice to assume that trips from i to j were equal, over a twenty-four-hour day, to those from j to i, that is $t_{i-j} = t_{j-i}$, and that origins equalled destinations in each zone over the twenty-four-hour day, thus simplifying the model and the computational process. That is, only one matrix, t_{ij}, was calculated as opposed to two, t_{i-j} and t_{j-i}. It was assumed that this operation would not seriously affect the projected travel patterns. Although, of course, this simplifies computation, it does mean that a non-directional matrix is produced, that is, that t_{ij} represents both trips originated from i and destined to j and those originated at j and destined to i. If directional flows were required, such as those in each direction in the peak hour, then separate origin-destination matrices were calculated, or assumptions made of the proportion of the non-directional flow t_{ij} that takes place in each direction during the peak hour.

Growth factor methods are now rarely used. One of the main disadvantages was that large-scale origin–destination studies with high sampling sizes were required in order to estimate the smaller zone-to-zone movements. Another fault was that high expansion factors were required for zones where substantial new development takes place. In this case any error in the original data collected on specific zone-to-zone movements was magnified in the forecasting process.

A fundamental fault with all growth factor methods is that they imply that the future resistance to travel will remain constant, that is, they do not attempt to measure the resistance function. The construction of a motorway system will radically change travel behaviour, but unfortunately growth factor methods of distribution do not incorporate changes in travel demand, brought about by network changes. By contrast, synthetic models attempt to relate trip behaviour to the generation and attraction of trips and the network resistance to travel.

3. (iii) *Synthetic models (gravity models)*[22, 23]

This group of models has been termed synthetic because existing travel data are analysed in order to set up relationships between trips and measures of attraction, generation and travel resistance. The very important advantage of synthesis is that not only can such a model be used to predict future trips but it can also synthesise the base-year flows without having to survey every individual cell in the trip matrix. The cost of data collection is thus considerably reduced. As a result, synthetic models have now largely replaced growth factor methods of distribution.

Within this group there are essentially two types of model, namely gravity models and *opportunity models*. Gravity models were the first models used after growth factor methods and have been extensively developed. In one form or another they are presently the conventional distribution models. They had their origin in sociological studies, and may be stated simply by:

$$t_{ij} = k a_j g_i f(c_{ij})$$

where a_j = attraction of zone j

g_i = generation of trips in zone i

$f(c_{ij})$ = travel resistance function

k = constant

The early studies measured the generation and attraction components in terms of respective zonal populations and employment. The resistance function was assumed to be related to an inverse function of distance, thus giving a similar relationship to that proposed by Newton in his law of gravitational attraction. The equation for trip distribution can be written:

$$t_{ij} = k \frac{P_i E_j}{d^n}$$

The sector trip data from the London Traffic Survey in 1962, summarised in Table III.7, can be used to demonstrate

TABLE III.7   London Traffic Survey sector trip data.

Sector	Car and cycle driver non-work generations	Car and cycle driver trips to central area	Distance of sector centroid from central area (miles)	Trips to Central area divided by total generation from sector %
0	428,038	21,099	11	4·9
1	313,365	19,730	11	6·3
2	81,962	2,279	16	2·8
3	319,520	10,903	11	3·4
4	306,426	92,492	3	30·2
5 6	Central area			
7	308,574	76,673	5	24·9
8	199,723	8,910	14	4·5
9	435,561	34,852	12	8·0

the validity of this relationship. It will be seen that trips to the central area from those sectors at similar distance from the central area are approximately proportional to the generations in the sector. Similarly, if trips from each sector to the central area are divided by the number of generations in that sector and this value is plotted against the log of distance to the central area, an approximate straight line is formed, the slope of which is the power of the distance in the resistance function. This latter example is shown in Figure III.1.

In the early studies[24] it was found that the power needed in the resistance function was not the same for all areas. It was also found that even within these areas the power was not constant for all types of trip. This was one reason for considering

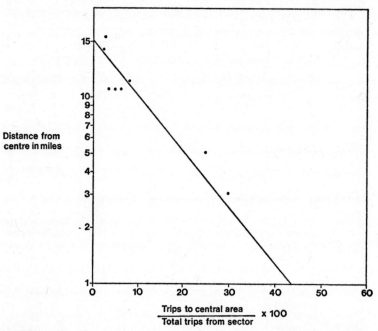

FIGURE III.1 **Effect of distance from the centre of London on trip distribution.**

trips separately according to their purpose, a concept which is now used extensively throughout all phases of the transport model.

As part of the development of the gravity model method of distribution, generations and attractions were introduced to replace origins and destinations. The definition of a generation is the home end (origin or destination) of a home-based trip or the origin of a non-home-based trip. Similarly, an attraction has been defined as the non-home end of a home-based trip, and the destination end of a non-home-based trip. It was

shown in the section on trip generation that the use of attraction
and generation could improve the accuracy of the trip end
model because of the close relationship between generation and
household characteristics and between attractions and land-use
parameters. It has also been found that the use of attractions
and generations in the gravity model gives a better fit with
observed data than simply using origins and destinations. The
use of these definitions also enable one non-directional matrix
to be estimated as opposed to two directional ones. Previously
two separate directional origin-to-destination trip matrices
were required to describe the journey from home to work and
the return journey from work to home. By using the concept of
attractions and generations only one trip matrix is required, a
non-directional matrix of generations (always the home end)
to attractions (always the work end). Should directional
matrices be required these can be calculated using the ratio of
the generation-to-attraction movement to the total two-way
movement from the survey trip matrices.

It also became clear in these early studies that empirical
formulation of the resistance function simply using some
inverse power of distance or time was inadequate in that the
synthetic matrices produced were still not reasonable repre-
sentations of observed trip matrices. It therefore became
common practice simply to calibrate the resistance function
directly against survey data. In the process, the resistance function became known as the distribution function and values of
this function became known as distribution rates or friction
factors.

Again, writing the gravity model equation: $t_{ij} = k a_j g_i R(c_{ij})$
where $R(c_{ij})$ is identical to the resistance function, though now
called a distribution function. Initial values of the function
$R(c_{ij})$ may be found by plotting the value of each trip interchange (t_{ij}) divided by its respective attractions (a_j) and
generations (g_i) against the respective zone-to-zone travel time
(c_{ij}). That is, by plotting values of $\dfrac{t_{ij}}{a_j g_i}$ against their respective
trip lengths (c_{ij}), the actual distribution function is obtained.
Trip distribution is then computed with these values $R(c_{ij})$, as
the distribution function, to give a synthetic trip matrix.

It is then necessary to check this synthetic matrix to see if it represents adequately the observed trip matrix. It has been common practice to do this by calculating from the synthetic matrix a synthetic trip length distribution. This synthetic trip length frequency distribution can then be compared with the observed trip length frequency distribution. If the trip length distributions do not compare well, new values $R^1(c_{ij})$ are used to calculate a new trip matrix, from which another synthetic trip length frequency distribution is plotted and compared with the observed. The process of trial and adjustments is continued until synthetic and observed trip length frequency distributions agree to within allowable limits. Because calibrating[25] a gravity model is such an important part of the quantitative forecasting process a simple example is included as Appendix A.

The first calibrated gravity models assumed that the distribution function was constant over the whole survey area, that is, that the distribution function could be applied equally to all zones. Although this assumption may well be reasonable for medium-size towns with a population of 100,000 or less, the assumption can break down in larger cities, where it has been found that an area-wide distribution may give poor representation of individual zone-to-zone movement. Even where the calibration procedure has been accurately completed on an area-wide basis, individual zone-to-zone movements may not necessarily agree with observed data. In practice, several very different matrices could be constructed having similar trip length distributions, total hours of travel and average trip length. To overcome this difficulty the gravity model has been modified by the inclusion of specific zone-to-zone adjustment factors in the larger transportation studies. This form of calibration is necessarily more laborious. First, area-wide distribution functions are synthesised by purpose, against base-year data, and adjusted to match the study area trip length distribution, person-hours of travel and average trip lengths. The next step is to estimate by trial and error the specific zone factors to make synthesised zone-to-zone movements more closely represent observed movements.

To do this on a zone-to-zone basis would of course be extremely laborious and so it has been common practice to develop factors for agglomerated zones or sectors. The trip matrix produced from the calibrated gravity model is compared, manually, with the survey matrix at a sector level. Then, by inspection, factors can be calculated to make both the observed and the calculated matrices match. The whole process of calibration is then repeated with these additional sector-to-sector travel factors. It has been suggested that these additional sector-to-sector factors can be related to socio-economic factors. However, the whole process is essentially arbitrary and does not directly reflect any known sociological phenomena. It is simply a further device for calibration.

In several of the larger transportation studies it has been found that central areas attracted trips from longer distances than did outlying zones, that is, different distribution functions might be applicable to each attracting zone or groups of attracting zones. An alternative method of calibration involves the use of numerous distribution functions for different areas of attraction. In this case the gravity model has been termed 'an interactance model'.[26]

In the London Traffic Survey[27] distribution functions were investigated over the whole of the survey area. The area was divided up into a number of areas, each area having similar densities of trip attractions per square mile. Plotting the observed distribution functions from each of the areas, they were found to approximate to the general equation:

$$F_k(c_{ij}) = ae^{-b_k c_{ij}} \times c_{ij}^{-n}$$

where b and n are specific constants associated with attracting area k; i varies throughout the survey area, and j lies within area k.

In practice, while it has been found by other research workers that this distribution function gives a more accurate description of travel than previous functions, it is often sufficient to include only the first term $(ae^{-bc_{ij}})$. The equation can then be rewritten:

$$F_k(c_{ij}) = ae^{-bc_{ij}}$$

or re-written as:

$$\text{Log}_e F_k(c_{ij}) = A - B(c_{ij})$$

In this equation, the important influencing factor is the constant B. A statistical investigation of this constant showed which groups of areas one particular distribution function would satisfy. For example, in the LTS, three separate areas (i.e. three distribution functions) were used, to estimate the trip distribution factor for work journeys. As in the previous calibrated gravity models, the interactance model distribution functions have to be calibrated for each of the selected attracting areas, subject to the criteria of average trip length and synthetic distribution and hours of travel agreeing with the observed data.

Calibration of the gravity model with sector-to-sector coefficients or the interactance model are rather complex procedures. Nevertheless, with both models, standard practices have been established so that satisfactory calibration can be made according to well-defined routines.

3. (iv) *Synthetic models: opportunity models*

One of the main criticisms that has been raised against the gravity model is that it does not directly reflect any particular pattern of individual behaviour. The search for some model more closely representing the selection process a person may follow before making a trip has led to the formulation of opportunity models based on the use of probability theory. An opportunity model may be simply described as follows: if there are g_i trip origins in zone i and t_{ij} trips from zone i to zone j, then any trip from zone i will have a certain probability of ending in zone j, which may be represented as $Pr(S_j)$. Trip distribution may be expressed as:

$$t_{ij} = g_i Pr(S_j)$$

Two different formulations for the probability function have been put forward, namely, the intervening opportunity model[28] and the competing opportunity model.[29]

The intervening opportunity model uses a probability concept which requires a trip to remain as short as possible becoming longer only as suitable destinations cannot be found at shorter distances. Consider an individual trip from zone i. It is first assumed that the likelihood of any attraction being suitable is a constant (L). All opportunities or destinations where the journey may end are then considered in order of travel time away from the zone of origin. The probability of the traveller accepting a particular destination $(P(S_j))$ in zone j will decrease the further j is away from the zone of origin. This probability is given by the expression

$$P(S_j) = e^{-LD} - e^{-L(D+D_j)}$$

where D = sum of attractions up to the zone before j
D_j = attractions in zone j

Thus, if there are G_i generations in zone i, the trip interchange between zones i and j is given by

$$T_{ij} = G_i(e^{-LD} - e^{-L(D+D_j)})$$

Most studies which have used the intervening opportunity model have stratified trips into long residential, long nonresidential, and short trips and L values have been computed for these categories. These L values have then been used to calculate a synthetic matrix from which the trip length distribution, average trip length and total person-hours of travel could be compared with those for the observed trip matrix. The forecasts have then been adjusted in the same way as in the gravity model until calibration has been satisfactorily carried out.

This procedure has been further sophisticated in the Pittsburgh Area Transportation Study[30] by developing distinct L values for short and long trips for each zone of origin.

A distinct disadvantage of the intervening opportunity model is that when used to forecast future trip interchanges, a future L value has to be estimated. It is only to be expected that, as more and more opportunities are available, the likelihood of being satisfied by any one attraction will fall. For example, if the same L value for short trips were retained for the design year, then there would be an increased number of short trips predicted by the model, because the number of opportunities increases in most zones. It is therefore generally assumed in the use of the opportunity model that the proportion of short trips in the future design year will be the same as that observed in the base year. A short L value is then computed which will produce a similar proportion of such trips in the design year as found in the base year.

The long trip L values can be determined by a similar argument. They may be expected to fall with an increase in population and number of trips. The maximum fall that could be expected would be by the ratio of base-year trip to future trips. The best estimate of future L values will lie somewhere between that of the base year and the base-year value multiplied by the ratio of base-year to future trip ends. The arbitrary choice of L factor is somewhat unsatisfactory, because the chosen L value has a crucial effect upon the forecast trip matrix.

In the competing opportunities model it is assumed that the probability that a trip, chosen at random from zone i, will stop in zone j will depend upon the ratio of the trip opportunities in j to the total number of competing opportunities within a given time boundary, including those in zone j.

That is
$$P(S_j) = D_j \bigg/ \sum_{k=1}^{m} D_k$$

where D_j = attractions in zone j

D_k = attractions in zone k

It has been found that in practice to use the the model to synthesise base-year OD patterns, subjective selection of time bands has been necessary. These same time bands are then used in the forecasting of future trip patterns and as such represent a form of calibration that has proved particularly difficult to carry out.

3. (v) *Comparison of alternative models*

It is instructive to compare the models which have been described under the following headings: operation and performance; philosophical concept; and computational ease and expense.

Considering operation and performance first, several studies have been carried out comparing one distribution model with another.[30] Many of these comparisons, however, have suffered either because the forms of the model used were not as developed as they might have been, or because other input data raised doubts on the validity of possible conclusions, or, lastly, from particular prejudice of the user. One of the most carefully carried out comparisons was that by the Bureau of Public

Roads[31] on Washington data. Two household interview surveys had been carried out in 1948 and 1955. Models could be calibrated using the 1948 data. Forecasts were then carried out to see how well the models predicted 1955 conditions. Basic 1955 data on trip ends were used rather than forecast trip ends, thus avoiding errors at the trip generation stage. Four models were tested, Fratar growth factor, gravity model, intervening opportunity and competing opportunity models. Some of the conclusions of this report bear repetition: 'The overall accuracy of the gravity model in base-year simulation and in forecasting ability proved to be slightly better than the accuracy of the intervening opportunity model. This fact must, however, be considered in light of the need for and use of socioeconomic adjustment factors in the gravity model for the work-trip calibration. In effect, more parameters were used in the gravity model calibration.'

With the use of these adjustment factors, the gravity model exhibited less error than the intervening opportunities model when trips by sector to the CBD were examined. However, the opportunity model was better than the unadjusted gravity model. It is not clear whether this is due to the conceptual basis of the models or to the trip-purpose stratifications used.

Due to the fewer parameters used, the intervening opportunities model proved slightly less difficult to calibrate. However, adjustments necessary in future L values reduce this advantage in making the forecasts. Considering all factors, the gravity and intervening opportunity models proved of about equal reliability and utility.

The Fratar growth factor procedure demonstrated a good ability to expand trips correctly for stable areas but showed significant weaknesses in areas undergoing land-use changes. Even by eliminating zones of completely new growth from the OD test data, approximately 10% of the total 1955 trips were lost through the expansion. This 10% amounted to a much more significant portion of the increase in trips between 1948 and 1955. The concentration of error in areas experiencing growth in trips point up the need for supplemental procedures to provide a base-year synthesised trip pattern in such areas. The magnitude of this problem, when examined in the light of the favourable results attained with the gravity and intervening opportunity models, indicates that the use of a synthetic model provides a more direct and efficient approach to trip distribution for growing urban areas.

In this study, it was found impossible to calibrate the competing opportunity model. Various time bands were tried, but no simple procedure could be devised which led to a satisfactory calibration.

The main conclusions of the Washington studies are probably true in general of most comparisons and are perhaps to be expected. The models are being applied to a highly complex situation. Even though individuals conform in their habits to generalised groups of behaviour, the models themselves are no more than approximations. It is not surprising therefore that a perfect simulation of trip behaviour has not been achieved.

Another argument that has been used in support of one model or another is that of philosophical concept. It is suggested that a model which describes human behaviour more closely is the more likely to achieve a better total synthesis. As an hypothesis, this is probably very true. However, when applied to support particular distribution models, this argument too can be fallacious in that while a model can be built which describes one individual's behaviour fairly closely, no one individual conforms in detail to a general pattern. It may be true that people attempt to minimise their travel costs, but the way each traveller estimates travel costs could be a particularly individual characteristic.

It has often been argued that the opportunity models represent the individual's decision process. At the same time it is stated that the gravity model is not a 'behavioural description' but a borrowed relationship which empirically fits observed facts. In fact, a closer examination can show a gravity model to be a special form of the demand model.

Recently, Wilson[32] has described how both opportunity and gravity models may be similarly derived, using a statistical mechanical approach, so that the apparent 'philosophical' preference for the opportunity model is not necessarily too important.

When comparing ease of computation and cost, the answer may depend on the extent to which calibration is taken and the form of model used. It is probably true that there is again very little difference, since all models discussed require calibration, all need iteration to balance rows and columns of the trip matrix and all require the same amount of numerical analysis to determine a value for each cell in the trip matrix.

Numerous other forms of distribution model have been suggested, some of which have been used with a modicum of success. None, however, can be said to be operational in the same sense as gravity models and to a lesser extent the intervening opportunity model.

3. (vi) *Treatment of external and intrazonal trips*

In any transportation study four types of trip requiring different forms of analysis may be studied. These are *interzonal trips* with both trip ends in different zones in the study area; *intrazonal trips* with both trip ends in the same zone; *external trips* with one trip end inside and one trip end outside the study area, and finally through trips with both ends outside the study area. These trips are generally treated in different ways in the distribution process.

The most common assumption concerning intrazonal trips is that the proportion of intrazonal journeys in the design year will be the same as that observed in the base year. Alternatively, some studies have assumed that all trips having an average trip length or time less than a particular value are intrazonal.

In the use of the intervening opportunity model, the more rational assumption has been made that zones which are comparatively well developed, that is, the more mature zones, will have much more stable trip patterns, particularly for short trips, whereas less mature zones obviously will change with increasing development. The assumption is then made that an L value is chosen which will keep the proportion of intrazonal trips at the constant level associated with more mature zones.

Clearly, any treatment of intrazonal trips is not precise. It can be argued, however, that intrazonal trips would be made on transport facilities within the zone and as such would make little use of the link system represented in the synthesised network. Thus intrazonal trips would predominately use the many intrazonal distributor roads, and will thus have little effect upon the design of the more strategic network.

D

All models discussed cater for interzonal trips. However, journeys with one or both ends outside the survey area cannot be represented simply using a synthetic model, because total trip ends are not usually known for external traffic zones. It has been common practice therefore in the large conurbational studies where external and through trips are in fact a small proportion of all trips, to use a growth factor technique to forecast future numbers of trips. These growth factors have been based on changes in population, employment and income *per capita* and have then been adjusted on a subjective basis to take into account increased travel owing to any specific new transport facilities that would substantially reduce journey times for these external trips. Where, however, there are major changes in the regional network, external to the survey area, it would be preferable not to have to use a simple growth factor technique but to forecast these trips using a larger-scale regional model.

3. (vii) *Choice of resistance function*

One point which should be considered is what resistance function should be used in assessing the way in which zones should be ranked away from a zone of origin. Both gravity and opportunity models employ this principle in the measure of travel resistance or the ranking of opportunities. In most transportation studies distribution models have used travel time. However, a better measure would be the total journey cost to the traveller. Cost, or perceived cost, may include both the monetary cost of travel and more subjective factors such as comfort, convenience, and the value placed on passenger time. In all cases zone-to-zone travel resistances are calculated using trip assignment procedures which will be discussed in the next section.

4. ASSIGNMENT

4. (i) *Introduction*

The purpose of the assignment stage of the transport model is to simulate route choice. It can be considered in two parts;

first, determining individual routes through the networks and subsequently loading these trips on to the paths selected. Loading of trips on to a network is a relatively simple task accomplished using normal accounting procedures. Standard programs are available and are therefore not discussed here. Route choice, on the other hand, is a much more difficult task and this will be discussed in greater detail.

It can be assumed that the traveller usually selects his route so as to minimise his travel costs for that journey. These would not necessarily be the real money costs, indeed they are usually less than the real costs, but they are the costs as perceived by the traveller. The basic assumption in all assignment procedures is that all trips have their origins and destinations at zone centroids and that individuals choose a particular route according to various parameters associated with travel costs.

Although perceived costs should ideally be used as the measure of travel resistance on a link they are difficult to use in practice because of the problem of associating values to some elements of the total perceived costs, such as the value placed on different standards of comfort and convenience. Most transportation studies have therefore developed route choice procedures simply using travel time as the measure of travel resistance on each link and at each intersection. This has the advantage of being relatively simple to measure and also appears to be one of the more important variables determining route choice. In addition it has been shown to be an important variable affecting the pattern of trip distribution.

Early studies in small towns decided routings on the basis of the engineer or planner's judgment followed by manual adjustments to fit the loaded flows to existing data. These trial and error procedures may have been satisfactory for very small networks where the number of alternatives for each zone pair was small, but in complex urban networks where the number of alternatives is large a quicker, cheaper method is obviously required. At the time when transportation planners were seeking such a solution, Moore,[33] who was concerned with a similar problem in the field of telecommunications, developed a procedure to solve the problem of routing the direct dialling of long-distance telephone calls. Many traffic assignment programs are based upon what is known as the Moore Algorithm.

4. (ii) *Moore's Algorithm*

It is worth describing this algorithm in some detail and, although shortest travel times are referred to, the method is, of course, applicable to any measure of link and intersection travel resistance. The following example illustrates the shortest route procedure using the network shown in Figure III.2. The problem is to build the minimum time tree for centroid 1.

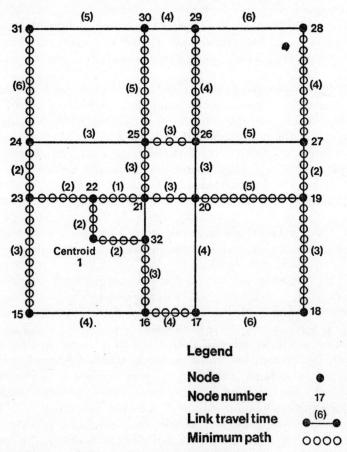

FIGURE III.2 Minimum time path calculation.

Starting at centroid 1, go to each connecting node and record at each node the travel time to it, i.e. $T_{1-22}=2$ and $T_{1-32}=2$. The node closest in time to the centroid (the home node) is considered next. In this example the times to nodes 22 and 32 are equal and the lowest numbered node, 22, is used in this situation. The cumulative time from centroid 1, through node 22, to all nodes directly connected to node 22 is then recorded, i.e. $T_{1-22-21}=3$ and $T_{1-22-23}=4$. Node 32, being the next closest in time to centroid 1, is now considered, i.e. $F_{1-32-21}=4$ and $T_{1-32-16}=5$. It can be seen that two routes have been calculated to node 21, the shorter $1-22-21=3$ is chosen and the other route $1-32-21$ deleted.

We now go to node 21 and find:

$$T_{1-22-21-20}=6$$
$$T_{1-22-21-25}=6$$

Similarly, from node 23

$$T_{1-22-23-15}=7$$
$$T_{1-22-23-24}=6$$

and from node 16

$$T_{1-32-16-15}=9$$
$$T_{1-32-16-17}=9$$

Again two routes have been calculated to node 15 and the shortest $(1-22-23-15=7)$ is chosen. This process is then repeated until all nodes have been reached via the minimum path from centroid 1. Figure III.2 shows the final minimum path trace (often referred to as a minimum time tree) for centroid 1.

A large number of computer programs[34] based on Moore's Algorithm are currently available both to build trees and to make the subsequent assignment of the trip matrix to the various links in the network.

These programs can be used for public transport networks but are best suited to road networks where more uniform operating conditions apply within a link. A considerably improved algorithm for use with public transport networks has recently been developed and will be described later in this section.

4. (iii) *All-or-nothing assignments*

When all the trips for a zone pair have been allocated to the links forming the minimum time path between the two zone centroids and the procedure has been repeated for all zone pairs, then an all-or-nothing assignment is said to have been made.

Experience has in fact shown that the all-or-nothing technique can lead to poor assignments. When two or more links or routes are close together and approximately in the same direction, then one route only has to be marginally quicker than the others to attract all of the trips to it. This sort of error may be partially remedied by sensible interpretation of the flows on each of the links. In some circumstances one may be concerned only with the volume of traffic along a corridor, as distinct from each of the routes forming the corridor, and in this case the all-or-nothing assignment is quite adequate.

It is helpful to examine why all-or-nothing assignments sometimes give poor results. Some of these reasons apply equally to all assignment procedures, others are peculiar to the all-or-nothing assignment.

1. Assignment procedures assume that all trips originate and have destinations at zone centroids. Clearly trips have their ends at points spread over the whole area of the zone and an assumption of this sort produces a poor simulation of the real situation. A further factor coupled with this assumption is that all travel takes place on the designated networks. Errors due to the omission of the less important roads, some of which may carry significant volumes of traffic, may often be important.

2. It has already been suggested that an individual not only considers travel time in selecting a route, more precisely he minimises perceived costs. If time is used as the only parameter, errors in assigned flows will be found because a driver will also have considered factors such as the number of turning movements and number of traffic signals he has to pass through; or, for a public transport journey, he may have considered the cost and number of boardings in addition to travel time.

3. Another factor which can lead to a poor assignment is

the use of an average perceived cost when obviously people assess the value of the parameters just described differently, i.e. each person places a different weight on distance, time or number of turning movements and by using an average value for each link in the network a poor presentation of traffic flows is inevitable.

4. Assignments are often made on the basis of average twenty-four-hour traffic conditions and in this situation inaccuracies may occur as traffic conditions, and therefore travel times, vary continuously over the day.

5. Not only do individuals weigh each of the elements within the total perceived costs differently, they also estimate the value of each element to various levels of accuracy. For example, a regular commuter may be able to assess the travel time on a route with a higher degree of accuracy than an individual making such a journey for the first time.

6. Finally, we are not able to measure travel times and the other elements of perceived costs to a high degree of accuracy. Inaccuracies made in journey-time measurement will tend to accentuate the problem of assigning trips to competing routes with small time differences.

Improved assignment techniques have been developed to counter some of these difficulties.

One possibility is to use finer zones and a finer network. This helps to reduce the effect of representing all trips starting from a zone centroid. It also helps to allow for the different weighting placed by individuals on the elements of perceived costs by reducing the size of group of people, thereby making the assumed average value more compatible with the individuals that it represents. An increase in the number of zones and the size of the network will of course increase the cost of computation considerably and is often, therefore, prohibitive.

Improvements can be made to the algorithm by allowing for other factors which affect route choice, for example, turning penalties. These could be measured as a time or cost penalty perceived by drivers at each of the intersections. Such time or cost penalties are frequently included in current studies.

Assignments can be made for several hours of the day, to take into account the variation in travel conditions over the day. Again, costs usually prohibit this, but separate assignments are often made for peak periods and off-peak periods as well as the twenty-four-hour period.

A further possible improvement would be to make assignments by category of person and this would tell us more accurately how different individuals weight elements of perceived costs. Here again, however, it would be costly to implement in the transport model.

An improved assignment procedure can be achieved using multipath proportional assignment. This method tends to help with all of the problems listed previously. This improved procedure involves computing a number of routes for each zone pair and attributing a proportion of the total number of trips between the two zones to each of the alternative routes. A very simple type of multipath proportional assignment is that using diversion curves.

4. (iv) *Diversion curve assignment*

The original use of diversion curve analysis was to estimate the proportion of a given traffic flow which would use a new road, e.g. the diversion expected from an all-purpose road to a motorway in the M1 study.[35] It is first assumed that for any given zonal interchange at least two alternative routes exist, that each route will have its own characteristics of distance, time, speed and level of service and that a driver evaluates each of these factors before choosing his route.

Diversion curves are empirical relationships constructed from data collected in surveys of the usage of alternative routes, e.g. a study may be made of the travel time saved by using route *A* as compared with route *B* and also of the proportions using routes *A* and *B*. (Diversion curves may also be used to determine the proportion using mode *A* compared with the proportion using mode *B* in a modal split analysis.)

Diversion curves have been developed using the following variables:

    1. Travel time saved
    2. Distance saved

3. Travel time ratio
4. Distance ratio
5. Travel time and distance saved
6. Distance and speed ratio
7. Cost ratio.

The diversion curves 1–4 (see Figure III.3) are the most simple, incorporating only one variable. These curves may be

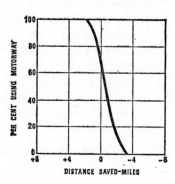

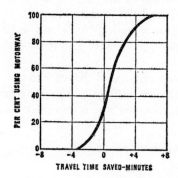

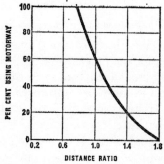

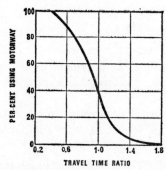

FIGURE III.3 Examples of diversion curves.

satisfactory in some circumstances, e.g. when considering the amount of traffic which will bypass a small town, but may be inadequate to deal with more complex situations.

A further development is to introduce two variables into the model of travel resistance, as for example in the California diversion curves.[36] These are based on a measure of travel time and distance saved, and as such provide a better explanation of how drivers choose a route. The principles stated in the California method are as follows:

1. Factors other than time and distance are ignored.
2. The method to be produced should be one which can be expressed mathematically.
3. The greater the travel time saved the greater the use.
4. The greater the distance saved the greater the use.
5. When travel time and distance savings are small some drivers will use the freeway (motorway) and some will not.
6. A few drivers will travel any amount of distance to save travel time, and some drivers will select the shortest route in terms of distance, however much travel time is consumed.

The model developed was as follows:

$$P = \frac{50 + 50(d + \tfrac{1}{2}t)}{(d - \tfrac{1}{2}t)^2 + 4\cdot5}$$

where P = percentage using freeway
$\quad d$ = distance saved in miles via the freeway
$\quad t$ = time saved in minutes via the freeway

(The curves are illustrated in Figure III.4.)

The principles stated above would appear intuitively correct, except the first one, of only considering the factors of time and distance saved, and even this may be a reasonable approximation in most circumstances.

If diversion curves are used it is usually necessary to consider separate networks, one with and one without the new network and calculate all-or-nothing costs or times on both networks, as input to the diversion curve. Reference is then made to the diversion curve to obtain the proportion of trips to be allocated to each route. Each proportion is then loaded by an all-or-nothing assignment to its appropriate network and two loadings added to obtain the final assignment incorporating the results of the diversion analysis.

Diversion curve assignments have normally only generated two alternative routes for each zone pair, but clearly in a

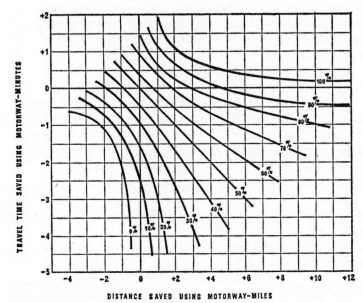

FIGURE III.4 **Travel time and distance saved diversion curve.**

complex urban network and particularly for the longer trips, there are likely to be more than two alternative routes available.

4. (v) *Multipath proportional assignment*

In a large urban area there may be a choice of many different routes between individual zones, and the trips between zones will be distributed over all the available routes. The most popular route will probably be the minimum time or cost route but there will be plenty of trips choosing routes that are slightly longer or apparently more expensive. There are two main reasons for this spread; first, imperfect knowledge (not all travellers will judge correctly which is really their cheapest route), and secondly, the effect of location within the zone (in reality trips start from a variety of points and the best route from the zone centroid may not be the best route from all points in that zone).

Where a number of alternative routes are possible, diversion curves which use only two alternatives may not necessarily give a much better assignment than a simple all-or-nothing loading. Multipath proportional assignment attempts to allow for this problem by loading proportions of the trips for each zonal interchange to a number of alternative routes.

One approach to this problem has been developed by Burrell.[37] In this model it is assumed that a driver does not know the actual link times, but that he associates with each link in the network a supposed time. The supposed time is drawn at random from a distribution of times, having as its mean the actual link time, and a mean deviation, which might be, say, 20% of the actual link time. (Actual link times are those measured in the survey stage and would, in fact, be mean link times from several measurements.) It is assumed that the driver then selects and uses the route which minimises the sum of his supposed link times.

It is further assumed that the supposed link times over the network remain constant for all the trips originating from one zone, so that in fact all the trips from any one zone are assigned on an all-or-nothing basis. However, trips from adjacent zones similarly assigned on an all-or-nothing basis will be assigned using other assumed values for the supposed link times. This route choice model therefore determines paths which are often quite different from those found by using the shortest time algorithm. A further development of this model would be to divide the trips from a zone into several equal parts, each part having its own tree built from a different set of supposed link times. Although this would involve more computer time it would give a better simulation of route choice behaviour. With this approach all of the reasons for a poor assignment discussed earlier are overcome to some extent except the final point (i.e. inaccuracies in travel time measurement).

As this multiple route model is a considerable advance on minimum time and diversion curve models, we will describe the method more fully. First, it is necessary to be able to choose at random a supposed link time from a distribution which has as its mean the actual link time. A reasonable assumption for the distribution of supposed link travel times is a normal distribution. For ease of computation in this model the normal distribution has been approximated using a constant distribution consisting of eight possible values. To allow for the fact that link times can be estimated more accurately for long links than for short links the maximum percentage variation permitted is greater with a short link than with a longer link.

Considering the supposed link times on a route which consists of several links, it is unlikely that the random numbers used in obtaining each supposed link time will cause each of them to take an extreme value from its distribution of possible values. Thus, for long routes, the total of supposed link times will, on average, differ from the total actual link times by a smaller percentage than for shorter routes.

This would appear to correspond well with what occurs in practice. For example, on a journey for which by the shortest route the travel time is five minutes, an individual might select a route taking seven minutes, which is 40% greater than the best time. On the other hand, it seems much less likely that on a journey for which the shortest route has a travel time of 100 minutes, an individual would choose a route taking 140 minutes.

The distinction between this model and one in which the n quickest routes would be determined is an important one and the following example should help to illustrate the main differences. In Figure III.5 the three quickest routes between C and H are as follows:

CDEH	100
CDFEH	110
CGH	115

If a multiple route model split the trips from C to H between the three quickest routes, then each of the three given routes would take some of the traffic, but the procedure of randomising the link times may well mean that the illogical route $CDFEH$ would never be chosen. This would be the case if, say, the actual link times were $DE = DF = FE = 10$ and we allowed a maximum variation of $\pm 20\%$ on a link time. The maximum possible supposed link times for DE would be 12, and the minimum possible supposed times for DF and FE would be 8, giving a total time for DFE of 16. With the random selection procedure from the range of supposed link times it is impossible for the route DFE to be quicker than the route DE.

However, it is apparent that the multiple route model could select the route CGH, and this leads to the apparent paradox

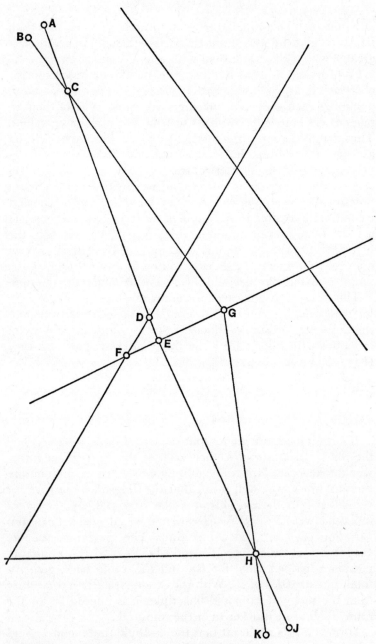

FIGURE III.5 Multiple route model example.

that some of the routes chosen between a pair of points may be slower than some of the routes which cannot be chosen. This is probably a very real situation; in the example it is unlikely that drivers would choose the route *CDFEH* because it is clearly longer than *CDEH*. On the other hand, it is much less obvious that *CGH* is longer than the other routes and some drivers may well select that route.

Two important features emerge from this discussion. First, the time of the selected route between *A* and *B* exceeds that of the quickest route between the two points by less than a given fixed proportion, and secondly, the time of the selected route between any two points *C* and *D* along that route exceeds the quickest time between *C* and *D* by less than a fixed proportion.

With the simplest application of this model, all trips from one zone are assigned to the same randomised network, so that all the trips originating from one zone follow the same route to a particular node. It does not, however, follow that all trips passing from one node to another will use the same route. Referring again to Figure III.5, all trips between *A* and *J* may use the route *ACGHJ* and all trips between *B* and *J* may use the route *BCDEHJ*. Thus, of the trips between nodes *C* and *H*, some will use the route *CGH* and others the route *CDEH*. In a complex network there may be many alternative routes between two nodes which are well separated and clearly the simple type of multiple route model may allocate trips to each of the possible routes.

The model described has been tested against an actual network with satisfactory results, and although it is apparent that the route taken by a particular trip may be arbitrary, in the sense that it is determined at random, nevertheless, the total traffic loadings on each link are found to be more accurate than those obtained from an all-or-nothing assignment. The assignments obtained from a multiple route model do, however, depend upon the assumptions made about the maximum variability ('degree of randomness') allowed. The calibration of the multiple route assignment model and our confidence in its results would, however, be greatly helped if some special surveys were carried out on driver route choice.

The further stages of development of this model will be to use these route choice methods to choose a number of alternative routes for each zone and to proportion the total number of trips originating in that zone to each of the selected routes. Although a multipath proportional assignment will give more realistic link loadings than an all-or-nothing assignment in unrestrained conditions, it has particular value in congested situations, which are discussed later.

4. (vi) *Public transport assignment*

Public transport networks differ fundamentally from road networks, as they comprise a system of fixed services following given routes generally at regular intervals. The assignment procedure developed for these networks follows the same principles as for roads in that traffic between two zones is assigned to the quickest or least costly route between those zones. However, in contrast to the road network (where only link and intersection times are included) the journey time includes link travelling times, waiting times at interchange points and walking times. Additionally, perceived time penalties can be added every time a new service is boarded in order to simulate a known passenger aversion to changing from one vehicle to another.

Much of the required network information is available from the operators' schedules. The relationship between average waiting time for a service and the frequency of service, however, does require calibration.[38] Observed waiting time functions fall between the two possible extremes of a random arrival of the vehicle, where waiting time equals the headway, and a strictly scheduled time of arrival of vehicles, where waiting time equals half the average headway. For high-frequency services, waiting time approximates to random vehicle arrivals and for lower-frequency services approaches more nearly half the headway of scheduled arrivals. One further point concerning waiting time frequency curves is that there is a maximum conceivable time beyond which people will not wait for a service but rather organise their time of arrival to coincide with service departure times. This feature is synthesised by giving a maximum waiting time to each curve, which is dependent upon the type of service considered.

The following example illustrates the main principles of public transport assignment.[39] The calculation of paths through a network is carried out in a number of simple steps, the complexity of the overall network being reflected in the total number of steps involved. As with private vehicle assignment the first stage is to select a home node and then calculate the paths from the 'home' to all other nodes in the network. As with road networks this is known as the 'tree' for that particular home node.

Against each node in the network there is detailed a certain amount of information concerning that node. This information for each node is stored in the computer and can be called a node label. The main information on the label is:

1. The node number
2. Time taken to the node
3. Number of boardings to reach that node
4. Service on which arriving
5. The node at which the service was boarded
6. The indicator: either o or +.

Figure III.6 illustrates the route-finding process in a hypothetical example. Having selected the home node, the position may be represented as shown under 'Zero Boardings' (that is, no boardings of services have yet been made). The 'home' node is indicated by the '+' sign. All other nodes have the indicator 'o' sign. In the next stage all the services through the home node are considered and for each node served by these routes the following changes are made. The indicator is changed from 'o' to '+' sign. The time taken to reach the node (including waiting and boarding time) is recorded together with the number of boardings made, the number of the service last travelled on, and the boarding node (in this case always the home node). The indicator on the home node is set to 'o' to show that all routes through it have already been examined.

If the boarding were to be limited to one, the process would then stop and a list of all nodes which could be reached from the 'home' node together with the time, number of boardings, service and boarding node taken to reach then could be tabulated. Because only comparatively few services would be likely to pass through the 'home' node, the total number of nodes involved, and hence the time spent over computation, would normally be small. Obviously, however, computation

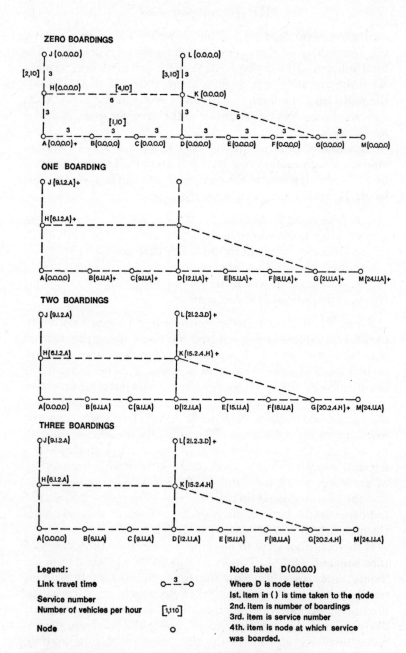

FIGURE III.6 Public transport route choice algorithm.

cannot stop at this point because journeys often use more than one service. It is when more than one boarding is considered that computation becomes considerable and repetitive, and the use of a computer becomes advantageous.

Using a computer program, therefore, the situation is examined for a second boarding. Clearly a second boarding may be made at any node reached in the one-boarding stage, that is any node with a ' + ' indicator but not the nodes where the indicator has been cancelled, in this case the 'home' node A. The program examines, therefore, all the services passing through each ' + ' indicated node in the same way as it did for the 'home' node in the first boarding stage. Nodes which have not been reached before are labelled with time of journey, number of boardings, service number and boarding node as before, and are indicated with a ' + ' indicator that the label information has been updated. If the program comes across a node which has been reached previously, it compares the time by the new route with that by the previous one. If the new time is greater than the previous one, it makes no change; if the new time is less, it substitutes the new time, number of boardings, service number and boarding node for the old ones and indicates that a change has been made. As each node reached in the previous computation using one boarding is examined in this way, the indicator against it is removed to show that all new services to which access can be obtained by means of an additional boarding from that node have been examined. If, after this has been done, the computer subsequently builds a shorter time path to the node and updates the label, the indicator is restored to show that the onward services need to be re-examined in the next stage.

The position is as shown in Figure III.6 under 'Two Boardings'. The algorithm has first examined node B, because it is a ' + ' indicator, and found there were no other services through the node. It has then cancelled the indicator and gone to C, where it has done the same thing. At D it found service 3 and set the labels at K and L. The algorithm would subsequently examine the fast service through H and would find at K and G that travel time was faster via services 2 and 4 than via services 1 and 3, and would reset the labels at K and G to show the path via H. It would also if necessary reset the indicators at K and G.

This process would then be repeated allowing three board-ings, the only point of interest here being that times to L are the same for 2 and 3 boardings in which case the first route calcula-tion, that is 2 boardings, would be selected.

At the fourth boarding stage, the indicated nodes would again be examined, but as no other services pass through these points, no further changes would be required, except that the indicators would be set to zero and tree-building would be complete.

It is interesting to note in the example above that, although it is quicker from A to G via H, the route from A to M would go on service 1 via C because the time incurred by the three boardings, via services 2, 4 and 1, compared with the one boarding via service 1 would make the former route uncompeti-tive. In practice, it is doubtful whether people would travel to G via H thereby saving one minute at the expense of having to make change at H. The introduction of a boarding penalty of, say, four minutes would keep all traffic to G and S on the route via C and would probably be more realistic.

Having built the complete tree for the one 'home' node selected, the whole process is repeated using each zone centroid on the network as a 'home' node.

This method results in all-or-nothing assignments. The advantages to be derived using multipath techniques may equally apply to public transport route choice models, although in only a very few conurbations is the public transport network likely to be sufficiently complex to justify the higher cost of multipath public transport assignment.

5. MODAL SPLIT

5. (i) *Introduction*

In the introduction to this chapter the factors an individual may consider when deciding whether and where to make a trip were discussed. Subsequent sections have described models to simu-late each phase in the procedure. The phase dealing with the choice of mode has deliberately been left until after assignment for two reasons. First, the implications of modal split on transport policy, particularly for the larger conurbations, are considerable, probably greater than those of any other part or output of the transport model. Secondly, modal split is not a definable single phase but has an effect at various stages in the individual's decision-making process, and therefore in various stages of the transport model. It is for this reason that a reader may be confused when looking at different transportation studies to find modal split occurring at different positions in the process.

In early studies[40] modal split was not considered at all because at that time it was not fully recognised to what extent transport modes were in competition. The early studies were simply interested in a forecast of road vehicle traffic and the impact of congestion was then not foreseen. In some very small-scale transportation studies it may still be adequate to consider only a private travel network but in large congested urban and regional situations many people will have a choice of travel mode so that the way in which people actually make the choice must be considered.

In recent years there has been an increasing interest shown in model-building for the modal split problem, to begin with in the USA and more recently in the UK. Some of this research has been to examine the modal split problem for a city or a conurbation as a whole while other researchers have been concerned at building models to simulate modal choice for individual journeys. Some of these latter models have been developed in isolation to the transport model and have investigated in great detail certain parameters affecting modal choice. Although these models in this form cannot be incorporated into the whole of the transport model, they have nevertheless provided considerable insight into the reasons for individual choice of mode.

Modal split models have been applied to the transport model in one of two forms. First, by relating the number of trip ends in a zone to certain journey origin characteristics, thereby introducing modal split before trip distribution (i.e. to stratify trips by mode in the trip generation equations). Alternatively, models of modal split have been incorporated after the distribution phase and have taken the form of diversion curves or regression type equations relating the percentage using public transport to the factors it is assumed individuals consider when choosing their mode for a particular trip. In the models assuming modal split before distribution parameters such as journey purpose and mode availability at the generation end are said to influence modal choice whereas in the models after distribution such factors as the relative trip times by the competing modes are said to influence modal split. Modal split decisions are in fact made at both the generation stage and in a subsequent search for a suitable destination (the distribution stage). Before, however, a more detailed discussion of the effect of modal split and its appropriate synthesis in the transport model is presented, it is worth while discussing the factors and parameters which determine modal choice.

5. (ii) *Factors affecting modal split*

The factors affecting a person's choice of mode are numerous and it would be difficult to incorporate all of them in the transport model. As an exercise, Wilson[41] has prepared an extensive list of the factors that he felt influenced an individual's choice. Many of the factors he considered, such as comfort and cleanliness, unfortunately cannot be directly incorporated into the transport model.

The earliest models, particularly in the USA, which were constructed to synthesise modal split, were introduced in the transport model at the generation phase and were based on such factors as car-ownership levels, distance from the central business district, and net residential density. Additional explanatory variables were later included to synthesise mode availability by assessing the relative accessibility of each zone by each mode.

A recent example is that of the early stages in the London Traffic Survey,[42] where an extension of the category analysis procedure (described earlier) was adopted to take account of relative accessibility to the various modes of travel for each zone. A number of household classifications were established in category analysis to take account of the three main factors influencing trip generation, namely: car-ownership, income and structure of the household (this gave 108 household classifications). A further number of categories defining levels of accessibility to each mode in this analysis were then added. Thus in phase II of the LTS bus accessibility of a zone was defined as a function of the number of buses passing through the zone, and an inverse function of the circumference of the zone. The accessibility by train was similarly defined by the number of trains stopping in the zone, the number of stations at which these trains stop and the area of the zone.

Three categories of each index were defined and these expressed low, medium and high accessibility to each mode producing a further six categories to be associated with each of the 108 classifications of household. Not all of the combinations of level of accessibility and household characteristics were found to be applicable, and so the total number of classifications was somewhat less than 108 × 6. Nevertheless a large number of household classifications still remained and the difficulty again arose of obtaining a reliable trip rate for each cell.

One of the earlier examples of including a modal split model after distribution is that of the Traffic Research Corporation in the Washington study.[43] In the Traffic Research Corporation (TRC) model, an attempt was made at introducing a variable which expressed the relative level of service offered by two competing modes. This was defined as the ratio of excess time when travelling by public transport divided by the excess time spent outside of the vehicle while *en route* from origin to destination. For a trip by public transport this would include the walking time to the nearest bus stop or station, the waiting time at the stop, any transfer time and the walking time to the destination. For a trip by private car the excess time would include the walking time to the parking place and the time to park or unpark the car.

In the TRC model a number of categories for each variable were established and diversion curves calibrated to express the percentage expected to use public transport in terms of the variables discussed. The typical diversion curves established by the TRC are shown in Figure III.7. The diversion curves are more complex than any of those described for traffic assignment because four variables are now being considered whereas the maximum number of variables included in diversion curve assignments was two.

The model gave best results when applied to work trips to

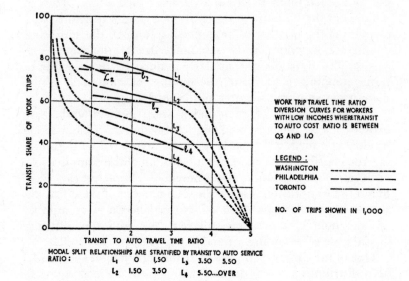

WORK TRIP TRAVEL TIME RATIO
DIVERSION CURVES FOR WORKERS
WITH LOW INCOMES WHERE TRANSIT
TO AUTO COST RATIO IS BETWEEN
0.5 AND 1.0

LEGEND :
WASHINGTON   ----------
PHILADELPHIA   ——————
TORONTO   —·—·—·—

NO. OF TRIPS SHOWN IN 1,000

MODAL SPLIT RELATIONSHIPS ARE STRATIFIED BY TRANSIT TO AUTO SERVICE
RATIO : L_1 0   1.50 L_3 3.50   5.50
          L_2 1.50   3.50 L_4 5.50....OVER

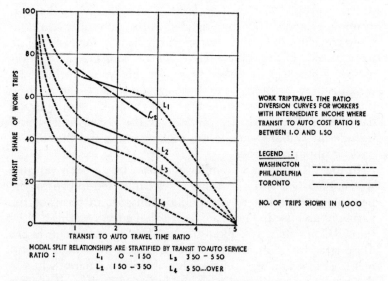

WORK TRIP TRAVEL TIME RATIO
DIVERSION CURVES FOR WORKERS
WITH INTERMEDIATE INCOME WHERE
TRANSIT TO AUTO COST RATIO IS
BETWEEN 1.0 AND 1.50

LEGEND   :
WASHINGTON   ----------
PHILADELPHIA   ——————
TORONTO   —·—·—·—

NO. OF TRIPS SHOWN IN 1,000

MODAL SPLIT RELATIONSHIPS ARE STRATIFIED BY TRANSIT TO AUTO SERVICE
RATIO : L_1 0 - 1.50 L_3 3.50 - 5.50
          L_2 1.50 - 3.50 L_4 5.50....OVER

FIGURE III.7   TRC modal split diversion curve.

the CBD. Less satisfactory results were obtained for non-work trips to the CBD and for trips to areas outside the CBD. Table III.8 lists the results.

TABLE III.8 Comparison of observed and diversion curve modal split predictions in Washington.

Type of trip	Trip purpose	Observed No. of trips	No. of trips given by model	Percentage trip difference
To CBD	Work	77,723·9	76,723·9	−1·36
—	Non-work	2,203·5	2,410·0	+9·37
Non-CBD	Work	45,529·4	38,459·2	−15·53
—	Non-work	2,607·1	3,423·9	+31·33

A further example of the use of diversion curves for modal split were those calibrated for use in the later stages, phase III of the London Transportation Study.[44] These diversion curves are of the simplest type incorporating one variable only, i.e. the percentage of trips between any zone pair using public transport was related to the travel time ratio. Separate diversion curves were produced for the central area and non-central area trips and three trip purposes. The curves for central area trips are shown in Figure III.8.

Studies carried out in isolation to the transport model have examined particular zone-to-zone trip movement in an attempt to isolate all the factors affecting modal split. In the main these studies have involved a diversion curve type of multivariate analysis and have generally only considered those factors affecting modal choice after a destination has been chosen. One of the first of these was by Warner[45] in which he found relative travel times and relative travel costs (actual costs were used and not perceived costs) to significantly affect modal choice whereas the income of the traveller was found to be unimportant. In a study by Quarmby,[46] of the journey to work in Leeds, it was found that overall travel time and excess travel time differences together with cost difference and a variable 'use of car for work' were the most significant variables influencing the choice of mode. The variable use of car for work is included to account for the person who must travel by car during the course of his work.

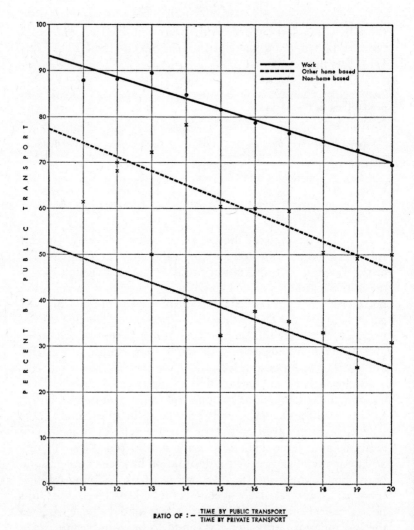

FIGURE III.8 London Transportation Survey modal split diversion curve.

5. (iii) *Modal split in the transport model*

The purpose of modal split analysis is in general to determine the trips made by public transport as opposed to those made by private car. In many cases of course public transport can carry large volumes of traffic at far lower costs than can be achieved with the private car. Where such situations arise, i.e. high population and employment densities in complex urban areas, it is clear that the relative investment in public versus private transport is a vital factor in transport policy. Because modal split is of such importance, this section will deal with the impact of modal split on the various stages in the transport model, and show how existing techniques can result in poor forecasts and how these techniques could be modified to give a more satisfactory measure, synthesis and therefore forecast of modal split.

The parameters affecting modal split fall into two groups, those associated with the origin or generating end of the journey such as journey purpose and mode availability, and those associated with the possible routes and journey destination such as relative travel costs or time spent parking. Thus if modal split is incorporated at the generation phase it will omit journey characteristics, and if included after distribution it will omit generation factors. Recent transportation studies have attempted to include the effects of both sets of parameters. At the generation stage, journey generation factors such as household composition and income have been included either by regression or category analysis. The effect of mode availability has been approximated by classifying households as car-owning or non-car-owning. It has then been assumed that the majority of trips by non-car-owning households will be by public transport and thus captive to the public transport network. The car-owning household trip ends have then been split into car and public transport trip ends by the means of zonal accessibility indices included either in the regression equations or as an additional category for category analysis. The subsequent public transport and private road journey generations have then been distributed using minimum cost or time functions by public transport and road respectively. In order to carry out this distribution it has been assumed that journey attractions can be divided for each zone into car and public transport journey attractions. This division has usually been made on the basis of observed public and private attraction ratios possibly modified to allow for expected changes in the future.

The subsequent zone-to-zone car-driver journeys have then

been split into car-driver and public transport trips using conventional diversion curve techniques calibrated against the base-year observations. The resulting car matrices have then been used to load the road network and the public transport journeys added to the captive public transport trips, and assigned to the public transport network.

Although this methodology is an advance on earlier studies, there are nevertheless certain criticisms. First, this method of estimating mode availability, though satisfactory for the base year, can result in poor forecasts if changes in accessibility are not accurately fed into both the generation and attraction categories. This criticism will be particularly true in conditions of congestion, though this point will be returned to in the following section. Secondly, travellers do not consider attraction at a particular zone of destination under the two headings of car-driver and public transport attractions. Thirdly, the carrying out of modal split after distribution will mean that the resulting public transport journeys will have been distributed using private car travel times. This error can be rectified by redistribution of these journeys using public transport travel times. Nevertheless, even if this is done there must be some inherent error in resultant trip ends.

These criticisms can be better demonstrated with the following example:

Consider a group of residents living in zone i. Suppose that within this group some own cars and have them available for their use, whereas others have not. Suppose also that a public transport system exists. The group of would-be travellers can be divided into three groups, one group having only public transport available, another having both public and private transport available and a third group who for one reason or another may only want to use the private car mode. Three sets of isotime or isocost lines can be associated with each group of traveller, those by public transport, those by car alone and those consisting of a minimum of the two (see Figure III.9).

The destination opportunities will be ranked in order of increasing cost or time in different order for the three groups of traveller. For the captive public transport user, central area destinations are available to him more quickly than the individual having only a car available, whereas of course the traveller

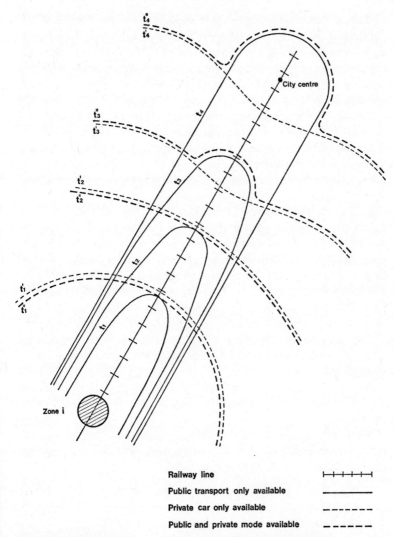

t″₄
t′₄

City centre

t″₃
t′₃

t′₂
t″₂

t″₁
t′₁

Zone i

Railway line	├─┼─┼─┼─┤
Public transport only available	———————
Private car only available	— — — — —
Public and private mode available	— — — — —

FIGURE III.9 Effect of travel cost on opportunities available.

using only a car has destinations available to him away from the town centre more quickly than the captive public transport user. The group who can choose public or private have of course the most opportunities available of all in any particular perceived cost level.

This illustrates how transport models may, after calibration, accurately synthesise a base-year situation, but could be in error in forecasting. First, by calibration of the generation rates for the base year, the breakdown of car-owning and non-car-owning households will approximate to car-available and non-car-available groups. That is, some car-owning households will generate public transport trips and likewise some non-car-owning households will generate car-passenger trips. However, if accessibility is not accurately included in the trip generation and attraction models, any changes in accessibility, particularly those caused by congestion, will not be reflected in the resultant modal split.

Secondly, the example illustrates how travellers within each modal opportunity group should be distributed according to the minimum travel costs or times associated with that group. In particular, residents with a choice of mode available should be distributed by the lowest cost mode and not as at present by the future cost on the mode that happened to be used in the base year. Thirdly, the example demonstrates that there is no real distinction between car-driver and public transport attractions. These last two criticisms also illustrate the errors introduced by using diversion curve techniques after distribution has been carried out.

Many of these criticisms could be overcome by the inclusion of modal split in the transport model as follows (see Figure III.10):

First, trip generations should be grouped by modal opportunity classes rather than by car-owning and non-car-owning groups. They may be defined as follows:

(a) people who have only public transport available to them
(b) people who wish to use only a car
(c) people who have a choice between public transport and car.

In practice only two groups may be required. If few trips occur in group (b) then they may be added to those of group (c) without incurring large errors.

At the distribution stage the three groups would be distributed using the respective minimum travel time of modes

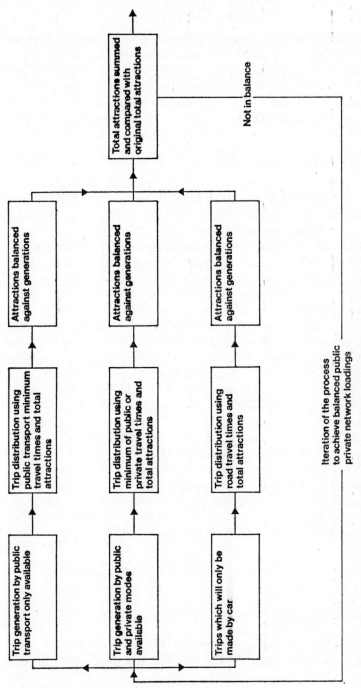

FIGURE III.10 Suggested method of including modal split in the transport model.

available for each group. Individuals in group (*a*) can be distributed using public transport minimum travel times and assigned to the public transport network without being involved in modal split at all, since these people do not have a choice. People in group (*c*) would be distributed by the minimum of public or private travel times. Those trips to zones using public transport travel times as a minimum would be added to the public transport trip matrix for assignment and those by private road to the road matrix.

In both cases, groups (*a*) and (*b*) would be distributed using total attractions in each zone. This does mean a rather more sophisticated method of balancing trip attractions has to be made. The method is demonstrated in Figure III.10.

Two last points must be discussed. In the larger urban studies, zone sizes will be relatively large. In these cases the assumption that for the group with choice of mode, journeys for each particular zone-to-zone movement must be by only one mode, car or public transport, cannot be entirely true even when further broken down by purpose. In these cases it may be that the group of travellers who have both public and private modes available, will have to be subjected to a further public or private mode diversion after distribution using some conventional form of diversion curve. The last point is that it is unlikely that the models, although calibrated, will result in balanced public and private network loadings with one run of the model process. The balanced situation will only be achieved by iteration of the procedure as illustrated in Figure III.10.

This methodology has been incorporated in recent studies[47] in the UK. The process has been carried out using a somewhat complicated two-mode distribution model. As yet (1971) an operational evaluation of the process in terms of a comparison of synthesis against observed travel has not been made.

6. Transport model and congestion

6. (i) *Introduction*

In our discussions so far on the transport model, we have always assumed that one key variable, the speed of travel on a link, is known in advance. Thus trip generation, trip distribution, trip assignment and modal split are all based on assumed speeds of travel. But in fact most link speeds are not independent of the volume of travel taking place on the link. In this respect all our 'forecasts' are forecasts of the *demand* for travel, assuming given conditions of movement. In practice this demand may not all be realised as the transportation system may not be able to accommodate all the forecast demand. Instead, the system becomes congested.

Congestion affects trip-making in an identical fashion, whether the trip is made by road or public transport. Congestion increases travel time and general irritation and inconvenience to the traveller, so that the total cost of the journey to the traveller increases. Generally speaking, the traveller will select a route which minimises his perceived costs of travel. As congestion increases so travel costs will increase until a point is reached at which the traveller may begin to try alternative routes in the hope of finding one having less congestion. Alternatively, the traveller may consider alternative modes. An example of this may be the long-distance commuter. Congestion will increase his total travel time by car, including parking time, to such an extent that he may change mode to public transport.

Congestion can, of course, reach such a point that to certain travellers the costs of the journey may outweigh the benefit derived from making that journey. These travellers, the marginal travellers, may then consider travelling to alternative destinations. Alternatively, the marginal travellers, to whom the benefits from making a particular journey are very small, may with increasing congestion decide to stay at home rather than take part in any activity involving vehicular travel.

It can be seen that congestion, because of its effect on travel time or perceived travel costs, affects trip-making at three stages in the transport model, namely, assignment and therefore mode of travel, distribution, and finally, generation. The transport model must be capable of simulating increasing travel costs with increasing congestion caused by increasing traffic. This section will deal with the capacity restraint models which relate travel time as a measure of travel cost with volumes o

E

traffic, and will further describe how the effect of the increased travel costs as measured by this capacity restraint model can be used in a transport model to synthesise the effects of congestion on all phases of assignment, modal split, distribution and indeed generation.

6. (ii) *Effect of congestion on assignment*

Let us first consider the effect of congestion on assignment. Capacity restraint techniques have been developed mainly for application to road networks although the concepts are much the same for public transport.

Before we examine the problem of traffic restraint on road assignment, we must know something of the mechanics of traffic flow. Most studies of traffic flow have assumed that the volume of traffic which can pass along a given length of road is affected mainly by one variable, speed. They have then set out to determine this speed/flow relationship. It should be remembered that this is oversimplifying a complex subject, but such approximations are probably justified when they merely represent one step in the transport model.

These speed/flow relationships were first determined for rural highways where a relationship was obtained between the average *running speed* along a road, the volume of traffic on the road and the average width of the road. The relationship as such ignored the effect of intersection delays. However, in congested urban areas, intersection delays may be more important than link running speed relationships. In general, therefore, it is better to consider the speed/flow relationships as two components, one related to intersection delay, and one to the running speed between intersections. It is often convenient to express this as a journey time/flow relationship, the journey time (t_{AB}) being expressed as the time from the beginning of link A to the beginning of the next link. We may then express

$$t_{AB} = X_{AB} + \frac{l_A}{r_A}$$

where X_{AB} = the intersection delay
l_A = the length of link A
r_A = the running speed along link A

Let us now look at the problem of delays at intersections (X_{AB}). First, we may assume that total vehicle delay is related to the type of intersection, the area of the intersection and the size of the approach flows. Much research has been done into the capacity and the calculation of delay at various types of intersections[48,49,50] and it is possible to compute average vehicle delay for each intersection in a network when the flows on the approaches are known. In a well-designed grade separated intersection, delays should not occur due to queuing or weaving but merely owing to the extra distance travelled on the slip roads. These slip roads can be represented as links in the designated network.

The relationship between the running speed of traffic (excluding delays at intersections) and the flow of traffic has been investigated by the Road Research Laboratory[51] and the following results were obtained:

Central urban roads $\qquad v = 31 - \dfrac{q + 430}{3(w - a)} \qquad 10 < v < 24$

Other urban roads $\qquad v = 42 - \dfrac{q + 1{,}000}{4(w - a)} \qquad 20 < v < 35$

Rural roads
(single carriageways) $\qquad v = 54 - \dfrac{q + 1{,}400}{6w} \qquad 24 < v < 45$

where v = running speed in mile/h
  w = carriageway width in feet
  q = traffic flow in vehicles/h
  a = effective reduction in carriageway width caused
    by parked vehicles

It would theoretically be possible to compute link and intersection delays separately with these formulae and those mentioned previously for intersections. However, it would be extremely difficult and costly to incorporate this detailed analysis of intersection delays into a large-scale transportation study network. It would be much more convenient to consider a journey time per link which includes some allowance for the intersection delays along the link. This approach has recently been investigated by Wardrop.[52] He assumed that most of the major intersections causing delays in an urban area are controlled by traffic signals of the vehicle-actuated type. Moreover, it can be assumed that these signals tend to behave like the fixed-time variety under congested conditions. Earlier work has shown that the relation between the reciprocal of delay and flow is approximately linear for fixed-time signals. If a system of signals is linked along a route, the effect would be to reduce delays on that route at each signal (except, of course, at the first signal) and it is therefore reasonable to assume that delays at a set of linked signals are related to flow in a similar manner to unlinked signals. The formula for a journey speed/flow relationship may now be derived from the formulae:

$$v_R = a(1 - q/Q) = \text{running speed}$$

and $d = \dfrac{b}{(1 - /q\lambda s)} = \begin{array}{l}\text{delay for intersection or set of linked} \\ \text{signals}\end{array}$

where λs is the absolute capacity of the intersection

If there are f intersections or sets of linked intersections per mile and the journey speed is v mile/h then:

$$\frac{1}{v} = \frac{1}{v_R} + fd$$

or $\dfrac{1}{v} = \dfrac{1}{a(1 - q/Q)} + \dfrac{fb}{(1 - q/\lambda s)}$

When the model was calibrated using data collected in London the result was as follows:

$$\frac{1}{v} = \frac{1}{31 - \dfrac{140}{w} - \dfrac{0 \cdot 244q}{w}} + \frac{f}{1{,}000 - \dfrac{6 \cdot 8q}{\lambda w}}$$

where v = journey speed (mile/h)
$\qquad q$ = total flow in road, both directions together (p.c.u./h)
$\qquad f$ = number of controlled intersections per mile
$\qquad \lambda$ = proportion of effective green time at intersections
$\qquad w$ = width of road in feet

This journey speed/flow relationship (see Figure III.11) is rather more sophisticated and therefore somewhat more unwieldy in use than previous relationships used for capacity restraint. To date, we are unaware of any case where this relationship has in fact been incorporated into a transportation model. However, the use of such a model may well be justified in the future especially if it were combined with the improved assignment techniques discussed earlier in this chapter.

An alternative approach to speed/flow relationships which

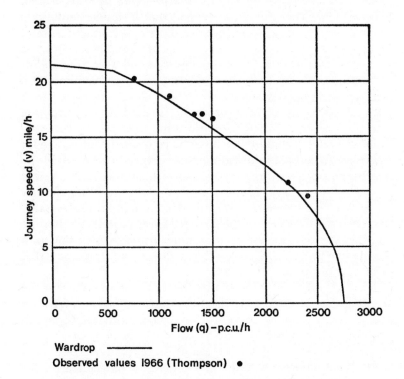

Wardrop ——————
Observed values 1966 (Thompson) ●

Comparison of relations between journey speed and flow – central London. Average carriageway width 42 feet.

FIGURE III.11 Journey speed/flow relations.

has several computational advantages when incorporated into the quantitative traffic forecasting approach has been developed by Thomson.[53] He argues that in complex urban areas link and even intersection speed/flow relationships have little meaning since the flow of traffic through an area is determined by the street characteristics and movement pattern throughout that area rather than by the problems of any one particular intersection. Instead he has developed relationships for larger areas in which the speed of traffic passing through that area is related to the volume of traffic in that area. To date, only a limited amount of information has been collected and empirical relationships developed for individual *area speed/flow relationships*. The evidence does, however, suggest that it should be possible to incorporate some allowance for the street characteristics of different towns into the formula so that eventually it should be possible to determine more universally applicable area speed/ flow relationships that depend on the street configuration within the area considered.

A repetitive or iterative procedure is needed to incorporate the effect of speed/flow relationships into the traffic forecasting model. The first step in any capacity restrained traffic model is therefore to compare the assumed travel speed (the input to the coded network) with the speed at which the traffic would actually be carried. If these are substantially different new estimates of link speeds are required as fresh input to the traffic model. The first effect of the changed speeds will be to alter the routeing or assignment so that some traffic avoids the most congested areas in favour of less direct but less congested alternative routes.

In Figure III.12, let q be the demand corresponding to the first estimate of speed v. The resultant point P will normally not lie on the speed-flow curve so that a new estimate of speed is required. Speeds would have to fall to the level v_0 (see Figure III.12) before the demand Q could be accommodated. However, if speeds were to fall, the demand for movement on the link would also fall. Hence the link speed to be assumed in the next assignment should lie between v and v_0. A speed v^1 is therefore assumed given by the formula $v^1 = v - k(v - v_0)$ where $0 < k < 1$. A value must be chosen for k and held constant for all links in a particular assignment.

Having estimated new speeds, new trees are built and the matrix again loaded. A comparison is then made between the new assigned flows (q^1) and the capacity (c) at that speed as before. The aim of these comparisons is to observe how the subsequent iterations converge to a balance-loaded network. Rather than looking at each individual link, the following information can be used:

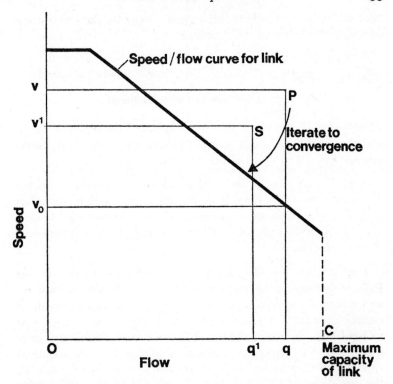

FIGURE III.12 **Example of use of speed/flow curve in adjusting link travel times.**

1. A listing of all links for which the flow/capacity ratio at the assigned speeds lies outside pre-set limits.
2. An analysis of assignment error, which reflects the difference for each link, between the assignment produced and the capacity of each link at the same speed. A ratio for the whole system can be calculated as the

$$\frac{\text{assigned flow (vehicle miles)}}{\text{capacity at the assigned speeds (vehicle miles)}}$$

If this ratio is close to 1, then on average speed and flow are in balance. It is, however, possible that this average may be composed of a series of links, some with much too high, and some with much too low speed. An absolute measure of the

success of the speed-flow convergence requires the calculation
of a slightly different ratio, namely

$$\frac{\sum\limits_{\substack{\text{all} \\ \text{links}}} \dfrac{\text{capacity at assigned}}{\text{speed}} + \text{mod.}\left(\dfrac{\text{assigned}}{\text{flow}} - \dfrac{\text{capacity at}}{\text{assigned speed}}\right)}{\sum\limits_{\substack{\text{all} \\ \text{links}}} \text{capacity at assigned speed}}$$

(The value of the error may be computed for all links taken
together and for various groups of links, e.g. motorways, links
within sections or rings of the area under study.)

3. The number of links for which the speed/flow point lies
   on the opposite side of the speed/flow curve from that
   of the previous assignment. This has been found to be a
   valuable indicator of the working of the convergence
   process.

Transportation studies are just beginning to incorporate this
form of iterative procedure, and at the end of this section we
will describe the results of one such study. Earlier methods of
capacity restraint[54] were less successful. One method tried was
to load trips in an incremental fashion, a fraction, say, one-
quarter of the trips, were assigned at the initially assumed
speeds. If it then looked as if certain roads would be overloaded,
the speeds were adjusted and a further fraction of the trips
assigned to the network at the new speeds. This method was
logically unsound in that it assumed that some traffic would
travel along a road at one speed while other traffic was assigned
to the same road at a very different speed. It also suffered from
the disadvantage that no allowance could be made for overall
congestion on trip distribution or generation. In practice, this
form of capacity restraint assignment worked well if only
isolated links in a network were overloaded. However, if a large
area had too much traffic assigned to it, some most unrealistic
routings could materialise as traffic tried desperately to reach
attractions in the congested area.

Capacity considerations could also affect assignments to
public transport. As congestion worsens, the service offered by
public transport tends to become less reliable. Passenger comfort is also adversely affected as soon as public transport services
become overloaded. It is, however, difficult to incorporate such

comfort and convenience factors into the general transport demand model. The effect of increased road congestion on bus services can, however, be easily incorporated into the transport model, by adjusting journey times to reflect the presence of congestion.

6. (iii) *Effect on modal split and distribution*

In practice one of the major effects of increased road congestion will be to alter the modal split between road and rail travel. As car and bus times lengthen, more and more travellers can be expected to divert from road to rail especially for journeys to and from work in the centre of the large conurbations.

In the previous section of this chapter on modal split, it has been suggested that most transportation studies have experienced difficulty in including the modal split sub-model satisfactorily within the transport model as a whole. When included before distribution, network effects have been ignored. Alternatively, when effected after distribution, effects on distribution have been ignored. It has been further shown in that section that modal split should in fact be considered at both stages, though in a slightly different way from conventional methods. First, the generation stage has required the subdivision by modal opportunity. Secondly, distribution then has to be carried out using minimum perceived travel cost functions for each modal opportunity category, thus rationalising modal split and integrating it with distribution.

The effect of increases in perceived costs due to congestion can easily be synthesised by iteration of these sub-models. As described above, new zone-to-zone perceived costs or times are first calculated allowing for the expected congestion on each link. These new journey times or costs are then used to redistribute trips within each modal opportunity category. This will necessarily not only change distribution but will also affect modal split. This effect will occur in two ways. Zones will be ranked in a new order of journey time away from the zone of origin. For example, with an initial underestimate of travel time on the road network, certain zones, possibly some in the central area of large cities, may be relatively poorly accessible by public transport, compared with other zones which can easily be reached by private car. However, higher costs, particularly in the peak period, such as parking or increased travel times on the road, may now cause these other zones to be much less accessible. The central area zones will then be ranked nearer to the zone of origin than previously and will thus on distribution receive a larger proportion of trips. In addition, the changes in perceived costs must be included in the modal split regression equation, to be used finally to correct the output from the distribution model. The net effect will be for a greater percentage of trips to be distributed to the central area and for a higher proportion of these trips to travel by public transport.

Clearly, this iterative procedure will not immediately close on a balanced public/private split of journeys. The whole transport model will therefore have to be repeated until balance is achieved between public and private networks.

6. (iv) *Effect on trip generation*

Finally, the effect of congestion on trip generation has to be considered. It has been suggested in the section on generation that both generation and attraction of travel are not independent of the transport networks, but should include the effect of network accessibility. It is therefore worth while considering the meaning of accessibility. Trip rate must depend upon the total number of opportunities available within a certain perceived cost of travel. As congestion increases so the number of opportunities available at a given cost of travel decreases, which reduces the demand for travel.

There is, of course, considerable evidence to show that household generation rates are affected by network accessibility. It was shown in the section on generation that distance from the centre of the urban areas was related to generation rate, and, as such, was some measure of decreasing accessibility. There is also evidence to show that attraction rates are equally affected by accessibility. For example, increasing car-ownership makes non-central areas very much more accessible. The result is in the large urban areas a larger growth rate of employment, shopping floor space, etc., for non-central areas as compared with central areas. As yet, however, the effect of network accessibility on trip generation rates has only rarely been incorporated in transportation studies. The effect of accessibility on trip generation and attraction rates clearly merits much more research, particularly since it is this area of the transport model which fringes with location and urban growth models.

6. (v) *Peak and off-peak*

The greatest demand for travel when the transport network becomes most congested is that of the peak period, and indeed, the peak within the peak. Any data derived from the transport model which may be used to help determine policy, or in the detailed design of transport facilities, should clearly consider the peak demand.

Several methods have been used to estimate peak-hour flows. Two approaches are possible, either estimating peak-hour flows from average daily volumes,[55] or alternatively the use of separate models run for peak and off-peak periods. The earliest methods of the first technique simply factored the twenty-four-hour matrix by an overall factor. A peak-hour factor was related to the average daily volumes for each of the various links in the road network. Data have been collected over a large number of years so that peak-hour percentages can often be adequately related to average daily volumes. It has, therefore, been common practice to factor the assigned twenty-four-hour linked volumes by specific peak-hour link factors. These factors have been, in general, of the order of 6% to 10% of the twenty-four-hour flow. Even a difference of 1%, however, can markedly change design considerations, particularly when dealing with large volumes; clearly, a close examination of peak-hour factors is most important. Further factors may also be required to convert the peak-hour flow into directional flows. Again, these factors have been based on past experience and particular data collected in the survey stage.

Although these methods can lead to design volumes, and although past experience has shown that in urban areas diversity of activities results in relationships between peak and average daily volumes, which are relatively stable, it is nevertheless to be expected that differing categories of trips and land use will have differing peak-hour characteristics. One of the most predominant factors governing the time of day a trip is made is trip purpose, and because trip purpose relates to land use, some methods of determining peak-hour matrices have used assignments by purpose. The assumption is made that trip purpose by time of day will remain relatively constant, that is, although the working week may perhaps be getting shorter, the majority of people will still travel to work in morning and evening peaks. It is assumed that trips for other purposes (shopping, school, etc.), where in fact there will be the greatest increases, will assume similar hourly patterns in the design year as in the base year.

These early methods of producing peak-hour matrices are quite sensible where network capacity restraints do not have a material effect upon expected flows. The methods themselves have in general been used with unconstrained assignments as a tool to forecast required facility capacity. In the more recent studies in the large urban areas, budgetary and environmental objectives have limited the size and number of road facilities. This in turn has made capacity restraint an essential sub-model in the total transport model. Congestion has been shown to affect all parts of the transport model. Clearly in the peak period, where travel demands are greatest, the effect of congestion is critical, and assessments of its effect on modal split, distribution, and generation as well as assignment are essential. It has been shown that the effect of congestion on the sub-model can be achieved by iteration of the whole of the transport model. It would appear, therefore, that in order to synthesise correctly conditions of considerable congestion, the whole transport model should be run for peak and off-peak conditions. Nevertheless, this procedure encounters model difficulties besides additional computation. For example, travellers in the peak period are prepared to suffer greater discomfort and travel costs than in off-peak conditions. Whilst these effects may be synthesised with particular speed/flow relationships, distribution functions and assignment algorithms, conditions cannot be simply divided into peak and off-peak categories. There will be a continuous change throughout the day. One example of this is the spreading of the peak-hour into the less congested periods. The synthesis of such effects will not only be very expensive, but also provide a considerable intellectual challenge. For the present, until new forms of synthesis can be achieved, perhaps using some incremental procedures, examination of traffic variations should be restricted to two or at most three peak and off-peak periods. In many studies it would appear natural to divide traffic into three components, peak-time traffic, average daily traffic between the peaks and off-peak (evening, night and early morning) traffic.

6. (vi) *Traffic congestion and road pricing*

In recent years, growing attention has been given to the idea of controlling the use of congested road space by some form of toll or *road-pricing* system.[56,57] This point is considered in the next chapter. At this stage it is only necessary to indicate that the effects of a road-pricing system on trip assignment, modal split, distribution and generation can easily be incorporated into the traffic forecasting model. In this case the road charge would alter the perceived cost of travel, affecting the demand for travel in the same way that a change in journey speeds can affect trip assignment, modal split, distribution and generation.

6. (vii) *An example of the effect of congestion on the traffic forecasting model*

An interesting example of the incorporation of congestion into the traffic forecasting model took place in the Bogota Urban Development and Transportation Study,[58] with which one of the authors was concerned. As part of this study, six alternative transport systems were considered for a town of $4\frac{1}{2}$ million people. These alternative systems included two different rail rapid-transit systems, a system of reserved busways, a system involving road pricing, a system in which road pricing was applied to a network which also included the smaller of the two rapid rail transit systems, and a no-change system in which the effects of minimum investment and the resultant heavy congestion were investigated.

Initially, public transport and private car matrices were obtained based on present-day traffic speeds. These matrices were then assigned to their respective bus and car networks (at present there is no short-distance rail traffic in the city) and it was found that the road system in the design year would be heavily overloaded, especially in the central area of the city. Speed/flow adjustments were therefore carried out. These adjustments were based on area speed/flow relationships for six areas in the centre of the town where there was a densely developed network of intersecting roads, combined with individual link speed/flow relationships used for the outer areas of the town where the street system was less dense. In each case it was assumed that a new speed could be assigned to each link or area which was halfway between the old assigned speed and the speed at which the forecast demand could have been accommodated.

The effect of the new speeds on trip distribution and generation was approximated by assuming an *elasticity of demand* for travel. It was assumed that the number of trips between two zones was related to a power of journey time or journey cost between the zones. This approach has a considerable advantage from a computational, and hence cost, point of view in that the forecast demand from zone i to zone j can easily be recalculated as a simple function of the change in journey time or journey cost between the two zones. This avoids the need for further costly iterations of the distribution and generation models. Thus it was assumed that the effect of congestion on road trips from zone i to j could be given by:

$$\frac{q'_{ij}}{q_{ij}} = \left(\frac{c_{ij}}{c_{ij}}\right)^e$$

where q'_{ij} = forecast demand from i to j
   q_{ij} = original demand from i to j
   c_{ij} = original cost from i to j
   c'_{ij} = new cost from i to j
   e = elasticity of demand for travel

This process was repeated for all six transport systems. The effect of congestion on modal split was allowed for, using diversion curves which related the traffic that transferred mode to the journey times by the alternative modes. It was found that three iterations of the speed/flow model were sufficient to obtain a close agreement between assumed speed and forecast demand. Some of the results of these comparative tests are given in Tables III.9 and III.10 below.

Table III.9 shows the differential effect of congestion in

TABLE III.9 Average speed in currently built-up areas forecast with different transport systems.

			Average speeds,* km./h.				
Speed flow area	Present day	Minimum road system	Road pricing	Maximum rail	Minimum rail	Minimum rail/road pricing	Busway
Area 1—northern suburbs	43·8	27·7	31·7	29·8	28·4	31·2	32·6
Area 2—northern inner suburbs	30·0	29·0	34·5	32·0	31·8	36·2	30·4
Area 3—north-west inner suburbs	29·5	23·5	28·5	26·0	24·6	26·0	26·7
Area 4—western industrial	29·6	19·2	26·2	23·6	22·7	29·3	25·0
Area 5—centre	20·2	11·5	18·6	17·0	17·0	23·0	15·2
Area 6—southern (poorer) suburbs	32·5	19·5	24·5	25·5	21·3	25·4	24·6

* Speeds refer to the daytime period from 7.30 a.m. to 7 p.m.

TABLE III.10 Forecast demand for transporation and proportion of demand satisfied.

Transport system	Car and taxi trips 000's/day			Public transport trips 000's/day		
	Basic demand	Percentage satisfied	Final demand	Basic demand	Percentage satisfied	Final demand
Minimum road system	1,324	78	1,035	4,112	92	3,813
Minimum road system controlled by road pricing	1,324	61	805	4,112	98	4,050
Rail mass transit (larger system) with minimum road system	1,324	83	1,100	4,112	102*	4,226
Rail mass transit (smaller system) with minimum road system	1,324	82	1,096	4,112	98	4,017
Rail mass transit (smaller system) with minimum road system controlled by road pricing	1,324	62	819	4,112	98	4,024
Busway with minimum road system	1,324	77	1,018	4,112	107*	4,425

* Extra trips were generated because of faster journey times possible if either the larger rail mass transit or the busway system were introduced.

reducing speeds in different areas of the city. The initially assumed speeds vary between 20 km per hour in the town centre to 44 km per hour in the northern suburbs. However, the final speeds fall to between $11\frac{1}{2}$ and 29 km per hour. It is interesting to note that the rail transit system is most effective in reducing congestion in the town centre and the poorer suburbs, and has less effect in other areas of the city although a good service was provided to all areas. Road pricing by contrast is capable of reducing congestion in all areas of the city.

Table III.10 shows the effect of congestion in reducing the demand for travel and the effects of new transit systems and new pricing systems such as road pricing on modal split. The first and fourth columns of Table 10 show the demand for car and taxi, and public transport trips, assuming that present-day speeds could be maintained in the future. In fact, as shown in Table III.9, such speeds cannot be maintained in the future and the other columns of Table III.10 show the final demand for movement with each of the alternative transport systems. If no transit system were introduced, only 78% of the initial demand for car and taxi movement would eventually be accommodated. Rather surprisingly, there is more car and taxi movement with the rapid transit system than without it, despite the diversion of a certain number of car trips to the transit system. The reason for this apparently strange result is that the transit system attracts a substantial number of bus passengers, thus reducing the frequency of the remaining bus services, which reduces road congestion and generates some new private car trips. It is also interesting to note that the net effect of the road-pricing system is to encourage more travel. It can be seen from Table III.10 that there are 210,000 fewer car trips with the road-pricing system. However, the resultant increased speed of movement on the road system generates 237,000 new bus passengers, including some passengers who divert from car to bus, thus giving a net increase of 27,000 trips.

It can be seen from Tables III.9 and III.10 that the effects of congestion on the trip-making pattern can be quite substantial. The example given above involved an 'elasticity of demand' approach to trip generation and distribution. This is a relatively simple and straightforward way of incorporating congestion into the traffic model. If it is considered necessary to include a complete distribution model at each iteration of the trip forecasting procedure, the work becomes much more complex and expensive.

6. (viii) *Conclusion*

The standard traffic forecasting model forecasts the traffic demand that would take place under given travel conditions. The first forecasts from a transport model are thus essentially demand forecasts and are not necessarily an accurate estimate of the traffic that would actually flow on a given traffic network. For many purposes, demand forecasts may be sufficient. Such forecasts highlight the areas and places where traffic growth is likely to be greatest and where traffic problems may become most acute. They do not, however, indicate in detail what is expected to happen within a given network. Hence, such demand forecasts are of little use for detailed design work. They are also of little use if we wish to estimate the benefits to be expected from a new transport system. In order to do this, it is necessary to have an accurate assessment of the traffic that would flow on a network if the new system were introduced and if it were not. This assessment can only be obtained by using an iterative traffic model which allows for the effect of congestion on all aspects of the traffic forecasting model.

CHAPTER IV

Prediction of the future use of transportation systems

1. INTRODUCTION

Most of the transport models and analysis procedures that have so far been discussed are judged, at least initially, and where necessary adjusted (or calibrated) on their ability to explain some past pattern of movement, usually the pattern of movement observed at the inventory stage of the study. Yet, as suggested in Chapter I, the objective of transportation planning is not primarily to explain past events, but rather to predict, and then influence, the effects of any policy or facility that might be introduced into the transportation system.

This chapter is concerned with methods of predicting the future use of transportation facilities. The transport model is an essential element in the predictive process. A transport model that satisfactorily explains the present use of the existing transportation system is an invaluable guide to the likely future use of any other transportation system. It is, however, vital to ensure that the correct information is fed into the transport model, and also to make certain that the model is adapted where necessary to allow for changed conditions in the future.

The forecasting phase of the transportation planning process can be divided into three separate but interrelated parts. First, prediction of the future demand for travel; next, prediction of the future availability of transport; and finally, prediction of the future use of the available transport.

It is essential in any field of planning but especially in urban and regional planning to understand clearly the distinction between the demand for travel and the use of any specific travel facility. The demand for travel is the desire of a specified community to obtain the advantages which can result from travel and is essentially an abstract idea. By contrast the use or flow on a specified line or between a specified pair of points is a hard statistic. In much of the literature on transport planning, this distinction has not been fully appreciated and the two terms have been used as if they were synonymous. This has been the cause of considerable confusion and has at times proved positively misleading. It is often stated that because there would, on certain assumptions, be a very high demand for travel between two points, this demand must somehow be accommodated on the transportation system connecting the points. This statement is based on the fallacy that there is some absolute quantity that represents demand. In fact, demand is always self-adjusting to meet the available supply.

The demand for travel is only one of many such demands or desires for the various goods, commodities or courses of action open to the population. Because of time and financial constraints, people have to choose between conflicting needs and desires. As we have mentioned earlier, to take part in an activity some travel is usually involved. The cost and time of travel have to be added to the cost of the activity itself to make comparisons. Thus a person's demand for travel depends on the relative costs of taking part in activities where these costs are inclusive of travel costs. Equally, it depends on how much time and money he has. This process of choice between alternatives can be represented graphically by the demand curve for travel shown in Figure IV.1 as *DD* which represents the number of trips *A* to *B* that would be made at a given cost by some given group. In Figure IV.1 the volume or amount of travel is shown on the *x* axis *Ox*, the cost of travel (taken in its widest sense to include both monetary and non-monetary costs) is shown on the *y* axis *Oy*. As the relative cost of travel decreases so travel will become relatively more attractive compared with the other options available and a person will choose to travel more. Conversely, as the price rises, he will choose to travel less. By itself, however, the demand curve does not indicate how much

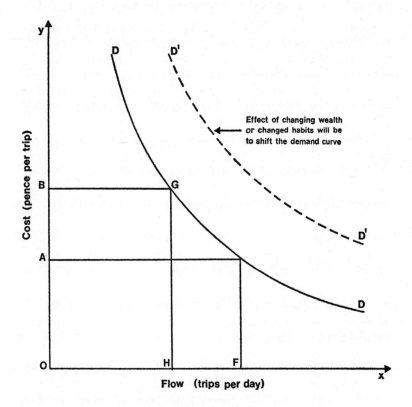

Demand curve: Showing variation in travel with journey cost.

FIGURE IV.1   Travel demand curve.

travel will take place. This also depends upon the cost of travel. If the cost of travel were *OA*, the volume of travel would be *OF*. If, however, the cost of travel rose to *OB*, the volume of travel would fall to *BG* or *OH*. A change in the cost of travel can therefore lead to a change in the use of a transportation system without any change in the real desire or demand for travel.

The nineteenth and twentieth centuries have seen a vast increase in travel, especially in the number of longer journeys that could not be covered in a few hours on foot. Some of this increase in the volume of traffic is due to an increase in the inherent demand for travel brought about by a larger population, greater wealth and changed habits (in other words due to a shift outwards, away from the origin of the demand curve). But much of this increase is due to the tremendous reduction in the cost of travel (in other words due to a movement down a given demand curve) brought about by the progressive mechanisation of transport and especially the advent of the railway.

Future changes in the nature and supply of transport facilities that could affect the cost of travel are considered in section 3 of this chapter. The next section, however, is devoted to changes in the inherent demand for travel as reflected by an outward shift of the demand curve shown in Figure IV.1.

2. FACTORS INFLUENCING THE FUTURE DEMAND FOR TRAVEL

There are several factors which will influence the future demand for travel within and through any area being studied. Of these the most important are:

1. The expected population within and adjacent to the area being studied. Not only the absolute size of the population but also demographic factors such as the age distribution of the population.
2. The wealth (income) or spending power of the population.
3. The opportunities made available by travel and also the needs that cannot be satisfied without travel. In particular the opportunities resultant from travel and the basic need to travel will be very dependent upon the spatial location of employment, shopping facilities and leisure activities relative to households.

These factors will affect not only the future demand for travel *in toto* but also the spatial distribution of such travel. In particular the future location of new housing and employment may radically change the existing origin and destination pattern of movements. Information about the future land-use pattern, that is to say the future distribution of population, industry, retail and wholesale outlets and other major traffic generators, is thus an essential input to the transport model developed to predict future travel in any area.

The future level and pattern of demand for travel is also dependent upon the future wealth of potential travellers. The future pattern of travel in any area will also be dependent upon the transportation system provided and the cost of travel on the system.

The factors mentioned above as influencing the future volume and pattern of travel are of course all related to one another. For instance, the future population in any area may depend upon the future employment in the area and future employment may depend upon changes in the future cost of transport. Yet if each factor is considered initially in isolation it should later be possible to check and allow for the repercussions of each upon the others so as to arrive at a final set of consistent conditions for the area being studied.

2. (i) *Predicting the future survey area population and employment*

The basic requirement of most transport models and indeed most planning models is information about the nature and number of households located in each zone. If an agreed physical plan has already been prepared for the area being considered such information may be given to the transportation planner. However, in many more cases the transportation planner may also be faced with the task of estimating the future population by zone. In these cases an essential preliminary to the zonal distribution of population is agreement as to overall survey area control totals. Such estimates can and have taken many forms depending upon the nature of the survey area being considered. Of these the quickest but generally least satisfactory is merely to extrapolate forward past trends.[1]

If the study area is tightly defined around or even within the perimeter of an existing conurbation or built-up area, the key determinant of its future population will be the planning decisions taken on the nature and size of any redevelopment contemplated within the study area. In these cases the future population of the study area cannot be determined without detailed local planning knowledge, so that population control totals are best fed into the transportation planning process by the respective local authority planning departments.

Unless the particular study being considered is itself a sub-study of a larger study, the study area chosen should preferably be sufficiently large to allow for any future expected growth in the built environment of the area being studied. An estimate can then be built up of the future study area population by considering the expected changes owing to natural increase coupled with net migration to or from the study area. Several studies have used such simple demographic techniques[2] to obtain estimates of future control totals for population, and an example is given in Appendix B.

It is of particular importance to know the future pattern of employment[3,4] within the study area because this is a key determinant of the level of travel, especially of peak-hour travel to and from work. The location of places of employment could radically affect the demand for travel and the consequent need to provide travel facilities in different parts of the study area. A study of the future employment potential is also an essential element of the whole planning process and may even be a main determinant of the future study area population.

The future level of employment depends upon two main factors; namely, the potential labour force available for employment, and the demand for the output that could be produced by those employed either in manufacturing, primary or service industries.

Local knowledge is probably the best source for estimates of employment in the near future in the study area. In particular, the managers of medium- and large-scale organisations should have a reasonable idea of the likely level of future employment in the immediate future and will know if any planned expansion or contraction of specific plants, offices or shops is intended. However, reliance on local knowledge has some disadvantages. In the first place local employers may often be over-optimistic in estimating desired future employment without making sufficient allowance for the actual availability of labour. Also insufficient allowance may be made for future improvements in productivity. Perhaps more importantly, there are obvious political difficulties in using and quoting objective assessments of the management's estimates of changes of employment. (Most managers are likely to consider good labour relations more important than objective input to a transportation planning exercise.)

Short-term employment projections should also make use of past employment statistics and trends. In this context the Department of Employment's Statistics[5] by employment exchange areas should prove particularly useful. The local planning authority is also likely to have a good idea of short-term trends and decisions which will affect the level and structure of employment within its area.

However, most large-scale transportation studies are concerned with a longer time period, usually between fifteen and thirty years into the future. In these cases more attention should be paid to longer-term phenomena, such as the decline in importance of certain basic heavy industries and the growing importance of service industries as a source of employment. One method of carrying out these longer-term employment forecasts is discussed in Appendix B. The basic approach is to assume that certain forms of employment serve an essentially national or international market and will be dependent upon developments in the national economy, while employment in other industries, particularly the service industries, depends on the size of the local population which it has to serve.

The future survey area population and employment are not independent but interdependent. If separate population and employment potential forecasts are produced, the two forecasts must at some stage be equated. After allowing for net commuting into the study area, the rest of the employment within that area must be filled from the resident labour force. If with the initially assumed population and employment this is not the case, then either the labour force must be increased or some of the potential employment must be diverted elsewhere. While the pressure of demand for labour in any given area may influence the number of people prepared to seek employment, much of the balance may have to be brought about by migration of people into the study area or employment moving out, or both. The whole problem of balancing population and employment is best explained with the aid of the specific example given in Appendix B.

It may perhaps be considered that the subject of population and employment forecasts discussed in the last few paragraphs and at considerably greater length in Appendix B is rather far removed from the subject of transportation. In some senses this is true. However, forecasts of population and employment are an essential input to the transport model. It could again be argued that whilst such forecasts are essential to the transportation planning process, they are better supplied by the local planning authorities. In practice, however, the local planning authorities do not usually try to make definite determinate future forecasts of the exact numbers to be housed or employed in their areas as far as twenty years into the future. Although the methods suggested in this book are relatively crude, they have the advantage that they can be executed with relative computational ease and may well prove acceptable for the purposes for which they are required. The estimates should of course be agreed and revised as necessary in consultation with the local planning authorities.

2. (ii) *The spatial location of population and employment*

The precise location of future population and employment is of considerable importance in the future trip forecasting process. This is basically a local planning operation and depends upon a detailed knowledge of local conditions. This work is usually carried out either under the auspices of or in conjunction with the local planning authorities. The first stage of the procedure is to estimate from the population forecasts the number and type of households in the survey area. The age-specific population forecasts described in Appendix B have considerable advantages over a plain population forecast, since such information can produce a much better estimate of the future number and type of households. In particular, by applying headship rates (the chances of an individual of a specific age and sex being head of a household) to the age-specific population, it is possible to make an estimate of the separate number of households[6] in the study area.

Once the future number and type of households has been determined the spatial distribution of the population may be assisted by the preparation of land-use maps or planning sieves[7] showing the present distribution age and condition of all property in the survey area, the nature and use of all un-developed land and also any future planning proposals and zoning regulations. From the planning sieve, it is possible first to isolate the areas where there is likely to be some demolition of residential property due to slum clearance, central area redevelopment, road expansion schemes or other planning proposals. The households so displaced must be rehoused. Study of the land-use map in conjunction with the local planning authorities should then be able to determine where the house-holds displaced and any further growth in the number of households will be located. Normally this will be a combination of some central area redevelopment, some infilling and increase in densities in suburban areas, new local authority housing often in fairly large-scale developments and finally private building often in small sites and at times at rather lower densities than most local authority building. The changes in the age and size of the population and consequent changes in household structure will also help indicate the type and con-sequent location of the new residential development in the study area.

The location of employment depends upon the nature of the employment. The changes in the expected level of employment in any existing large-scale manufacturing industry should first be estimated, preferably after consultation with the companies. Although new large-scale industry may require special site requirements (e.g. a large area of relatively flat land, room for future expansion, adequate power and water supplies, the ability to dispose easily and cheaply of any waste and effluent) most light industry is nowadays relatively footloose.

In the absence of restrictive planning controls, office employ-ment tends to be concentrated around good communications centres, and as close as possible to other office developments so that advantage can be taken of common services. Thus, in the past, office development sprung up around the main railway stations, usually on the edge of the shopping areas of the cities. In the future, there may be much more development around key road intersections in the suburbs which can easily be reached by private transport from the surrounding area. This type of location will be especially favoured if there is also a reasonable public transport service between the new office and the city centre.

Employment in wholesale distribution was originally concentrated mainly around the canals and railway goods yards. In the future, it can be expected to be concentrated much more towards the outskirts of towns especially in places which can combine good road and rail communications. Employment in retail distribution is to a large extent dependent upon the location of the population. It is also, however, very much influenced by the local planning policies for the area. If the local planning opinion is not hostile, large-scale out-of-town shopping centres may develop, especially close to certain key road intersections. Otherwise such employment is likely to be fairly concentrated in a few shopping centres, although the prospects for individual shopping centres can be very dependent upon planning policy.

The final location of population and employment may not be independent of the transportation system provided for the area. Indeed one of the aims of a transportation study is to influence the location of population and employment so as to obtain the maximum benefit from the available communications system. It is natural to suggest that it ought to be possible to develop models to predict the resultant changes of land use that would be associated with improved transportation facilities. Work on these lines has been carried out, especially in the United States,[8,9] the aim being not only to predict changes in land use but more ambitiously to suggest optimum combinations of land use and transportation networks. To date, the practical results obtained from this research have been limited. It is probably fair to say that this type of research is most likely to prove useful in the planning of new towns and cities, but will be less useful where developments within an existing conurbation are being considered. In these latter cases the influences of local geography, politics and history may be at least as important a determinant of the future land use as any changes in the conurbations transportation system. With the present state of transportation planning, a fixed distribution of population and employment has to be fed into the transport model as input. As a result of testing the repercussions of the input, some modifications to the input may be suggested, and this is an important aspect in the interpretation of the results of the traffic forecasting process. Until a clear relationship between accessibility and trip generation has been demonstrated the process of distributing population and employment must in the last resort remain somewhat arbitrary.

2. (iii) *Forecasts of the future growth of income*

The future growth in personal wealth is likely to be one of the key determinants of the future demand for travel. The richer

Table IV.1   Effect of income on travel.

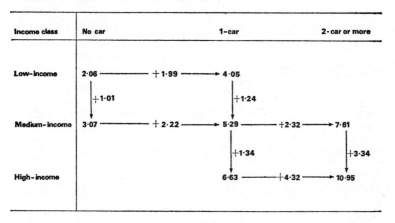

Income class	No car	1-car	2-car or more
Low-income	2·06 ——— +1·99 ——→ 4·05		
	+1·01	+1·24	
Medium-income	3·07 ——— +2·22 ——→ 5·29 ——— +2·32 ——→ 7·61		
		+1·34	+3·34
High-income		6·63 ——— +4·32 ——→ 10·95	

people are, the more they will be able to afford to travel and the more they will be able to do or buy as a result of travel. The increase in travel resultant from increasing affluence was discussed in Chapter III and is demonstrated in Table IV.1 which shows the results of a home-interview study. It can be seen that people belonging to higher income households make on average more vehicular trips per day than people from lower income households. This is true both of people in car-owning and non-car-owning households. This effect of income on trip rates could be due to the omission of walking trips, as discussed in Chapter III.

One of the major results of increased income is of course greater expenditure on cars. The rapid growth in car-ownership in the last ten to fifteen years is due in no small measure to rising incomes which, for the first time, have enabled most households in the country to have enough money to buy a car. It is also clear from Table IV.1 that once people own a car they make far more vehicular trips than they did previously.

In order to assess the effect of increasing wealth on the demand for travel, it is necessary to forecast its future rate of growth, that is to say the future growth in purchasing power that is obtained after the inflationary element (or fall in the value of money) has been subtracted from any increase in

TABLE IV.2 **Changes in real per capita national product: UK and selected countries.**

Country	Period	Average annual growth per capita	Period	Average annual growth per capita	Per capita income in 1968 US dollars
United Kingdom	1922–1938	2·2			
	1950–1960	2·3	1960–1967	2·3	1,451
Belgium	1950–1960	2·2	1960–1968	3·8	1,696
France	1950–1960	3·4	1960–1968	4·3	1,927
Germany					
(Federal Republic)	1950–1960	6·8	1960–1968	3·2	1,682
Italy	1950–1960	4·9	1960–1968	4·2	1,149
Netherlands	1950–1960	3·3	1960–1968	3·8	1,604
United States	1950–1960	1·1	1960–1968	3·6	3,578
Japan	1950–1960	6·5	1960–1968	9·1	1,122

Source: UN Statistical Year Book, 1969.

monetary income. Thus, since the war, although average income per head has risen by about 5% per annum, there has been relatively steady erosion of the purchasing power of money so that in absolute terms (here defined as at constant 1958 prices) real income has only risen by 2·3% per annum. While this growth rate is (see Table IV.2)[10] substantially greater than that achieved in any earlier period, it is considerably less than that which has been achieved in most advanced industrialised countries.

It is of course hazardous to predict the growth of any economy over a long time span such as the twenty-year periods often considered in transportation studies. Published estimates are usually limited to periods of two or three years into the future and any more distant estimates can be no more than inspired guesswork. At present (1971) the most fashionable guess for a long-term growth rate of national income would be about 3% per annum or 2·3% per head. But in a few years' time the climate of opinion as to future growth rates may have radically changed (either towards more optimistic or more pessimistic forecasts).

A given growth in total national income does not necessarily imply a similar growth in income per head in any particular area. This will again partly depend upon changes in the age-specific population within the survey area, so that if the percentage of non-earning households increases by more than the national average, there may well be a lower than average increase in income per household.[11] Probably the best way to calculate the increase in income in any area for trip estimation and car-ownership projects is to assume that the income of heads of households of a given age increases by the national average, although in certain areas, especially presently depressed areas, growth in income per employed resident may be slightly faster than the national average as some of the present regional differences in income are narrowed.

The important relationship between income and trip-end estimation was stressed in Chapter III. Usually this relationship is based on information collected as the result of a household interview. It is not always certain exactly what is meant by the phrase 'household income'. Ideally income statistics should include the total income (earned and unearned) of all members of the household, and for consistency should be given before deduction of any form of taxation. This ideal, however, is not usually attained, especially as questions on income often have to be phrased with some delicacy. However, for the individual deciding on the number of trips to make and whether or not to own a car, it is disposable income, that is, income after taxation, and not pre-tax income which is important.

2. (iv) *Forecasts of the future growth of car-ownership*

The most important factor influencing the level of car-ownership in any area is almost certainly the income of the residents of the area. As can be seen from Table IV.3 the results of several studies have all indicated that car-ownership is very sensitive

TABLE IV.3 Car-ownership related to income.

Area	Number of interviews	Date	Percentage car-owning households by income group					
			£0–500	£500–1,000	£1,000–1,500	£1,500–2,000	£2,000–2,500	£>2,500
London	50,000	1962	4·4	25·7	44·0	66·3	80·5*	†
West Midlands	21,000	1964	5·0	30·1	57·5	72·6	85·1*	
East Central Scotland‡	1,000‡	1966	5·4	30·5	50·1	63·8	72·6	
Hull‡	‡	1967	2·4	26·7	50·8	71·3	77·4	96·4

* Income range: £2,000–£3,000 for London; >£2,000 for West Midlands.
† Income range: >£3,000 for London.
‡ A small sample was used to adjust the shape of the household car-ownership curves found in London and the West Midlands to allow for local variation (see Section III.2. (ix)).

to income especially in the range £1,000 to £2,000 (mid-1960s prices). There will, however, always be a small element of the population which will not want to own a car either because of personal preference, age, debility or some other impediment. In consequence there will be some point above which increasing income is more likely to affect the number of two- or multi-car-owning households than the total number of car-owning households in general.

In the past fifteen years there has been a very rapid increase in car-ownership, and some gloomy forecasts have been made of the effects of ever increasing car-ownership leading to complete congestion of all our roads, with all the 'traffic

TABLE IV.4 Car-ownership per head in selected countries (persons per car).

Country	1953	1960	1962	1964	1966	1968
United Kingdom	18·0	9·7	8·0	6·5	5·7	5·0
Belgium	23·5	12·1	10·1	8·1	6·3	5·3
France	21·6	8·4	6·8	5·5	4·7	4·3
Germany						
(Federal Republic)	43·8	12·4	9·0	7·0	5·7	4·6
Netherlands	55·4	22·0	16·2	11·4	8·3	6·5
Italy	75·7	24·7	16·6	10·9	8·2	6·5
United States	3·6	3·0	2·8	2·7	2·5	2·4
Sweden	16·2	6·2	5·3	4·6	4·1	3·8

Source: Derived from UN Statistical Yearbook, 1969.

grinding to a halt'. This is of course complete nonsense, since people will not buy cars if there is no obvious use for them, and any system of this nature will eventually reach an equilibrium at some degree of congestion short of permanent saturation. It is worth pointing out that car-ownership is dependent upon the provision of associated facilities such as roads and parking spaces; however, except in the centres of the largest cities, conditions have not yet reached and probably never will reach the extreme state where lack of road or parking space exerts a severe downward influence on the level of car-ownership. Cars will still be used to reach out-of-town destinations more accessible by car. Table IV.4 shows the growth in car-ownership per head in selected countries and areas. It will be seen that in 1968 car-ownership per head in the United States or even in Sweden or France was significantly higher than in the United Kingdom.

F

There are also marked regional variations within the United Kingdom.

Two different approaches have generally been used to predict future levels of car-ownership. The simplest approach is just to examine past trends, and in particular to compare conditions in the United Kingdom with conditions in the United States. Thus in the London Transportation Study[12] it was assumed that car-ownership in London in 1981 would be similar to levels already achieved in metropolitan Boston, Philadelphia and New York. A similar type of analysis is that put forward by Tanner[13] which basically assumes that car-ownership will reach saturation level in the year 2010 and that the rate of growth to that date can be assumed to follow a logistic curve based on the present rate of growth in car-ownership per head (see Figure IV.2). Tanner's estimates suggest that the rate of growth

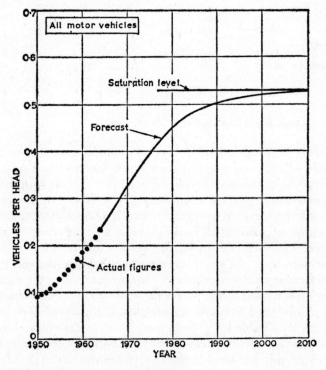

FIGURE IV.2   Forecast of car-ownership.

of car-ownership per head will continue close to the present rate until the early 1980s and then tail off rapidly.

The other method sometimes used to forecast car-ownership is a form of cross-sectional or category analysis. The basis of this method is first to predict the future changes in the number of households in various categories, such as households with two employed residents and a total household income of between £2,000 and £2,500. It is then assumed that the future level of car-ownership of people in such a category will be the same as the present level of car-ownership in this category. Such a method has obvious dangers: in particular there may be a high correlation between social class and income. If people of different classes or different types of occupation have different tastes and habits it may be unreasonable to assume that the level of car-ownership within a given income category will remain constant as the composition of that income group changes. Nevertheless, this method of cross-sectional or category analysis is probably better than an approach based solely on the extrapolation of past trends. Local variations in different areas that are not explained by differences in wealth can easily be recognised and allowed for. Thus if car-ownership in a particular zone is, say, 10% lower than the expected value given the distribution of population categories in that area, this discrepancy may be due to specific local characteristics such as a high residential density and associated high public transport accessibility which will continue into the future. The number and nature of the categories must in part be based on the size of the initial statistical sample collected during the household interview survey.

In many recent studies[14] car-ownership has been based on this cross-sectional analysis. However, an additional factor known as the car-ownership trend factor has been introduced to allow for the fact, first demonstrated by Wootton and Pick,[15] that car-ownership, as opposed to car-use, appears to be rising at a faster rate than can be explained by rising incomes. There are two reasons for this. First, there has been a relative drop in car prices. Secondly, the present generation are more car orientated than their predecessors. There is thus a secular trend factor. The younger members of the population are more likely to buy a car than their parents were, given the same real income. The size of the car-ownership trend factor is a matter of individual judgment. In some recent studies, it has been assumed that car-ownership as distinct from car-use will be based on a cross-sectional analysis assuming that average real incomes are rising at a rate 1·5 to 2·5% faster than actually expected.

2. (v) *Forecasts of the future growth in commercial vehicle traffic*

The first stage in predicting the growth of goods traffic is to forecast the overall growth of the transport of goods by all modes, and then to split the growth of goods traffic between the competing modes. The growth in goods traffic must be related to the overall growth of the economy, although there may not be any direct constant relationship between the growth in gross domestic product and the total ton-mileage of goods traffic carried. Indeed, as a nation's GDP grows, the proportion accounted for by basic but bulky raw materials such as coal drops, and the proportion made up of commodities with a high value-to-weight ratio such as electrical goods or of a service such as television which involves little commercial transportation rises. Thus the growth of commercial goods traffic could be considerably lower than the growth of total national output. However, there is an important counterbalancing factor and that is the tendency for fewer and bigger centres of production. Products are produced in one place, but designed to serve regional, national or international markets instead of, as previously, more local markets.

Unfortunately, relatively little research has been undertaken to isolate these trends or predict likely future developments. Table IV.5 below shows the growth in commercial ton-mileage both in total and by mode in Great Britain.

It will be seen that over the period from 1958 to 1968 the total growth in goods carried was over 32%, an annual rate of growth of 2·8% per annum. This is almost identical to the growth of total national output over that period. It is arguable whether a similar relationship will hold in the future.

The relatively slow overall growth in goods ton-mileage conceals a marked difference in the fortunes of the individual modes. Over the ten-year period 1956 to 1966, the goods ton-mileage carried by road almost doubled. During the same period goods traffic by rail fell by about one-third. Between 1960 and 1966 there was also a very rapid growth in pipeline traffic. The future modal split of goods traffic is a crucial question at the moment in many countries. The future profitability and possibly even existence of certain railway lines is dependent upon the level of goods traffic that they carry. In this country the future pattern is likely to be very different from the period between 1956 and 1966. The development of freightliner systems should ensure that the railways are rather

TABLE IV.5   Goods transport in Great Britain.

	1956	1958	1960	1962	1964	1966	1968
Total (ton miles × 10⁶)	54·9	53·6	58·7	61·1	66·6	67·9	70·8
Road	23·2	25·2	30·1	33·6	39·0	41·5	44·0
Rail	21·5	18·4	18·7	16·1	16·1	14·8	14·7
Coastal shipping	9·9	9·7	9·5	10·8	10·7	10·6	10·6
Inland waterway	0·2	0·2	0·2	0·2	0·1	0·1	0·1
Pipelines	0·1	0·1	0·2	0·4	0·7	0·9	1·4

Source: Ministry of Transport.

more successful in carrying goods traffic than they have been in the past.

The urban transportation planner is more likely to be interested in forecasting the growth of road than rail or other forms of transport for goods. With the rapid growth of car-ownership, commercial vehicles are becoming a decreasing proportion of the total vehicle mileage in any area. The likely change in commercial vehicle mileage is still, however, of considerable importance. Most commercial vehicle mileage, as opposed to the bulk of private motoring, makes a direct contribution to the national economy and to the country's Gross National Product. Government investment in major highway projects has been particularly geared to improving roads, including connections to the docks, which are important to commercial vehicles. It is necessary to have a good estimate of the growth in commercial vehicle traffic which generally requires a rather different kind of transportation facility than is needed by private vehicles.

Unfortunately, there is as yet (1971) no officially laid down suggestion as to the likely future growth in commercial vehicle mileage. Comparison with levels in the United States is probably not very relevant to other countries because of the vast difference in the geographic and economic circumstances of the USA as compared with most other countries, especially the United Kingdom. Recent studies[16] have postulated rates of growth of goods vehicle traffic of just over 2% per annum for both heavy and light commercial vehicles. The forecast of future goods vehicle mileage is, however, an area where rather more research could produce very useful results.

3. DESIGN OF FUTURE TRANSPORT FACILITIES

The previous section has dealt at some length with factors such as population, income and employment which directly affect the future demand for travel. Let us now consider the provision of transport facilities. Expected changes in transport facilities, together with the changes in income, population and employment previously discussed, combine to determine the final usage of any transportation system.

The most important factor in planning a future transportation system is the relationship between transport and general town planning and development. Any major change in the basic transportation network is in the long run likely to have a profound effect on the pattern of development.

This relationship can be illustrated in the location and growth of most towns. Figure IV.3 is a dramatic illustration of the growth of London from 1800–1958. London's inception at the first crossing point of the Thames can be seen as the response of land use and development to the transportation network. The growth of London from Roman times until the eighteenth century was concentrated along the river, the Thames being the chief artery for London's merchant trade. The great expansion of London in the nineteenth century, not just along the river but in all directions, was stimulated by the advent of the railway, the horse bus and tram. The rapid growth of London parallel with the lines of the electric trams and tube railways is the most dramatic example of the connections between transport and general land-use development. Not only did residential development follow the transport lines but office and shopping development tended to concentrate at the major transport interchanges, especially at the railway stations. The process is still continuing. Recent examples include the rapid growth of population along the line of the Southend and Clacton railway electrification systems.

Nevertheless this relationship should not be overstressed. The transportation planner is just as much the prisoner as the master of land use. In most conurbations, the main centres of attraction have been determined over a long period of time, and will continue to exert a predominant influence on the pattern of traffic demand. Although the transportation planner may be able to influence the pattern of development in the outer suburbs, the most difficult and most expensive problems to solve are found near the city centre. All attempts to solve these problems may, however, reinforce the very pattern of development that causes the problem.

In this situation it is virtually impossible to suggest optimum forms of transport network or city development. Every town must adapt its transportation system to its own circumstances. Although some general research work[17] has been carried out on the optimum form of road network and the most advantageous form of city development, these studies are of limited relevance when planning the transportation system for an existing conurbation, although they become much more relevant to the design of completely new cities. However, all transport models require some form of network as input. The transportation planner has to decide what this network will be. Usually the practical possibilities to be investigated are limited. The existing transport network in the study area is known, and certain other improvements are so firmly committed that they will certainly be carried out whatever the outcome of the transportation forecasting procedure. Beyond this point there is initially no substitute for inspired guesswork. The planner will decide what alternative proposals are worth studying and feed them in as input to alternative runs of the traffic forecasting model. The results of the model can then be used to evaluate the alternative proposals and on the basis of this evaluation further tests can be carried out with modified or refined networks. It is thus possible by examining the results of successive tests to progressively refine and improve the assumed trans-

FIGURE IV.3   Growth of London.

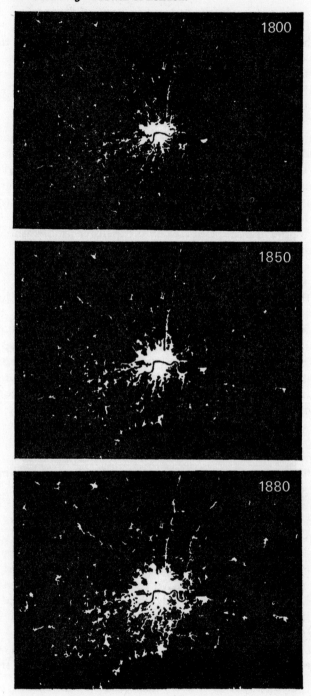

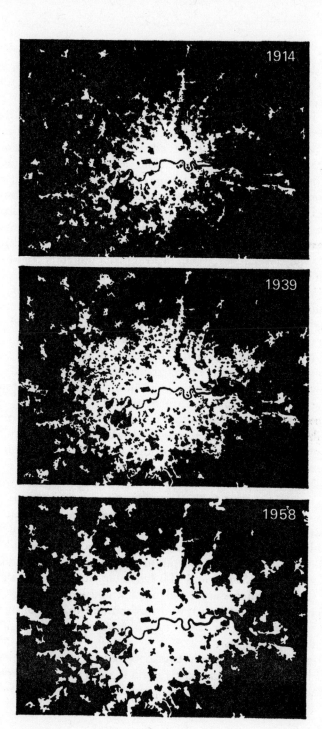

portation network. This is not cheap, however, and in consequence the initial networks considered should be as realistic as possible.

It is important to remember when designing the initially assumed transport network that funds for transport facilities are not unlimited. There is no advantage to be gained from designing a transportation system costing several hundred million pounds, if there is no hope of obtaining so much money. In some of the earlier transportation studies some ambitious road investment proposals were produced, which later proved quite impossible to finance. For this reason the Ministry of Transport now recommend that transportation studies should consider solutions that cost less than an agreed budgetary constraint.

An immediate result of the budgetary constraint is that it may not be possible to accommodate all the demand for travel by private cars. Not unnaturally, in view of their evolution in American city planning, most land-use transportation studies have until recently concentrated on travel by private car. It has been considered axiomatic that sufficient road space will have to be provided to carry the expected growth in traffic. This attitude is now changing. The large expenditure voted for such projects as the Bay Area Rapid Transit Scheme[18] or the underground extensions in London and other cities show that the importance of public transport as an alternative to the otherwise ubiquitous and overpowering domination of the private car is at last being realised. In Britain the Buchanan[19] report on traffic in towns highlighted the enormous expense and destruction which would be required to cater for full motorisation in large towns and cities. Although it might be possible at a price to provide for unrestricted use of the private car in Newbury, such a solution would be intolerable if not impossible in Leeds or London. The more recent British transportation studies such as the London Transportation Study and the Leicester Study[20] have shown that it will be necessary to plan for a considerable degree of travel by public transport, and furthermore that to bring this about it may be necessary to impose severe restrictions on the use of the private car.

The best form of public transport system in any particular conurbation will depend partly upon the size and density of the city and partly on the present public transport system in the area. An interesting theoretical design and costing study[21] recently carried out has suggested that for all except the largest and most densely developed cities the most efficient and economic form of transport would be provided by a bus system. Busways would operate in the city centre rather like a conventional railway service but with fairly frequent stations, while further out the busway would feed into a more flexible and conventional bus system. Other studies have compared the advantages of different forms of railway system.[22] These studies have generally concluded that modern forms of conventional duo-rail systems are better than any of the forms of monorail currently available.

Given the financial limitations on future investment, the existing road system must be used as wisely as possible. Traffic management schemes[23] may therefore have a big part to play in getting the maximum advantage from a city's proposed road network. They should therefore be included as input to the transport model. The practical application of traffic management schemes is outside the scope of this book. It is, however, worth mentioning that all town planning schemes should if possible strike a reasonable balance between the supply of parking space and the capacity of the road network to feed the parking provided. In particular, street congestion may be alleviated by a parking policy which limits the number of parking spaces available at peak hours. In this sense the roads to an area and the parking there are complementary goods and one should not be considered without the other.

A form of traffic management that may at times be particularly advantageous is restricting parts of certain streets for the use of buses.[24] The theoretical advantages in reduced congestion and quicker journey times that could be derived from restrictions on the use of the private car supplemented by the provision of different types of bus service have been well described by Webster.[25]

4. FUTURE POLICIES

It has probably become clear from the preceding section that any transportation infrastructure can be used in many different ways. In transportation planning it is therefore necessary not only to predict the demand for future transportation, and compare this with a proposed transportation system, but also to assess how any such system could be controlled. The control of a transportation system can be divided into two parts, legal or regulatory controls and fiscal controls.

Regulatory controls are usually introduced to protect the public or certain sections of the community. The prime justification for many of these controls, especially the earliest regulations such as speed limits, and construction and use regulations, was public safety. But much early regulation, especially in the field of public transport, was designed to protect the public from the abuse of monopoly powers and franchises granted by central and local government to certain transport undertakings. In recent years there has been a tendency to introduce further regulations to protect the quality of the environment. Thus experiments have been carried out with one-way street systems designed to prevent through traffic from entering selected residential areas; heavy commercial vehicles have been prevented from entering city centres except to load and unload, and more recently specific regulations have been adopted to control the level of noise emitted by road vehicles. Regulatory controls have also been used to increase the volume of traffic that can pass through an intersection or area. Finally regulation has been used as a policy to beat or ameliorate the effects of congestion. Thus parking restrictions, clearways, priority lanes for buses may all be used to speed or increase the flow of peak-hour traffic.

Fiscal controls may serve three main purposes. First, they create revenue, e.g. vehicle licence duty, purchase tax, public transport fares, and the charge on toll bridges. The second main purpose may be to redistribute income, e.g. concessionary fares policies for old-age pensioners and cross-subsidisation of rural bus services from the profits on more urbanised routes. Such policies can also be used to regulate the supply of transport facilities to match the expected demand. The first two of these aims are determined more by considerations of the general need to equate as fairly as possible the demand for goods and services in the whole economy to the general productive capacity of the economy, and so should not be too influenced by factors solely determined on transportation planning grounds. It should not, however, be forgotten that any change in fiscal policy such as an increase in the tax on petrol or the cost of travel over a toll bridge is bound to affect the demand for travel.

The third aim of fiscal policy to regulate the supply of transport facilities is, however, an integral part of the transportation planning process. Thus the scale of charges and permitted length of stay at parking meters can and should be adjusted so that the demand for parking spaces does not exceed the supply. Similarly, it may be reasonable to operate a differential fares policy on public transport so as to induce certain passengers to use services when demand is otherwise relatively slack and to avoid those periods when demand is heavily peaked. A final example of a possible form of fiscal control is some form of road pricing.

The theoretical argument for road pricing,[26,27] that many road travellers impose costs on others which are greater than the benefit the travellers gain from travel, is by now fairly well established, if not so well accepted. The basic advantage of a road-pricing scheme is that people who really need to use a scarce supply of road can outbid people who need to use the road less. At present such people with a real need to take advantage of the fast and efficient service that is potentially offered by road transport cannot do so at peak hours in congested cities because the roads are clogged up with less essential users, many of whom place a relatively low value on their own time.

Whilst the practical and theoretical arguments are by now fairly well understood, the technicalities of implementing road pricing have been much less clearly established. The Smeed Report suggested that direct road pricing was technically feasible, and work is continuing at the Road Research Laboratory on alternative control systems. In the longer term it may be desirable to introduce some form of road pricing as one possible input to the transportation model.

5. FORECASTS OF FUTURE USE

The previous two sections have been concerned with the demand for movement, and the facilities that may be provided to cater for this demand. The transport model must combine these two aspects and determine the resultant pattern of movement when a given transport network operating in a specified manner is subject to a predetermined pattern of demand.

Most transport models are developed to predict present-day trip characteristics and it is worth examining in some detail how well an existing transport model can predict this future pattern of movement. The immediate answer to this problem is that the model predictions will be best when the future transport pattern in the area is not too dissimilar from the present. So long as trip generation, modal split and distribution are expected to remain fairly similar to the present pattern, the models calibrated to match the existing traffic flows can be expected to give a good estimate of future flows.

Many of the earlier transportation studies were based upon a simple analysis of predicting the demand for travel assuming that traffic could move as freely in the design year as the calibration year. However, it was found that the resultant demand was too high to be accommodated on the networks. In these circumstances a traffic model is required that allows for some element of restraint to be included as part of the model. These capacity restraint models were discussed at the end of Chapter III.

Of the four main stages of the normal traffic model, the trip generation and distribution formulae are particularly likely to be influenced by changed traffic conditions, whereas modal split and assignment should be less affected. The traditional trip generation formulae for most transportation models have allowed for changes in demand due to such factors as changes in the numbers and wealth of the population and the spatial distribution of population and employment, but they have assumed that the cost of travel will remain approximately constant, or if not, that trip generation is independent of the cost of travel. In fact, trip generation is likely to be affected not only by demand factors such as changes in household income and composition but also by supply factors such as parking availability, government taxation policy and the available supply of public transport and road space. At present, not enough research has been carried out to discover how these supply factors influence trip generation, and further work is required on the relationship between trip generation and trip accessibility. Studies such as the London Transportation Study and the example from Bogota given in the previous chapter which have assumed changed trip generation as a result of changed traffic conditions have based their assumptions on plausible but unproven guesses as to the effect of traffic congestion on trip generation.

Trip distribution is more likely than trip generation to be affected by changed conditions. The standard trip distribution procedures allow for a changed spatial pattern of generations and attractions, but they are usually based on the assumption that trip length is a function of journey time and of journey distance. However, if the average journey time and the average journey costs between all points in an area alter drastically, either because of new urban motorways or because of increased congestion or an inadequate road network, the distribution of trips may not be based on the same time or cost distribution function as before. It is even more difficult to predict the exact change in the trip distribution function that might result from changes in journey costs, so that for planning purposes, in the absence of any further evidence, the distribution functions will probably remain unaltered in the future. However, the mathematical relationships assumed in the distribution process have not as yet been shown to represent real physical relationships but only approximate truths that can provide a useful predictive tool, provided future conditions do not alter too drastically.

In view of this uncertainty as to the effect of changed network conditions on trip generation and distribution, one is tempted to despair. If so little is known about the basic relationships of trip generation and distribution, why continue with the traffic forecasting exercise? The answer to this problem is that, despite all their faults and uncertainties, these forecasting procedures can still help predict patterns of movement, which is useful for policy decisions. The basic distribution and generation equations may be far from accurate and forecasts of the expected traffic flow throughout a city may be too high or too low. However, the quantitative results are sufficiently accurate to compare alternative transport systems and give a good estimation of the relative importance of alternative possible investments. This subject is discussed in more detail in the final chapter, when we consider the value of the traffic forecasting process.

Although it is difficult to predict the effects of changes in the supply and cost of travel facilities on generation and distribution, the effects of future changes in relative journey costs on the future pattern of modal split and assignment are somewhat easier to assess. Provided the traffic model incorporates some form of iterative procedure by which road speeds and flows are balanced, the methods of assignment used to represent traffic flows in the calibration year should be satisfactory even under conditions of greatly increased congestion. Modal split is especially dependent upon changes in the supply and cost of travel between specific points, including changes in the relative costs of private motoring and public transport fares. For any particular point-to-point movement, the relative cost (including times costs) of a journey can be radically altered by a new public transport service. For this reason modal split analyses which rely on diversion curves based on journey cost characteristics by private and public transport, but applied separately for different household and income categories, are greatly to be preferred to simpler analyses which determine modal split at the trip generation stage. So long as the diversion curve analysis is applied on a journey cost basis separately for different income groups, these curves will probably still hold good in the future irrespective of changes in the transport services provided.

The complexity of the problem of obtaining a balance between demand and supply can be illustrated by a specific example. In Phase III of the London Transportation Study,[28] the demand for travel was first estimated on the basis of an assumed set of journey speeds for travel by public or private transport. The estimated demand was based upon a form of cross-sectional analysis by income categories to determine trip generation, separately for car-owning and non-car-owning households, thus approximating to a simple form of modal opportunity grouping. Trip distribution allowed for future changes in land use and consequent trip generations and attractions and assumed a fixed time-based distribution function. Modal split was based upon diversion curves applied separately for all point-to-point movements by car-owning households and the information from the household interviews. The resultant demand was, in certain areas, far greater than the capacity of the road networks being tested. In these circumstances it was assumed that the speeds on the motorway links (initially the most heavily overloaded links) would be reduced (equivalent to some degree of queuing to join the network) until these links were equally overloaded with the basic street system. This process is akin to one of control of demand by network congestion, if it is assumed that the demand for travel is some function of the speed of travel. In the particular case of the London Study, it was assumed that the result of increasing congestion was to leave the trip distribution function in time terms unaltered, consequently shortening the trip length distribution measured in terms of distance travelled.

At the point at which the motorways and ordinary streets were both equally overloaded, it was thought better to introduce restraints such as parking controls than to allow congestion to increase until reduced speeds eventually led to an equilibrium between demand and supply. That is relating generation and attraction rates to an estimate of accessibility. It was also assumed that car-owners who, because of the policy of restraint, were unable to use their cars would act like non-car-owning households and make some, but not all, of the curtailed car trips by public transport thus again crudely following a modal opportunity procedure and a relationship between generation rates and accessibility. This process reflects a positive regularity or fiscal policy designed to equate the demand to use a network to the available volume of traffic that the network can efficiently hold.

The process adopted in the London Transportation Study is only one of several capacity restrained assignments and/or distribution techniques that have been used in different circumstances to simulate the eventual volumes of traffic on links where the inherent demand, if present-day cost conditions continued, would be too great for the network to contain. The capacity restrained assignment and distribution techniques described in Chapter III are still in their infancy. The example of the London Transportation Study is not put forward as a model solution to this problem, as it is based on a very special set of assumptions, but simply to show some of the difficulties involved in balancing supply and demand. The interrelationship between demand, supply and cost must be recognised. The demand for travel is not normally some absolute volume that must be satisfied. If the means to satisfy the volume of demand does not exist, the potential demand must be regulated. It can be regulated by deliberately reducing the attractiveness of travel, or by the natural process of ever-increasing congestion with increased journey costs and decreasing trip attraction and generation. Whatever the transport network supplied, the eventual demand will balance the supply either because of regulation or because of a high level of congestion. Costs must in the end adjust so that demand balances supply.

It is clear that the models outlined above to obtain a balance between supply and demand are much more complex than the simpler model which simply predicts the demand pattern, assuming specified cost conditions. In many circumstances the extra complexity of the complete model may not be justified as the demand forecasts obtained from a simpler model may be adequate for traffic planning purposes. It is, however, necessary at an early stage in the transportation study to decide which type of model will eventually be required. This will probably depend upon the range of alternatives. The greater the changes expected the more flexible the model will have to be. The form of model required for future forecasting needs to be calibrated, using present-day information. Hence the ultimate form of traffic model required for traffic forecasting should be determined before any attempt is made to calibrate a model to reflect present-day traffic characteristics. In our opinion it is generally advisable to prepare a flexible model which can be used to predict traffic movements under a wide variety of conditions, even if this flexibility is achieved at the cost of a reduction of apparent accuracy of base-year calibration.

CHAPTER V

Evaluation

1. INTRODUCTION

The major reason for developing a transport model is not just to predict the future, but to influence the future and help the planner decide which of several alternative policies should be preferred. To do so, one must evaluate the results of different plans and policies, and this means one has to examine carefully the possible consequences of each of the plans.

It was suggested in Chapter I that the output from the traffic forecasting model should be examined under four headings: numerical, operational, environmental, and economic evaluation. The numerical evaluation checks the computational validity of the forecasts. The aim is to ensure that the output obtained from the traffic forecasting process precisely reflects the input assumptions.

There are two possible sources of error, both of which can easily be overlooked when studying the computer output from a transportation study. The first of these is programming errors. In the traffic forecasting process, most traffic forecasting programs need time to be developed. Once the basic theory of the program algorithm has been devised, slow and laborious work is required to prepare a 'clean' version of the program. Unexpected errors are always creeping into the process of program development and it is not always easy to detect these errors. At times a computer print-out will be produced which appears valid, and only a close scrutiny of the details of the output or a chance comparison with some other output will reveal an unsuspected fault in the computer program. Great care should be taken in checking the output of any new computer program, however simple, designed as part of the traffic forecasting process.

The other possible source of error is in the input information. Sometimes the error is so extreme that it is immediately obvious from the output. At other times it is more difficult to detect. It is strongly recommended that all input information should always be printed out in full, so that the evaluator can check the accuracy of the input information. The most common faults in the input information are punching errors on the cards fed into the computer. It is vital not only to have checks built into the programs, but also to scrutinise all input data. For example, a common error is the omission of links from the coded transport network. This is often difficult to detect and can have serious repercussions.

2. Operational evaluation

The principal concern in most transport studies has been with the operation of the transport network. Could the roads take the traffic without unreasonable delays? Would the conditions on the railway network be acceptable or would the trains be grossly overcrowded? This of course depends upon a detailed examination of the traffic flows and travel speeds on different parts of the network and an understanding of the capacity limitations of different types of transport systems. A full discussion of this subject would require a treatise on basic highway design, traffic engineering and railway operating practice which lies outside the scope of this book.

Two points should, however, be mentioned. The first is that design standards are often determined by peak-hour traffic forecasts. The output from a transport model is often, although not necessarily given, in the form of twenty-four-hour flows and volumes. These may be of little direct use for design purposes although they are often essential for economic evaluation. However, it is always possible to convert from twenty-four-hour flows to peak-hour flows, either by assuming a percentage traffic demand during the peak hour or by means of a more detailed analysis which carries out separate assignments by trip purpose, or indeed separate runs of the model for peak and off-peak periods. This is discussed in more detail in Section III.6.

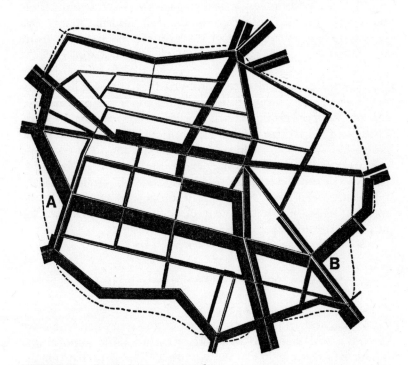

FIGURE V.1   Loaded street network.

The other point is that the results from transport models should not always be interpreted too literally. Figure V.1 shows part of a city street network and the associated coded road network. It can be seen from this diagram that there are two parallel routes from *A* to *B*, both of which could serve basically the same function. The assigned network, however, shows 1,000 vehicles using the more southerly route and 10,000 vehicles using the more northerly route. In practice of course this does not necessarily mean that the exact split between traffic along these two competing routes will be as assigned but rather that 1,000 vehicles will be assigned between the two competing routes. How much traffic, in fact, uses each route may depend on such factors as signposting, lighting and the form of priority given to each route at the junction at *A* and *B*. If the model were substantially refined it would no doubt be possible to obtain a computer print-out which gave the correct volumes on each link, but for many purposes such information is not required, and in most other cases it can be deduced from the print-out when supplemented by small sample traffic counts.

It should be remembered, however, that network link flows are not the only output from transport models. For example, the output concerning car-driver trip ends can be used to evaluate the parking policy assumptions. If the synthesis of congestion has been included in the model then the resultant effect on generation rates may have implications on land-use policy. The use of data from transport models has unfortunately up to now been too concerned with the transport network and too little concerned with how data might be used to formulate new policies and other alternatives.

3. ENVIRONMENTAL EVALUATION

The next important stage of the evaluation process is the environmental and aesthetic impact of any suggested transport plan. This is obviously a matter of considerable importance. There is a limit to the price we are prepared to pay for an efficient transportation system. No one would normally be prepared to demolish part of a fine twelfth-century church or an outstanding row of Elizabethan houses in a picturesque village just to make way for a road improvement. But equally the price to be paid for preservation should not be too high. While it would certainly be worth spending £500,000 to avoid an important national monument, it might not be worth spending £50,000 to avoid a couple of half-timbered houses which although of some interest and antiquity are not basically dissimilar to thousands of other such houses scattered throughout the country.

It should be clear from this last paragraph that environmental evaluation is to a large extent a matter of judgment, and it would be impossible to lay down hard-and-fast rules appropriate to all circumstances. What is unique in one place and therefore worthy of preservation may be too commonplace in another area to be of any real interest.

Environmental planning is, of course, concerned with far more than the simple question of where it is desirable to remould the physical environment to make room for transport improvements. It also looks at the immediate effect of traffic on the area through which it circulates. Two of the most serious effects of increased traffic circulation may be noise and danger to pedestrians. By careful planning and a certain amount of preventive engineering such as noise barriers, guard rails to separate pedestrians from moving traffic and the provision of safe pedestrian crossings, these problems can to some extent be alleviated although they cannot usually be completely solved. No amount of clever engineering is likely to make a village street through which a continuous stream of heavy traffic passes a pleasant or safe place to live in.

At the moment techniques for measuring the effect of transport systems on the environment are not well developed. The only factor which is easily measured appears to be noise[1] and certain studies include an assessment of the degree of damage or improvement in noise levels in particular areas. It will probably always remain extremely difficult to carry out quantitative evaluations on any other environmental factors, except perhaps atmospheric pollution which it should be possible to measure.

Environmental evaluation is essentially a matter of judgment on what is desirable and tolerable. Before any proposal is rejected on environmental grounds two specific questions must be answered. The first is, if we reject the plan, are we sure that the best alternative (which may in fact be to do nothing at all) will not have an even worse effect on the environment? The second is, if we reject the plan on environmental grounds, is the environment worth the entire cost incurred to ensure its preservation? A good example where these criteria apply is the case of airport location. Almost inevitably any airport will have a detrimental effect on the immediately adjacent environment.

Thus, before rejecting an airport site on environmental grounds one has to show (assuming that we do need an airport) that there are alternative sites where the environmental disadvantages of the airport would be less pronounced. Again, if extra capital expenditure is incurred to improve the quality of the local environment one has to ensure that the money is well spent. It may be much better to compensate people for loss of environment than incur the extra capital cost required to prevent the loss of environment. Thus rather than re-align an airport runway at a cost of £10 million so as to avoid flying over the top of a town of 20,000, it might be much better, and more acceptable to the people of that town, to spend only a quarter of the sum on urban renewal, slum clearance, or the provision of a new school, hospital or park that is urgently required. There is always some price that is too great to pay for the preservation of any environment. The difficult question is to decide what this price is. In the last resort, the question can only be solved by the politician acting as the community's representative. The politician will be in a much better position to make this decision if he has all the facts before him, and he must try to assess the immediate effects on the local environment if the scheme goes through, and also the effect and cost of rejecting the scheme.

4. Economic evaluation

4. (i) *Principles of cost-benefit analysis*

The final stage of the evaluation process is commonly known as cost-benefit analysis or economic evaluation, although it would be better to call it quantitative evaluation. The term economic evaluation is unfortunate because of what is sometimes implied by the word economics. Economics may be linked with production and the belief that the aim of the economic evaluation process is to measure the increase in a country's productive ability that will result from a transport improvement. This aim might be worth while, especially in less developed areas of the world, but it is not the aim of the economic evaluation process, which simply helps decide whether the community really wants the improvement in question. One reason for the improvement might be to enable industry or commerce to operate more efficiently, but equally the community may want a road for reasons of leisure—going to the beach, climbing a mountain, playing cricket or engaging in some other totally unproductive activity. There is no basic distinction between economic evaluation and evaluation in general, although in practice there can be a distinction between quantitative and non-quantitative evaluation.

The aim of the evaluation process is to decide whether a plan is worth while, but this not easy to do. This is the specific problem studied under the heading of *Welfare Economics* and a fairly extensive but generally inconclusive literature[2] related to the problem has developed. There is agreement that a change which leaves some people better off without making anyone worse off is worth while. This is, however, hardly a fundamental conclusion and in real life such an ideal situation in which everyone gains but no one loses occurs all too infrequently.

Another criterion (the Kaldor–Hicks criterion)[3] that has been put forward is that a change is worth while if the people who gain from the change could adequately compensate all the losers. This is the criterion generally adopted for cost-benefit analysis. Both costs and benefits are measured in terms of the money people would be prepared to pay to avoid the cost or obtain the benefit. If the total price people would be prepared to pay for the benefits from the change exceeded the price people would be prepared to pay to avoid the costs of the change, then the potential gainer could compensate the potential losers and still retain some benefit. In other words, if the price people would pay for the benefits exceeded the cost of providing the benefits, the scheme would be considered worth while. But in certain circumstances this criterion could be considered inappropriate. This is because while the gainers from the scheme could compensate the losers, it is most unlikely that they will in fact do so. A change which made a millionaire £1 better off but cost a poor man 50p would satisfy the Kaldor–Hicks criterion, but might generally be considered highly undesirable. A pound is worth far more to a poor man than to a rich man. In fact, to interpret the results of a cost-benefit analysis, one should consider not only the overall net benefit but also the distribution of the benefit between different sectors of the community.

Despite the uneven distribution of income, two alternative justifications may be put forward for the standard benefit–cost comparison. The first is that while in any one scheme some people will gain and others will lose, if enough schemes are implemented which satisfy the Kaldor–Hicks criterion, the chances are that altogether most people must gain, some quite appreciably, and hardly anyone is likely to lose. A second possible justification is that if the Government (and hence the community) does not like the eventual distribution of benefit, it can, by taxation, redistribute some of the benefit so that the gainers are in fact forced to compensate the losers. The best justification for using the price people would be prepared to pay as a pseudo-monetary measure of costs and benefits is probably to combine both these arguments, and say that if changes with a positive net benefit fail to provide a satisfactory distribution of benefit, the Government can adjust its taxation policy so that the combination of tax changes as well as other changes leaves all sections of the community better off.

It is now time to move from the rather abstract discussion of the principles of cost-benefit analysis to consider how in practice it can be applied to the evaluation of alternative transportation plans. The basic aim of evaluating any proposed transportation improvement is to compare the expected benefits with the initial cost of introducing the scheme. The standard process is to express the annual benefits of a scheme as some fraction or rate of return on the initial or capital costs.

The main factors which should be taken into account can be listed as follows:

Capital costs

Construction costs
Land costs
Delays and inconvenience during construction

Annual benefits

Transport user benefits
Public transport operators' benefits

Governmental benefits

External economies and diseconomies (all other costs and
   benefits)

(Changes in accident costs, if not included elsewhere)

Changes in maintenance costs.

Each of these factors is now considered in more detail below.
It is, however, worth pointing out that the definition of the
fourth item in the list of annual benefits implies all other
benefits (or costs) not included in the other items and thus
ensures that the list of annual benefits is all inclusive.

4. (ii) *Capital or initial costs*

To build a new road, large numbers of men, as well as
materials and machinery, and a certain amount of land are
required. If the road were not built, the same resources could
be used to construct new steelworks, houses, hospitals, schools,
pubs or whatever else the community decided it wanted. The
real cost of constructing the new road is the cost of the alternative benefits that have to be sacrificed in order to provide the
road. This cost is often known as the opportunity cost of capital.
The benefits rejected would normally (in a full-employed
economy) take the form of alternative goods that could otherwise have been produced either for present consumption or to
increase future productive capacity.

In a centrally planned economy it would be extremely
difficult to estimate the alternative benefits rejected by the
decisions to build a road, but in a market economy the price
that has to be paid for any factor of production probably
represents the maximum price that anyone else would be
prepared to pay for this factor of production in some alternative
use and hence the benefit forgone. Thus the price paid for the
factor is the cost of using the factor for road construction rather
than anything else. For most factors of production, the money
paid for the factor can be used as a measure of its inherent
alternative use value or opportunity cost.

There is one possible exception to this rule and that is the
price paid for land. In many cases the land required for a new
road or rail improvement is already owned by the organisation

which intends to use it. This does not mean that there is no cost associated with using the land, because if it were not pre-empted for the transport improvement it could be used for housing, say, or school playgrounds. It is the present potential alternative use value of the land in question which should be imputed as part of the cost of the improvement. The actual price paid for the land, perhaps in the distant past, is a historical fact of no immediate present significance. There is another reason why land costs should be considered separately from other construction costs, and this is that unlike construction costs, land costs do not represent an immediate use of resources but rather the capitalised value of the alternative use value or rent of the land in question; thus only a percentage of the land cost is really felt in any one year. This distinction can be of considerable importance when considering the overall strain on the national economy of additional expenditure on transport investments.

Another factor which can in many ways be considered as an initial cost is the effect of construction works on the traffic flow and general environment in the area. In certain circumstances the potential delays to traffic during construction are important, especially if they occur for several years before any benefit is received. In many cases the design or staging of a scheme is substantially influenced by the need to keep traffic delays down to a minimum. The cost of such delays can usually be calculated by the approach that is put forward in the following sections. However, in practice, these costs have not been included as a specific quantitative item in the evaluation process. As well as causing delays to traffic, any large-scale construction work may have an adverse effect on the environment. Such factors as noise, dust, visual intrusion and general unsightliness are, however, extremely difficult to quantify in monetary terms.

4. (iii) *Benefits to individual transport users*

The benefit to individual transport users should include all the benefits initially received by transport users. If, as the result of a new motorway, the cost of carrying a lorry-load of goods from A to B falls by £1, this is the benefit attributed to individual transport users. It is true that through the competitive process, a proportion of this benefit will be passed on to whole-salers, retailers and ultimately consumers, but if one accepts the basic postulate of all cost-benefit analyses that a pound is just as valuable whoever is the ultimate beneficiary, there is no need to follow through all the advantages and disadvantages of the competitive process.

The benefits to individual transport users result from a reduction in the cost of trips. These costs can be considered as falling into two distinct categories. First, there is the direct transportation cost of travel which for the user is the cost that he has to pay for travel. In the case of public transport this is simply the fare paid. For the private motorist the direct cost of travel should comprise costs such as petrol, oil, tyre wear and maintenance that are a direct result of travelling. But in addi-tion to these direct costs of transport there is also the time spent in travel together with any discomfort or inconvenience.

It is perhaps worth examining what is really meant by the phrase 'the value of time' commonly used to help justify trans-port investment problems. Time is not a commodity like bread that a person voluntarily chooses to consume. Whether he likes it or not a person consumes twenty-four hours of time every day. The choice open to him is not how much time he consumes, but rather how much time he is prepared to devote to any specific purpose. This means that when one is valuing time spent on travelling one is inherently valuing time spent in one use rather than another. It is for this reason that it may be acceptable to value time differently for different trip purposes.

A more detailed discussion of current thinking as to the appropriate value to place on time savings is included in Appendix C. This appendix also contains a discussion of the value commonly assumed for direct vehicle operating costs.

It is easiest to assess the benefit users receive from a new travel facility by considering the reduction in the cost of their travel brought about by the new facility. There are two possible approaches to this problem. So long as the improved travel facility does not substantially influence the pattern of movement in the area, it is reasonable to consider the total user benefit simply as a reduction in the cost of carrying a fixed matrix of traffic. An example of this fixed matrix evaluation is given in Appendix E.

In situations where a complete transportation model is applied it is often assumed that the trip matrix will be different for two separate plans that have to be compared. It is then no longer possible to evaluate the two alternative plans simply by comparing the total cost of moving the traffic. An increase in the total cost of moving the traffic could reflect a disbenefit because of worsening traffic conditions, or alternatively it could indicate a positive benefit, a reduction in the cost of movement encouraging people to spend a greater percentage of their total income on travel, to take advantage of the benefits of cheaper travel. It is not sufficient to compare two alternative transportation systems merely on the basis of the resultant user cost of travel without also considering the associated user benefits of the movement that takes place. This elementary point has often been forgotten in the past evaluation of transportation studies.

An analysis which allowed for this problem was developed as part of the cost-benefit evaluation of the London Transportation Study.[4] It was shown that in normal circumstances the direct benefit (or loss) to individual travellers as the result of a new transport facility was given by the formula:

$$B = \tfrac{1}{2} \sum_{ijm} \left(q_{ijm} + q'_{ijm} \right) \left(c_{ijm} - c'_{ijm} \right)$$

where q_{ijm} = volume of traffic flowing from i to j by mode m at a user cost of c_{ijm} with the old plan

q'_{ijm} and c'_{ijm} are similarly defined for the new plan

To calculate the user benefit derived from any improvement, it is first necessary to obtain estimates of the traffic that would flow between any pair of points by a given mode, if the new facility were or were not introduced. The mean of these two figures is then multiplied by the resultant cost differential (cost without − cost with) and this total is summed over all possible movements by all possible modes to give the total direct user benefit. The derivation of this formula is described in Appendix D which deals in more detail with the application of variable matrix evaluation techniques to the output from traffic forecasting models.

4. (iv) *Benefit to public transport and car park operators*

The benefit (or loss) to public transport operators from any new or altered transportation system can in principle easily be calculated as the change in net receipts (that is the change in total revenue, less any increase in total operating costs) as the result of operating one system rather than the other.

It is sometimes possible when considering public transport investment proposals to simplify the evaluation process by ignoring the transfer payment represented by the fare paid and merely comparing user time and comfort savings with any change in the total cost of operating the service. Any change in the fare paid for a specific point-to-point journey is a benefit (or cost) to the traveller counterbalanced by an equal but opposite loss (or gain) to the public transport operators. This short-cut procedure can, however, break down when considering newly generated traffic.

In principle, the benefit to car park operators can be considered in exactly the same way as the benefit to public transport operators. If the cost of parking is considered as a cost when assessing the individual traveller's benefits, the corresponding receipts must be considered as a benefit to car park operators. The capital cost of providing any extra parking spaces that may be required when comparing one plan with another plan should also be calculated.

4. (v) *Benefit to Central Government*

One potentially substantial item of benefit that should be considered when evaluating alternative transportation plans is the benefit received by the Central Government from increased road-user taxation. In most studies and official publications on the evaluation of benefits from road improvements, all costs are given net of indirect taxation on the grounds that such costs merely represent a redistribution of wealth between travellers and the Central Government without any real resources expended. While this is perfectly true as regards the benefits derived from a road improvement by existing traffic, it no longer holds where generated traffic is concerned. In fact, generated traffic is generated just because sufficient benefit will be derived from a trip to cover all the costs incurred on the journey and this includes the cost of taxation which is a cost to the individual but a benefit to Central Government. Consequently, when a new trip is generated, both the individual and the Government gain some benefit, despite the indirect taxation the traveller has to pay, and the benefit to both should be separately calculated.

With the approach suggested in this chapter, this point is automatically covered by including indirect taxation as a cost to the individual road user. A separate assessment then obviously has to be added, for the benefit received by the Central Government from increased taxation. It is slightly less obvious what this benefit should be. If both the volume of travel and hence total expenditure in travel increase as a result of better and cheaper communications, then if people generally receive fixed wages for working fixed hours, expenditure on some other commodity has to fall. However, there will probably have been an element of indirect taxation in the alternative expenditure so that the net gain to the Central Government will be less than the apparent extra indirect taxation collected from increased travel. In the London Transportation Study this point was allowed for by assuming that only three-quarters of the total receipts collected from increased indirect taxation in fact represented a real increase in total indirect taxation collected.

4. (vi) *Accident costs*

Increased road safety is often an important consideration in the design of new road networks. It is, however, questionable whether a reduction in accidents can be valued in the same way as other benefits from road investment. In fact, some elements such as accident damage to vehicles and property and medical expenses of the injured can be related to the direct monetary costs involved, but the other costs such as pain, grief and suffering which result from accidents are much harder to value.

It is normal practice to include an allowance for savings in accident costs as a benefit from a road improvement scheme. The current valuation suggested by the Department of the Environment[5] is to value the average saving from a reduction of all accidents by considering the expected reduction in personal injury accidents from a road improvement and applying a standard figure currently (1971) taken to be £1,150 per personal injury accident. The figure is supposed to include an allowance for the large number of damage-only accidents, personal injury accidents and for the far fewer fatal accidents. The valuation placed on fatal accidents is, however, essentially arbitrary.

4. (vii) *Changes in maintenance and other costs of operating the road system*

The extra costs required to keep open new roads should be assessed either as a standard annual average cost, or if a more complicated time discounted calculation is used, maintenance and other irregular costs can be considered as part of a fluctuating stream of future costs. The costs of operating the road system should include not only surfacing and general maintenance but also such factors as lighting, salting, gritting and snow removal as well as general traffic control and surveillance.

The cost of maintaining and operating a public transport system will have already been considered as part of the net change in benefit to public transport operators.

4. (viii) *Other annual costs and benefits (not quantified)*

Apart from the annual costs and benefits mentioned above, there are certain other important annual costs and benefits which cannot readily be quantified. Many of these have already been mentioned in the brief discussion on environmental evaluation which considered the effect of major transportation facilities on adjacent environment. However, such factors as changes in noise level and in the pattern of visual intrusion are even less readily quantifiable in monetary terms than some of the other benefits such as value of time and accident costs which have already been considered in this chapter. It is therefore suggested that pending any new advances in this field no attempt should be made to directly include such factors in the quantitative economic evaluation process.

G

4. (ix) *Comparison of costs and benefits*

The final stage of the economic evaluation process is to compare the calculated costs and benefits. There are various ways of making this comparison, and the most appropriate method will depend upon the particular circumstances behind the investment being evaluated.

The simplest form of evaluation comparison is to consider the one-year rate of return on the investment. This is calculated very simply as follows:

$$\text{rate of return in year } N = \frac{\text{annual benefit in year } N \times 100\%}{\text{initial capital cost}}$$

Table V.1 illustrates this type of calculation for a typical road investment scheme.

TABLE V.1   Economic evaluation of small town bypass.

Annual benefit (1974)	
User benefit	100,000
Benefit to public transport operators	2,000
Government benefit	−5,000
Savings in accident costs	10,000
Less increased maintenance costs	−3,000
Total	104,000
Capital cost	500,000

$$\text{Annual rate of return (1974)} = \frac{104,000}{500,000} \times 100 = 20 \cdot 8\%$$

The great advantage of this type of calculation is its simplicity. The annual rate of return means that in the specified year, the annual benefit will be 20·8% of the initial capital cost. Obviously the higher this rate of return is the better. A project with a 50% rate of return could be considered to cover its initial costs in two years and is generally preferable to a project with only a 10% rate of return which would take ten years to cover its initial costs. Theoretically a project can be said to be worth while if the rate of return is greater than the opportunity cost of capital, that is to say if the rate of return on the proposed project is greater than the minimum rate of return that could be obtained from any other competing alternative use of the capital invested in the project. Unfortunately it is much less certain what the correct value of this opportunity cost of capital really is, so that even if one could accurately measure all the true costs and benefits associated with any particular investment, one could not say that the investment is worth while if the rate of return is greater than $x\%$, and not worth while if the return is less. The figures quoted by the Treasury (currently 8%) as the minimum return required on a cost-benefit analysis should be viewed not as a hard-and-fast line above which any investment can be justified but merely as a rationing device designed to prevent or delay the implementation of those investments which apparently give a very inadequate return for the effort invested in them.

In these circumstances one might reasonably ask what purpose is achieved by carrying out a rate of return calculation. There are two answers to this question. In the first place, irrespective of the value placed on the absolute level of rate of return, the relative rates of return provide a useful ranking device in choosing between alternative schemes of a similar nature. The second point that can be stressed is that while we have no real idea what the true opportunity cost of capital is, we can with a fair degree of confidence say that it probably lies within the range of 5–25%, so that if a project has a rate of return of over 50% we can say there is a very strong case in favour of that project, whilst if the return is much less than 5% we can equally say that the project looks a very poor prospect.

One further general point should be made about all rate of return calculations (whether the simple annual rate of return considered above, or the more complicated time discounted returns considered in the next few paragraphs) and that is that it is not always the project with the highest rate of return that should be favoured. This point is illustrated in Table V.2.

It can be seen that scheme A has a higher rate of return than scheme B. However, scheme B is also considerably more expensive than scheme A, and column 3 of Table V.2 calculates the marginal or (additional) benefit on the extra investment in plan B as opposed to plan A. The resultant marginal rate of return on investment in B over A is still relatively high and provided this exceeds the opportunity cost of capital or the appropriate minimum investment rate the extra expenditure in plan B compared with plan A is definitely worth while, even if overall plan B has a somewhat lower rate of return than plan A.

The major disadvantage of the one-year rate of return as calculated above is that it makes no allowance for events in other than one year. It does not allow for the time stream of costs and benefits over a number of years. Not only does this mean that its use is misleading when considering investments

TABLE V.2 **Comparative evaluation of alternative road schemes.**

	Scheme A	Scheme B	Marginal return B/A
Initial cost (£)	500,000	1,000,000	500,000
Annual benefit (£)	200,000	325,000	125,000
Rate of return (%)	40	32·5	25

which may have an uneven time profile of benefits (such as a junction improvement in the middle of a town for which a bypass will be completed in five years' time), but also it does not adequately reflect the fact that present-day costs and benefits are of greater importance than more distant costs and benefits. Thus a saving of £1 in one year is worth more than £1 saved one year later since the initial saving could be invested and in the intervening year generate some extra return. Similarly it is normally desirable to delay recurring costs as long as possible so that scarce capital effort which could give an immediate return is not expended before it is really required.

The simplest way of allowing for a variable time stream of costs and benefits is to discount all future costs and benefits by an appropriate rate so as to calculate the 'net present value' of the proposed investment. Thus if B_i = annual benefit in year i, C_i = costs incurred in year i, then the equivalent benefits and costs in year 1 would be $\dfrac{B_i}{(1+r)^{i-1}}$ and $\dfrac{C_i}{(1+r)^{i-1}}$ so that the net present value of a whole stream of costs and benefits can be defined as

$$\sum_{i=1}^{n}\frac{B_i}{(1+r)^{i-1}}-\frac{C_i}{(1+r)^{i-1}}$$

where r = the discount rate

n = the number of years considered.

If this expression is positive, the project is said to have a net present value, and by implication the project is generally considered worth while. The disadvantage of the net present value approach is that it is necessary to determine the discount rate r. In the common situation where a fixed budget allocation has to be expended in a given time period, too low an assumed discount rate will mean that too many projects have a positive net present value for them all to be financed from a fixed budget. Conversely too high an assumed discount rate would result in too few projects having a positive net present value to utilise all the available budget allocation.

A much more satisfactory method of allowing for the future stream of costs and benefits is to calculate the *internal rate of return*[6] on the proposed investment. The internal rate of return is defined as the discount rate at which the time stream of costs and benefits would be equal, or in other words the discount rate at which the net present value would be zero. Mathematically this can be defined as the internal rate of return r and is given by

$$\sum_{i=1}^{n}\frac{B_i}{(1+r)^{i-1}}-\frac{C_i}{(1+r)^{i-1}}=0$$

Calculation of an internal rate of return (which is usually found by a process of successive approximations) has the great advantage of avoiding predetermining any discount rate. As with the simple one-year rate of return one can generally say that the higher the internal rate of return the more worth while the investment.

While all forms of time discounted benefit-cost comparisons have some undoubted advantages, they suffer from the big disadvantage of not directly answering the question of whether a scheme should be executed immediately. A positive net present value or a high internal rate of return implies only that it is better to carry out the investment at the proposed time rather than never carry it out. But, especially with road investment schemes, there may be many proposals which could have a relatively attractive internal rate of return owing to high long-term benefits from the road scheme, even though in the short term provision of the road investment is not really required. It is thus essential when carrying out an internal rate of return calculation to calculate what is often termed the first-year rate of return. This is defined as the annual rate of return that would accrue immediately on completion of the scheme (assuming that there was no time lag between the completion of the investment and the full adjustment by road users to the facility). If the first-year rate of return is low on an investment that appears to give a high positive present value this means that although the scheme is in the long term worth while, it would be better to delay its implementation. In fact in these circumstances it can be shown that an even higher internal rate of return would have been obtained if it had been assumed that the project were to be started a few years later.

Table V.3 is an example of how to calculate the internal rate of return for a particular road improvement. The first row of Table V.3 shows the estimated capital costs of the project and the year in which they are expected to arise, while row 2 shows the resultant stream of benefits (including negative benefits in years 1 and 2 because of delays during construction). A series of discount rates are then tried until a rate is found at which the costs when discounted are approximately equal to the benefits when similarly discounted. Row 3 of Table V.3 shows the multiplier by which future costs and benefits have to be deflated to provide present-day equivalents, assuming discount rates of 18% and 19%. The resultant costs and benefits are then given in rows 4 and 5. At a discount rate of 18% the time stream of discounted costs is a little less than the time stream of discounted benefits (giving a net present value in year *0* of +£87,000) but at a discount rate of 19% the costs exceed the benefits. The internal rate of return therefore lies between 18% and 19%.

This particular example also shows the potential danger of basing results solely on the internal rate of return. Although the project gives an apparently reasonable internal rate of return,

TABLE V.3 Calculation of internal rate of return on a transport investment.

Year	0	1	2	3	4	5	6	7	8	9	10	11	12	13	14	15	16	17	18	19	20	Total
(1) Capital cost £'s ooo's	−1,000																				+667*	
(2) Annual benefit	−100†	−100†	100	100	100	500‡	550	600	650	700	750	800	850	900	950	1,000	1,050	1,100	1,150	1,200	1,250	
(3) Discount factor @ 18%	1·000	0·847	0·718	0·609	0·516	0·437	0·370	0·314	0·266	0·225	0·191	0·162	0·137	0·116	0·099	0·084	0·071	0·060	0·051	0·043	0·037	
@ 19%	1·000	0·840	0·706	0·593	0·499	0·419	0·352	0·296	0·249	0·209	0·176	0·148	0·124	0·104	0·088	0·074	0·062	0·052	0·044	0·037	0·031	
(4) Capital costs @ 18%	−1,000	−847																			+25	−1,822
discounted @ 19%	−1,000	−840																			+21	−1,819
(5) Annual benefits @ 18%	−100	−85	72	61	52	218	204	188	173	157	143	130	116	104	94	84	75	66	59	52	46	1,909
discounted @ 19%	−100	−84	71	59	50	210	194	178	162	146	132	118	105	94	84	74	65	57	51	44	39	1,749

Net per cent value at 18% = +£87,000
19% = −£70,000

∴ Internal rate of return ≃ $18\frac{87}{157}\% ≃ 18·6\%$

* Residual value assuming a thirty-year life.
† The negative benefit reflects delays to traffic during construction.
‡ The jump in benefit is due to completion of a complementary investment.

it gives a low first-year rate of return. It can easily be shown that if the project were delayed for a further three years so that it was completed before year 5, the internal rate of return would increase to 26·5% while the first-year rate of return would then be 25% (in year 5) rather than 5% (in year 2).

In recent years it has become standard practice to calculate the rate of return on transport investment schemes before they can qualify for a government grant. A standard procedure[7] has been laid down for the evaluation of inter-urban road schemes (see Appendix E, Example 1). The calculated returns are not expected to be extremely accurate and are certainly not used as the sole criterion on which investment discussions are based. The economic evaluation procedure is, however, particularly useful in choosing between alternative schemes of a similar nature, such as the choice between alternative alignments for a new motorway. The results can also be used to give some indication of the relative returns on different forms of transport investment such as the benefits from rural as compared with urban road investment, or the advantage of investment in a rapid transit line as compared with an urban motorway. However, the results, particularly in urban areas, can be very sensitive to the accuracy of the traffic forecasts on which the economic evaluation must be based. Some examples and problems with the practical application of the economic evaluation procedure considered in this chapter are discussed in Appendix E.

CHAPTER VI

Conclusions

1. Introduction—the planning process

In earlier chapters we have discussed the techniques and the philosophy underlying each of the main elements of the transportation planning process. The purpose of this chapter is to take stock, review the progress that has been made to date, and the potential for future development so that an assessment can be made of the use of analytical techniques within the transport planning process.

In recent years attitudes to planning have tended to polarise towards two extremes. One school of thought has assumed that everything could be solved analytically. Mathematical models should be developed to assess the implications and repercussions of any proposed course of action. Uncertainty and risk in so far as they existed would be built into the equations. Decisions could be based on expected values obtained from statistical distributions, and risk aversion factors would be introduced to prevent the model giving too extreme an answer. On the other hand, there has been the school of thought which assumed that there was no substitute for plain common sense. Decisions should be taken by people who knew how to take them, and any attempt at scientific justification for predetermined prejudice was an unnecessary waste of effort.

One of the main reasons for this divergence of opinion was the arrival of the electronic computer which opened up vast new horizons for problem-solving, for the first time making it possible to apply a rigorous mathematical approach to many planning problems. As a result new techniques such as the transport models were developed to solve problems that previously could not be tackled analytically. Not surprisingly, these early mathematical models had to be based on a set of simplifying assumptions, which were often so simple that the experienced planner was rightly unwilling to accept that the mathematics of the model had any meaning in real life. Fortunately there are now signs of a reconciliation, and each group is beginning to appreciate the other's point of view. The model-builders are becoming less dogmatic and less confident of their ability to solve all problems, while the results of completed studies have begun to convince more and more planners that there is at times something to be gained from a detailed analytical examination of transportation movements within a specified area. One of the aims of this book is to help bridge this gap to show where the mathematical approach can be used to greatest advantage as the servant rather than the master of the decision maker.

In recent years the quantitative approach to problem-solving has become increasingly popular. In transport planning, the mathematical approach has become the rule rather than the exception. Investment decisions are based on transport models and economic rates of return rather than on the earlier criteria of measured flow and apparent capacity limitations. However, if the 1960s could be described as the time of hope, the early 1970s may become known as a period of reappraisal and awakening to reality. The Commission of Inquiry into the Third London Airport and the Greater London Development Plan Inquiry are likely to stand out as landmarks in the history of transportation planning. They were set up at a time when it was widely felt that all problems could be solved if sufficient time and effort were devoted to a rigorous assessment of the alternative points of view. In both cases it has since become abundantly clear that the final decision cannot be reduced to a set of mathematical equations. There will always be a need for value judgments. Conclusions must be based largely on informed common sense. It is, however, essential that the decision-maker should be adequately informed. It may not be possible to determine scientifically the answer to major planning problems,

but there is no doubt that the decisions on London's third airport and future transport policy will be based on better
information and a truer appreciation of the implications of any
course of action if the decision is taken with a rigorous analytical
framework which provides the background to brief the decision-
taker.

This advantage, however, has only been achieved at a cost.
Both inquiries will have been long and expensive. The time
spent awaiting decisions not only creates immediate problems
of planning blight but can also have a very damaging effect in
slowing down the pace of all future planning. This could
become extremely serious if all important investment decisions
have to be subject to as detailed an examination as that
required to locate London's third airport. There is also a real
danger in too much public participation in the planning process. Decisions will be influenced by public pressure although
the public will often not appreciate the full significance of the
course of action they are pressing to see adopted. The conser-
vationist will see the immediate advantage of conservation, but
cannot assess the cost in terms of alternative benefits forgone by
conserving a particular environment. Moreover, certain sectors
of the public are particularly vocal and well organised, and this
has to be taken into account when assessing the real strength
and nature of community preferences. One of the main tasks of
the moment is to obtain the right balance between rigorous
analysis, informed common sense, prompt decision-making and
appropriate public participation. The part that the transportation planning process can play in this synthesis is discussed in
this chapter. First, let us consider what has already been
achieved.

2. ANALYTICAL TRANSPORTATION PLANNING IN THE UNITED KINGDOM

Analytical transport planning in the United Kingdom has
followed two main streams, one based on area-wide traffic
models, the other concerned directly with the assessment of
individual projects.

2. (i) *Model-based studies*

Traffic models were originally imported from the United States and were first applied in some of the major conurbation studies (e.g. London, Glasgow, Belfast). The studies were in many instances carried out by British firms of consulting engineers but American experts were retained to direct the studies.

It quickly became apparent that these studies had been designed for a very different environment to that usually found in the United Kingdom. The standard techniques brought over from the United States included the extensive use of household interviews to obtain trip generation and distribution rates. Modal split was based on regression equations using data from the household interview surveys and trips were separated into private or public transport before distribution. A journey time distribution function was abstracted from the household interviews and then calibrated until it could be used to reproduce the present pattern of movement throughout the study area. Future trip rates were based largely on expected changes in zonal population, income and car-ownership and these trips were then distributed, to design-year networks using the same distribution function as that obtained in the base year. Primarily as a result of the trip production procedures, a substantial increase in the demand for movement by road was predicted, a demand which would not normally be met given the future resources available for road investment. The early transport models therefore played a valuable part in making people realise that the standard engineering solution of providing for the expected future demand was financially impractical. However, these first generation land-use transportation studies proved of only limited use as a guide to future transport needs. New policies for transport planning and new techniques of transport analysis were both urgently required.

If the policy-makers had realised the immediate limitations of these expensive new techniques they might have been less willing to finance these studies. It was perhaps fortunate that they did not appreciate the cumbersome nature of the conventional transport model, the limited range of questions it could answer and the relatively high cost of investigating a series of alternative transport policies, because in practice the by-products of the transportation studies were found to be at least as important as the detailed answers obtained directly from the work. Long before the studies were finished, decisions were being taken that had been influenced by the data collected and the general insight gained from the partially completed analysis. The data collected in Phase I of the London Traffic Survey has been much more widely used and has had more effect on strategic planning in Greater London than could ever have been envisaged when the study was inaugurated.

The need to input a closely defined future situation also forced the study area planners to consider closely the way in which they wished to control or promote development. This lead to a growing awareness of future problems and the transportation studies often served as the catalyst and framework around which a coherent set of long-term proposals for future development were evolved.

While these early large-scale transportation studies were limited in their ability to forecast traffic flows in congested conditions, they did give a good indication of the future pattern of demand. This was invaluable in stimulating and informing the discussion on long-term transport strategy in densely populated urban areas, and often proved useful in assessing the demand for alternative roads considered for construction in the near future.

Finally and most importantly, the studies acted as a training ground for passing on American techniques and expertise to British transport planners. This knowledge of the traffic forecasting model was an essential first step in developing fresh methods designed more specifically to answer the particular problem of obtaining the best return from the limited funds available for investment in urban and rural transport infrastructure.

2. (ii) *Project evaluation studies*

The second main stream of activity in transport planning has been more directly concerned with project evaluation. Two of the earliest and most important of these studies were the London–Birmingham Motorway Study, and the Victoria Line Study. In both cases the projects called for large capital sums, and followed a long period in which there had been very little investment in major new transport facilities.

These studies differed from the land-use transportation studies in that relatively more attention was paid to assessing the costs and benefits that could be derived from the projects being evaluated. In particular both studies showed the importance of the value of travel time in assessing the return from new transport investments. In neither case could it be argued that the study was a major factor influencing the decision to go ahead with the projects. The London–Birmingham Motorway Study was not completed until after a firm decision had been taken to build the motorway and the Victoria Line Study suggested that the case for investment was at best marginal. Nevertheless both studies proved of major importance in the future development of transport planning in the United Kingdom.

The London–Birmingham Motorway Study and other work carried out at the Road Research Laboratory formed the basis on which the returns on all inter-urban road schemes could be compared. The Ministry of Transport, under pressure from the Treasury, introduced standard methods of assessing the rates of return on road schemes. Counties and local authorities found in the second half of the 1960s that their favoured plans had to be shown to give a good economic rate of return. While some authorities no doubt became adept at cooking the books, other authorities and the staff at the Ministry of Transport headquarters found they now possessed a useful tool by which they could assess the merits of alternative proposals. As a result a number of wasteful investment proposals have been rejected whilst other schemes have been modified and improved in the search for an adequate rate of return.

The Victoria Line Study also played an important part in the development of urban transportation planning because it highlighted the need to obtain an appropriate balance between public and private transport. The Study and its subsequent discussion clearly showed the danger of basing road investment on the apparent demand to use unpriced roads at the same time as rail users were expected to pay the full costs of any new investment. The Study showed that road and rail transport policy were inextricably mixed. One of the main beneficiaries from new rail investment were existing road users whose journey costs were reduced because some motorists had switched to public transport. A good case could therefore be put forward for further investment in public transport facilities even if these schemes were not financially viable. Similar arguments to those put forward in the Victoria Line Study have subsequently been used to justify further investment in underground railway lines especially in the London area.

2. (iii) *Evaluation-orientated transportation studies*

The two types of approach are now increasingly combined. Most recent transportation studies have concluded with some form of project evaluation including the calculation of economic rates of return on alternative schemes. In particular some of the regional transportation studies have provided a consistent and soundly based set of traffic forecasts which can then be applied separately as required to evaluate the merits of alternative transport proposals. Thus a major output from the Land Use Transportation Study for East Central Scotland was a comparative economic assessment of twelve different major inter-urban road schemes. The information obtained from the main area-wide transportation study was also subsequently used as input to further project orientated studies which determined in more detail the design standards and most favoured alignment to adopt for two of these twelve schemes.

These developments by which the two streams of activity are merged are extremely important. The earlier transportation studies overemphasised the importance of traffic forecasts and were not designed for the more important task of project evaluation. By contrast some of the early project orientated studies such as the Victoria Line Study suffered because of inadequate information on the traffic flows in the area served by the line. An objective for the future is to find the right balance between these two facets of the transportation planning process.

2. (iv) *Achievements of the analytical approach*

Before considering the future use of the transportation planning process it is worth considering what has been achieved to date.

The most obvious benefits from the quantitative approach have been found in the planning of inter-urban roads, where road investment is now assessed on a sounder basis. As a result some roads are currently under construction that would not otherwise have been started, while the commitment of public funds to several unnecessarily extravagant road investment schemes has been prevented. The long-term planning of the major trunk motorway network is also being assisted by the use of transport models to predict the expected flows and rate of return from a variety of different motorway configurations.

The transportation planning process may, however, have had an even more profound effect on the future of urban transport planning. The present debate on urban transport is much better informed than it would otherwise have been. The need for a policy of management to control traffic in large urban areas may have been demonstrated by exercises such as the Buchanan Report on Traffic in Towns, but appreciation of the problem was greatly enhanced by the work of the London Traffic Survey and its successor the London Transportation Study. The cost implications of trying to cater for the full demand for movement by private transport became clear, and the need for some control on movement by private car in the centres of the largest conurbations was made apparent. In the dialogue that followed, the limitations imposed by available investment resources became more widely appreciated. The major conurbation studies have thus served as important focal points for the exchange and development of ideas.

The achievements of the last decade include the development of a new breed of transport models designed more closely to answer the problems of the moment. Technical advances include the introduction of synthetic trip end estimating procedures, multiple route assignments, use of speed/flow equations as part of the transport model, and the development of a suitable method for the economic evaluation of alternative transport networks. By the end of the period, new models which included an allowance for the effect of traffic congestion on trip distribution, generation and modal split as well as assignment were just beginning to appear. One of the main objectives of these improvements has been to make transportation study a better tool for evaluating alternative transport policies.

The experience gained over the decade has led to several organisational and computational advances. Data processing techniques have been improved so that computing costs have been substantially reduced. Standard information on trip rates by household category has been collected from a variety of different household interview studies, thus reducing the size of sample required in any one particular study. As a result of these innovations it is now possible to achieve much more from a given transportation study budget than would have been possible ten or even five years ago.

A review of the recent history of transport planning in the United Kingdom would not be complete without mentioning the dramatic increase in knowledge and understanding of the transport planning process that occurred in the late 1960s. In 1965 numerical transportation planning was a little-known skill confined to a few university departments, one or two local authorities and a handful of consultants. By the early 1970s the situation was quite different. A large number of transport studies had been completed and the techniques used and results obtained had been widely discussed. Many local authorities had set up traffic engineering or transport planning departments. This wide spread of technical understanding has been particularly valuable in helping those in positions of responsibility to assess the strengths and weaknesses of the quantitative approach, and should mean that analytical techniques will in future play an important part in the development of transport policy, not only at a national but also at a regional and local level.

3. THE FUTURE USES OF ANALYTICAL TRANSPORT PLANNING

The transport planner may face a variety of different problems. At a national level the planner may be concerned with broad strategic issues such as the future pattern of inter-regional motorways, or the national trunk railway network. At a local level, the planner will be concerned in greater detail with such problems as parking provision and access to the town centre. The information and the degree of detail required at these two levels is so different that no one transport model is likely to prove appropriate in all circumstances. Almost all planning will, however, follow the same general pattern of survey, analysis and model-building, forecasting and finally evaluation. The emphasis placed on each of these four main stages of the transport planning process will, however, depend upon the nature of the problems being considered.

The ideal approach might eventually result in a series of interlocking studies carried out to differing degrees of detail. A national study would be used to provide control totals for input to a regional model, while the output from the regional models would in turn be used as input to conurbation and local models. Eventually, a two-way process might develop, with information transmitted up and down between the local and national levels.

Within this hierarchy of planning, national models would serve two main functions. They could be used to help formulate national policy on such questions as the most appropriate modal split between road, rail, sea and air for inter-regional goods traffic. They would also be used to provide input on through trips to more detailed regional models.

National models might play a major part in determining future rail, air and ports policy. Recent experience, however, suggests that road planning may be better carried out at a regional level. The average distance travelled on most main roads is relatively short, much shorter than the average journey by main line rail. Any model designed to forecast traffic flows on specific inter-urban routes must therefore be based on a relatively fine zoning system, and a fairly detailed road network. The national model would therefore have to contain several thousand zones and tens of thousands of links. Even if computer programs were developed to analyse data on this vast scale, it would still be immensely difficult to control the zoning and coding of a national study. For this reason it may be better to develop a national roads model from the output of a series of regional models.

In the meantime, there is a need for some national co-ordination of all transport studies. The Department of the Environment have already put forward a system of national zoning which should be incorporated where possible in all regional and local studies. There is a need to agree on standard definitions for many of the terms and concepts used in the transport planning process. Once this has been done, a national data bank should be established to collect, codify and summarise the information obtained from past household interview and commercial vehicle studies. This could be used in conjunction with census information, and a small sample household interview, to calibrate future trip generation models. At present this form of synthetic trip end estimation procedure relies on an arbitrary collection of data from some of the earlier transportation studies, and a strong case could be made for a central organisation which would receive all future interview information and use the data to see that the trip end prediction equations are continually updated.

National studies will be supplemented by more detailed regional studies. The area covered by a regional study may vary, depending upon the characteristics of the area and the objectives of the study. Large regions such as the economic planning regions may be divided into sub-regions, while the problems within the major cities and conurbations of the region should be considered in separate studies.

The transport planning process is particularly well suited at a regional level for the analysis of inter-urban road movements. At this scale, a zoning system can easily be prepared, which isolates the relative position of cities, towns and villages, and a coded network can be prepared which suitably represents the ease with which movement can take place between these zones. This network should be coded in sufficient detail to include all the major inter-urban routes outside the main conurbations. If possible, the external cordon of the region should follow natural barriers, such as the coast or the top of a range of mountains. If such natural barriers cannot be found, better results may be obtained from two smaller regional studies than one large study.

One of the main advantages of regional studies is that the results can easily be assessed, and a consistent pattern determined for transport planning within the region. More difficult problems are faced when applying the transport model to the development of a land-use planning strategy. The potential viability of new town developments or out-of-town shopping centres can be assessed in terms of their relative accessibility to other centres of population and employment. At the same time, the effect of such centres on the proposed regional road network can be forecast. As a result, alternative locations or modifications to the design may be put forward to reduce the demand on certain routes. A recent regional study was specially designed to assess the transport costs and benefits associated with alternative locations for long-term urban development within one economic planning region.

Regional studies can also be helpful in determining the major demographic and employment trends which are likely to influence the future development of the region. This information is required as input to the regional model but also proves of great value for general regional planning. For example one recent study showed that there was little likelihood of the study area population increasing sufficiently to match all the individual local authorities' expansion plans. It is often found that the rigorous quantitative discipline imposed by the need to quantify explicitly land-use information later proves of great benefit for other planning purposes.

It has generally been found that the major regional studies have had a continuing value. It is often possible to use simple adaptations and approximations to the initial model to evaluate a succession of alternative road investment schemes, so assisting in the continuing design of the regional road network. The regional study may also be used to provide information on through and external trips as input to more detailed local or conurbation studies. The example of the regional study for East Central Scotland, discussed earlier in this chapter, shows how regional studies can have a continuing influence on decision-making. The main study not only showed the high priority that should be given to one particular route, the East Fife Regional Road, but also served as the base for a more detailed route alignment study. As a result, construction of this route is likely to start on a different alignment, and at a much earlier date than had been intended before the regional study.

The most important contributions from analytical transportation planning will continue to be made in the major conurbations, where the most difficult transportation planning problems are found. We have already discussed the part played by the early conurbation transportation studies. While these studies clearly outlined the problems, they could not be used to evaluate alternative solutions, as they were not designed to allow for the effect of congestion on travel habits. In the third phase of the London Transportation Study, an attempt was made to grapple with this problem. However, the techniques adopted were incorporated into the transportation study at a late stage, and also suffered some of the defects of a pioneering study. Nevertheless, the study did suggest new avenues to be followed in the analysis of conurbation transport problems, whilst the results obtained, if far from perfect, were still of considerable value.

As a result of recent technical advances, the prospects for the future look encouraging. The main improvement is likely to occur in the synthesis of the effects of congestion. Speed/flow equations will be incorporated into the transport model, and the effects of congestion on assignment, modal split, trip distribution and generation will be analysed more closely. In the future, urban transportation studies may devote relatively more of their resources to the analysis of a variety of different transport solutions. Models will be developed which are designed to test a wide range of alternative policy options, and less emphasis will be placed on the precise representation of the existing *status quo*.

There will also be scope for the development of local models within the framework of regional or conurbational studies. At the present moment, several London Boroughs are carrying out more detailed studies within the framework given by the main conurbation study. These studies are unlikely to be quite as complex as the larger conurbation studies although, to be worth while, the local pattern of movement must be studied in great detail. These studies are likely to play an important part in the design of the local environment, and will be extensively used to evaluate the effect on traffic movement of creating environmental areas with traffic-free precincts. They will also be used as an aid to the detailed design of local roads and car parks, and may also be useful for detailed public transport and land-use planning. The possible effect of major traffic generators, such as new hotels, could be assessed in advance, and steps taken to see that these developments are located in places where good access can be provided.

4. TECHNICAL DEVELOPMENTS

The previous section has shown that there is considerable scope for the use of analytical transportation planning. As a result, further analytical advances can be expected. New techniques will be developed to speed up the process of computation, and to increase the complexity of problems that can be analysed. One of the most glaring limitations of the present process is the inadequate and cumbersome nature of the models used to analyse public transport networks. It can only be hoped that further research and further experience will lead to the development of rather simpler public transport models, that can be more easily and cheaply incorporated in the main transportation study process.

Transportation planners are becoming more familiar with the problems of applying traffic models to congested urban situations. In the future, there should be little difficulty in developing a new set of models for use in densely populated areas. These models will be designed to test a wide range of alternative solutions such as road pricing, parking controls, or discretionary fares policy for public transport, as well as the construction of new or improved roads and railway lines.

The basic models are not, however, likely to deviate radically in concept from the procedure set out in this book. Changes are more likely to take the form of adaptations and modifications to existing processes, rather than the development of completely new concepts, although the advantages of these changes may be great.

One of the most justified criticisms of many recent transportation studies is that they have fallen between two extremes. They were too detailed to give cheap and immediately useful answers, but not sufficiently refined to give accurate answers that could generally be relied upon as a base for evaluating alternative transport policies. The experience gained from the first transport studies should and will be used to devise new procedures. Future models will pay more attention to detail in certain places, where this has been found necessary, while in other parts of the model less detail may be required than has in the past been customary.

In this chapter we have paid particular attention to the analysis and model-building stage of the transportation planning process, which we feel is the central core of the whole process. If the transport model cannot reproduce accurately the existing pattern of traffic movement, then little faith can be placed on any subsequent evaluation of results obtained by applying the traffic model at some future date. Nevertheless, it is necessary to achieve a balanced emphasis in all the stages of the planning process. The model-building stage is not an end in itself, but only a means to an end. There is no point in achieving a superb representation of present-day traffic movements, if insufficient funds are available to use this model for forecasting and evaluation. The art of quantitative transportation planning is to ensure that each stage of the study process can be used to maximum effect.

At the survey stage, too much detail is often collected in the hope that it may later prove useful. This natural tendency should be resisted, as it is an early symptom of one of the major diseases from which the transportation planner has suffered to date. Studies should normally be designed backwards from their end point, rather than forwards from their starting point. The survey and model-building stages of the process should normally be built into the study after a decision has been taken as to the objectives of the study, and the range of alternative policies that may have to be considered. Obviously, there must be some feedback between the model capabilities and the targets set for the study, but to design a study around the model-building capabilities and the survey results that happen to exist will severely limit the range of alternative policies that can be considered. At the survey stage it is also usually better to obtain a small amount of high-quality data than a larger amount of data of dubious quality.

We have already discussed the most needed developments at the model-building stage of the process. There is little that can be said about the forecasting stage of the procedure. Improved techniques for demographic and economic forecasts might lead to some improvement in the accuracy of future forecasts.

However, the future is always uncertain, and so long as the input to the transport model generally reflects the likely course of future developments, little may be gained from any further refinement. It is usually not too important for the design-year forecasts to reproduce accurately conditions for one particular year, so long as they will reflect the geographical spread of traffic problems at some future date not too far removed from the nominal design year.

A more useful avenue for research may be to develop means by which the sensitivity of the model result to a wide range of alternative assumptions could be forecast. These sensitivity analyses could then be used to test the effect of a wide range of different forecasts and different assumptions as to the values placed on certain journey cost characteristics. So far as is possible, new and improved techniques are required to dis-aggregate partial results from within the mass of the transportation study. This would enable the costs and benefits of selected proposals to be assessed more easily from the results of area-wide transportation studies. The development of sub-models to further process and modify the output from the larger-scale transportation studies could be a particularly fruitful field for research.

It is also important to develop better methods for the evaluation and interpretation of the output from transportation models. Within its own very narrow limits, the comparative economic evaluation of journey cost savings may be reasonably satisfactory, although further research is needed into such factors as journey time savings and the value placed on passenger comfort. There is, however, a real need to develop a framework for assessing the environmental implications of alternative schemes. There is also a need at all stages of the process to develop better monitoring processes to check that the results of the transportation model are valid, and that there are no network coding or other punching errors.

5. Conclusion

Throughout this book we have tried not only to describe the current procedures used in analytical transport planning, but also to indicate both the strength and the limitations of the available techniques. We have shown that existing methods can be costly, are often based on unproven relationships, may not be internally self-consistent, and usually produce answers which require careful interpretation. We have not claimed that the transport planning process provides the perfect answer to all problems, but we hope that we have not overstressed the limitations of present techniques.

Analytical transport planning is a relatively new science, which has needed time to develop. By its very nature, it is an inexact science, in that it tries to predict the activities of large numbers of individual people who will not conform to any precise mathematical laws. The science has both suffered and gained from being accepted in its infancy as an important tool for determining transportation planning policy. Techniques have developed fast as a result of this exposure to the real world, and the science has gained much. Unfortunately, it has also suffered from over-exposure. Large sums of public money have been spent on transportation studies, which have then proved inadequate for the tasks allotted to them. As a result, a reaction could set in.

This would be unfortunate. Although studies may seem expensive, the cost of not studying may in fact be much more expensive. Most transportation studies cost very much less than 1% of the cost of the new facilities they are expected to evaluate. One small suggestion can therefore pay for the whole cost of a study. The present analytical approach may have many faults, but it still gives useful insight into the implications of alternative policies and leads to many suggestions and improvements.

In this concluding chapter, we have shown how in the recent past analytical transport planning has evolved. We have shown how techniques of traffic forecasting have improved, and how studies are becoming increasingly orientated towards the evaluation of alternative policies. We have indicated the way in which the process could continue in the future. In the long term we are optimistic that the transportation planning process will play an important part in the development of future transport policy, both at a national and at a regional level, and in most larger towns and cities.

An example of calibrating a gravity model

It is not necessary to begin calibration with the exact values of the distribution function $R(c_{ij})$ calculated from the survey data because values giving the best fit are only obtained by iteration of the calibration procedure. It has been common practice either to take values of $R(c_{ij})$ from other studies of a similar town size or as an approximation to use simply the observed trip length distribution. In the latter case it has been common practice to plot the percentage of trips within journey time ranges against respective journey time on logarithmic paper and a smooth curve fitted from which initial values of $R(c_{ij})$ are selected. The logarithmic trace simply enables a better estimate of values of $R(c_{ij})$ to be made by somewhat flattening out the distribution function. This method has no mathematical signification except to say that the trip length distribution is vaguely related to the actual distribution function.

It would, of course, be mathematically correct to calculate first, values of the distribution function from

$$R(c_{ij}) = \frac{t_{ij}}{a_j g_i}$$

and to use these values as a first estimate. However, it has been shown that even if this method is used several iterations are required before a good fit can be achieved. Indeed, calibration can be achieved by initially assuming values of unity for the distribution function although, of course, in this case many more iterations are required. For these reasons, therefore, it has been common practice to use as a first estimate of $R(c_{ij})$, values from the trip length distribution.

The first step is to record the percentage of survey trips within given time intervals, as shown in Table A1, column 2.

TABLE A1 Relative distribution rate computation.

(1) Trip length (mins.)	(2) Per cent of trips OD	(3) Rate No. 1	(4) Per cent of trips Run 1	(5) Adjusted rate $\left(5 = \dfrac{2}{4} \times 3\right)$	(6) Rate No. 2	(7) Per cent of trips Run 2
0	10·13	1,580	3·11	5,149	5,150	9·67
1	0·44	1,480	0·36	1,899	4,000	0·87
2	3·31	1,400	1·69	2,739	3,100	3·35
3	7·18	1,330	4·06	2,352	2,400	6·92
4	11·79	1,250	6·71	2,190	1,900	9·95
5	10·91	1,160	8·84	1,438	1,438	11·02
6	10·93	1,050	11·09	1,039	1,050	11·27
7	9·38	925	11·79	735	780	10·20
8	8·78	790	11·37	606	580	8·69
9	6·60	660	10·71	406	420	7·24
10	5·22	530	8·25	335	315	5·28
11	4·60	415	7·18	266	240	4·49
12	3·20	340	5·57	195	185	3·31
13	2·14	265	4·04	140	145	2·37
14	1·97	170	2·29	146	115	1·70
15	1·16	118	1·35	102	94	1·17
16	0·73	80	0·76	77	79	0·83
17	0·59	54	0·36	88	68	0·51
18	0·40	37	0·22	67	60	0·40
19	0·21	26	0·11	50	53	0·25
20	0·23	19	0·07	62	49	0·19
21	0·11	15	0·03	48	45	0·11
22	0·00	13	0·03	—	43	0·09
23	0·04	10	0·01	40	41	0·06
24	0·02	8	0·01	16	39	0·03
25	0·00	6	0·00	—	37	0·02
Over 25	0·00	5	0·00	—	34	0·02
TOTAL TRIPS	49,133		48,842			48,843
PERSON HOURS	5,369		6,381			5,340
AVG. TRIP LENGTH (mins.)	6·56		7·84			6·56

These percentages are then plotted on regular graph paper against respective travel times (Figure A1). The purpose of the regular graph is to provide a base for visual comparison of trip length frequency distributions. Next, values of the distribution function $\dfrac{t_{ij}}{a_j g_i}$ are estimated and tabulated against their respective zone-to-zone travel time (c_{ij}). A smooth curve is drawn (see Figure A1) on the semi-logarithmic graph and from this curve the initial approximations for the relative distribution rates are obtained (see Rate No. 1, column 3, Table A1). These rates are used together with the zonal generations and attractions in the gravity model equation to calculate a synthetic trip matrix. The trip length frequency distribution calculated from the synthetic matrix is recorded in column 4, Table A1, and again these points are plotted on the regular graph paper. This synthetic trip length frequency distribution is compared visually with a survey trip length frequency distribution as also are total number of trips, total person-hours and average trip length in minutes. As can be seen, the synthetic trip length distribution obtained from this calculation does not compare favourably with the survey trip length distribution (see Figure A1). In addition, synthetic person-hours of travel differ from the survey person-hours of travel by some 19% and average trip lengths differ by 20%. The Bureau of Public Roads has suggested that as a criterion for calibration trip length distribution, person-hours of travel and average trip lengths should agree to within plus or minus 3%. In this case, therefore, a further synthetic matrix calculation is necessary. The new distribution rates are calculated as follows:

1. The initial rates (Rate No. 1) are adjusted by the ratio of survey per cent of trips to synthetic per cent of trips (column 5, Table A1).
2. These adjusted rates are plotted on semi-logarithmic paper and a smooth curve is fitted to these points.
3. From this curve, the new distribution rates are obtained (column 6, Table A1) and used in a second calculation of a synthetic trip matrix.

The trip length frequency distribution of a second synthetic matrix is recorded in column 7, Table A1, and again compared

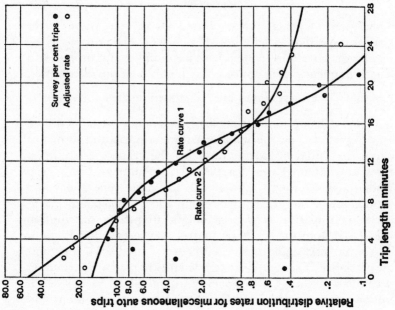

FIGURE A.1 An example of calibrating a gravity model.

with a survey trip length frequency distribution (see Figure A1). Synthetic and survey trips differ by less than 1%, as do person-hours. The survey and synthetic average trip length distributions are almost identical, thus the criterion for successful calibration of the gravity model has been satisfied.

APPENDIX B

Population and
employment forecasts

This appendix is divided into three sections. First, estimates of the future population of the study area; secondly, estimates of the study area employment potential; and finally, the reconciliation of the population and employment forecasts required to obtain balance between population and employment.

I. POPULATION PREDICTIONS

The first stage of the population forecast is to estimate the change in the study area population that would result from natural increase up to the design year, often fifteen to twenty years ahead. To do this, it is necessary to know the age and sex distribution of the base-year population. The national census, usually taken in the second year of each decade (i.e. 1951, 1961, 1971), supplemented recently by the 10% sample census first carried out in 1966, includes information on the age, sex and marital status of the total home population of the United Kingdom. This information is presented in the published tables for each local authority. More localised information for individual census enumeration districts can be obtained if required on application to the General Register Office at Titchfield in Hampshire.

Once the age and sex structure of the base-year population

has been established, the future population by natural increase can be found by the method known as 'cohort analysis'. The Registrar General publishes estimates of expected future mortality rates for five-year age-groups (or cohorts) by sex. These can be used to estimate the future population aged fifteen and over in, say, fifteen years' time. The population aged less than fifteen has to be estimated from the combination of future expected fertility and mortality rates. The fertility rates are expressed as the likelihood of a woman of a specific age giving birth to a child in a given year.

Table B1 shows an example of the population forecasts included in one recent Land Use Transportation Study. In this case, rather than carry out complete calculations from scratch of the effect of expected future fertility and mortality rates, use is made of the published future population forecasts made by the Registrar General. Column 1 of Table B1 gives the present study area population by age-group. Column 2 gives the 'mark-up factor' to obtain the expected population in the age-group fifteen years more senior, in fifteen years' time. It is taken from the Registrar General's national population forecasts as the ratio of the population in group x to $x+4$ in the base year to the expected population in the age-group $x+15$ to $x+19$ in fifteen years' time. It therefore assumes that the study area experiences the same age specific fertility and mortality rates as the rest of the country (and also that it contributes or receives a share in emigration and immigration from the country proportional to its present share of the age-group or cohort being considered). Column 3 which gives the future study area population in the design year aged fifteen and over is obtained simply as the product of the first two columns. The population under fifteen is assumed proportional to the women of childbearing age in the survey area. Thus, if f_i is the fertility rate for women aged i, the population aged l in the survey area is:

$$el \sum_i f_i W_i^l$$

where W_i^l = the women aged i in the study area l years before the design year

el = the likelihood of a child surviving in i years

Table B2 shows how to calculate the children of age seven in the survey area in the design year. In certain areas it may be

H

TABLE B1 Population forecasts for the survey area.

Male aged	Population (base year) column (1)	15-year life expectancy* column (2)	Male aged	Population (design year) column (3)	Female aged	Population (base year) column (4)	15-year life expectancy* column (5)	Female aged	Population (design year) column (6)
0– 4	17,347	0·985	15–19	17,087	0– 4	17,148	0·987	15–19	16,925
5– 9	18,342	1·018	20–24	18,672	5– 9	16,968	1·023	20–24	17,358
10–14	17,738	1·020	25–29	18,093	10–14	16,775	1·039	25–29	17,430
15–19	15,290	0·987	30–34	15,091	15–19	15,143	1·015	30–34	15,370
20–24	14,970	0·966	35–39	14,461	20–24	13,920	0·967	35–39	13,461
25–29	13,859	0·961	40–44	13,318	25–29	13,391	0·951	40–44	12,735
30–34	15,212	0·952	45–49	14,482	30–34	15,326	0·957	45–49	14,667
35–39	11,021	0·927	50–54	10,216	35–39	10,868	0·953	50–54	10,357
40–44	10,279	0·887	55–59	9,117	40–44	9,800	0·933	55–59	9,143
45–49	9,547	0·814	60–64	7,771	45–49	9,887	0·897	60–64	8,869
50–54	9,669	0·708	65–69	6,846	50–54	10,049	0·846	65–69	8,501
55–59	10,185	0·575			55–59	10,594	0·760		
60–64	8,023	0·421			60–64	9,497	0·626		
65–69	7,983	0·267	70+	12,239	65–69	9,449	0·443	70+	20,998
70+	11,355	0·065			70+	20,114	0·140		
			0– 4	21,967†				0– 4	20,857†
			5– 9	21,061†				5– 9	20,074†
			10–14	19,776†				10–14	18,970†
TOTAL	190,920			220,197	TOTAL	198,929			225,715

* Includes allowance for net overseas migration into the study area.
† See Table B2 for specimen calculation of children under fifteen.

TABLE B2 Specimen calculation: population aged five in survey area (design year).

Female aged	Population (base year)	10-year life expectancy	Female aged	Population (design year minus five)	Fertility rate per 1,000	Five-year survivorship rate	Children aged 5 (design year)
5–9	16,968	1·000	15–19	16,968	58·55	0·978	971
10–14	16,775	1·040*	20–24	17,446	165·37	0·978	2,822
15–19	15,143	1·025*	25–29	15,522	164·89	0·978	2,503
20–24	13,920	0·980	30–34	13,642	92·01	0·978	1,227
25–29	13,391	0·963	35–39	12,896	43·35	0·978	547
30–34	15,326	0·969	40–44	14,851	11·29	0·978	164
35–39	10,868	0·972	45–49	10,564	0·81	0·978	9
TOTAL							8,243

* Includes allowance for net overseas migration into the study area.

unreasonable to assume that national age-specific fertility and mortality rates apply and in this case the fertility and mortality assumptions can be adjusted to take into account local conditions by weighting the expected change in population by an area compatibility factor. The present-day area compatibility factors, which compare local and national age-specific fertility and mortality rates, are readily available.

The expected design-year population by natural increase must subsequently be adjusted to allow for the effects of migration from the survey area. The reasons for migration are highly complex, but often the basic reasons for migration are the search for accommodation or employment. Thus, the future level of population in any area will depend not only upon population forecasts but also upon some balance being struck between the population forecast and the employment forecast for that area. Present-day migration is mainly in search either of employment or of a suitable place in which to retire. Since such trends cannot be altered overnight, it is often useful for population projection purposes to consider the result of a continuation of past migration trends.

In order to estimate the future repercussions on the study area of migration, it is necessary to know not only the absolute volume of migration but also the age and sex distribution of the migrant population. This is of particular importance when planning and considering the impact of migration into new towns or growth areas, where the immigrant population is likely to be largely composed of young married families in age-groups with high fertility and low mortality rates. By contrast, migrants who leave an area on retirement will come from age-groups with relatively high mortality and extremely low fertility rates.

The need to analyse population projections separately by age was indicated by one study which showed how the percentage of the population of working age can change drastically. In this particular case, the study area has a very unusual population structure due to the effect of past migration out of the area. This structure will be further influenced by the expected future migration into the new towns planned for the study area. The net result was that the proportion of the total population that was of working age fell by about 10% whilst there was a big increase in the percentage share of school children in the population.

2. EMPLOYMENT PREDICTIONS

The study area employment potential is made up of two separate components. Some employment is generated by the need to serve the local population. Other employment serves a wider regional or national market. It is the latter which is said to make up the economic base of the area and which is essential to the area's long-term economic prosperity. However, before it is possible to estimate local employment, it is first necessary to consider expected trends in national employment both in total and for specific industries.

The first stage in the prediction process is, therefore, to determine the total increase in national employment. The Registrar General publishes estimates of the expected change over time in the 'activity rates' which indicate the likelihood of a person of a given age and sex seeking full-time employment. These estimates are based partly upon recent trends and partly upon expected changes such as raising the school-leaving age. It is a simple matter to apply these activity rates to the Registrar General's forecasts of future population, so obtaining a control total of the future national labour force available for employment. This can be compared with the base-year national labour force to give an estimate of the potential increase in national employment by the design year.

The next stage in the process is to estimate the future growth in employment by different types of industry. This is a hazardous process and for any given industry is liable to considerable margins of error as the result of unforeseen technological developments. Nevertheless, the most important factors such as the decline of some of the older basic industries like the coal-mining industry and the rise of other newer industries, particularly the service industries, are well known. Nevertheless, neither government nor private research organisations are particularly eager to undertake this type of long-term forecasting, although a detailed industrial employment forecast was included in the book *The British Economy in 1975*, published by the National Institute of Economic and Social Research. The basic information on which these forecasts are based is, however, now rather dated.

Some transportation and planning studies, in particular the South Hampshire Study, the West Midlands Study and the East Central Scotland Study, have based their employment forecasts on a somewhat similar approach to that followed by the National Institute. A number of separate industrial employment categories are determined, usually orders or suborders of the standard industrial classification. The numbers employed in these industries are usually taken from Department of Employment records. Estimates are first made of the expected growth in employment in each industry, using all available evidence including an analysis of past employment trends and any known information on the likely levels of future output and productivity in each industry. The resultant forecast employment by industrial category is first checked at the national level to see that the total change in forecast employment is equal to the change in the forecast labour force available for employment (including an allowance for any expected changes in the average level of unemployment). If necessary, a percentage adjustment is made to the original employment forecasts by industrial category so as to obtain a balance nationally between total employment and the labour force seeking work.

The national forecasts can now be applied locally. The base-year employment by industrial category is usually obtained in the United Kingdom from the Department of Employment's ERII returns although the results of any employment survey conducted locally as part of the study can also be used. The industrial categories are divided into two components. Employment in the industries which serve a regional or national market can initially be assumed to be based on the national forecast growth rates in employment for that industry. The locally dependent employment by contrast is forecast by assuming that the categories which serve a local market will obtain a growth in employment proportional to the national increase in employment in these categories modified by the ratio of the percentage increase in local population to the percentage increase in national population. An example of these calculations is shown in Table B3. Column 1 gives the base-year study

TABLE 53 Survey area employment potential.

Code number	Industrial description	Base-year employment	National growth ratio to design year	'Basic' design-year employment	Addition due to population differential	Design-year employment potential
1	Agriculture, fishing, etc.	6,074	0·76	4,622		4,622
2	Coal mining	27	0·30	8		8
3	Mining and quarrying	169	0·75	127		127
4	Food processing	8,230	0·98	7,975		7,975
5	Drink and tobacco	788	0·90	708		708
6/7/8	Chemicals and allied industries	12,281	1·10	13,620		13,620
9	Iron and steel	2,706	0·78	2,097		2,097
10	Non-ferrous metals	1,463	1·29	1,881		1,881
11	Engineering and electrical goods	7,008	1·23	8,620		8,620
12	Shipbuilding and marine engineering	4,487	0·78	3,477		3,477
13	Motors and cycles	3,283	0·90	2,948		2,948
14	Aircraft	5,692	1·00	5,692		5,692
15	Railway locomotives and rolling stock	322	0·37	118		118
16	Metal goods (n.e.s)	4,399	0·93	4,078		4,078
17	Textiles	805	0·89	713		713
18	Leather, clothing, etc.	2,332	0·86	2,003		2,003
19	Building materials	1,692	0·94	1,596		1,596
20	Pottery and glass	636	0·87	556		556
21	Timber and furniture	5,615	1·05	5,873		5,873
22	Paper, printing and publishing	3,381	1·09	3,699		3,699
23/24	Rubber and other manufacturing	1,506	1·25	1,878		1,878
25	Construction	11,204	0·96	10,711	140	10,851
26	Gas	971	0·90	872	10	882
27	Electricity	1,564	1·18	1,846	26	1,872
28	Water	243	1·06	258	4	262
29	Transport and communications	20,523	0·87	17,937	25	17,962
30/31	Distributive trades	27,956	1·09	30,593	287	30,880
32/34	Insurance, banking and services	37,965	1·18	44,799	551	45,350
33	Public administration and defence	9,093	1·07	9,775	107	9,882
	TOTAL	182,415		189,080	1,150	190,230

area employment by industrial category. Column 2 shows the national mark up appropriate to that industrial category, assuming a national balance between employment and the available labour force. Column 3 gives the employment potential assuming the national growth rate can be applied locally, whilst column 4 shows the effect of the difference between local and national rates of population growth in the locally dependent industries.

There are, however, some disadvantages in applying national forecasts indiscriminately to local industries. Specific make-up of the local industries within any one industrial category may be very different from the national pattern and in these circumstances the national forecasts can give a false picture of expected local development. The study area forecasts should, therefore, take account of any particular local trends. Thus, if one industry has been growing much faster (or more slowly) in the study area than nationally, then it may be wise to assume that such a pattern will continue in the future. It is also possible that a major employer within the study area may have specific plans for expanding or contracting his labour force and this could significantly affect employment in the study area. This can only be discovered from local knowledge and in all studies it is desirable to interview the management of large-scale employing organisations to ascertain whether they have any such plans and if necessary adjust the employment forecasts to match.

The prediction of the local employment potential thus relies on a mixture of national and local trends. National trends are first examined and a balance obtained between national employment and the available labour force. In the light of this information, forecasts are then made of the study area employment potential, assuming that industries which serve a national market generally reflect national employment trends, while employment in industries which serve a more localised market is more dependent upon the expected growth in the study area population.

3. RECONCILING THE POPULATION AND EMPLOYMENT PROJECTIONS

Since the study area employment potential is forecast separately from the future study area population and labour force, the two estimates have to be reconciled. The design-year study area employment must equal the final study area labour force including net commuting to and from the study area, and making a small allowance for unemployment (the labour force includes all those actively seeking employment and not only those actually in employment).

Either the population or the employment forecasts or more probably both sets of forecasts should be adjusted to achieve a balance. If, for example, there appears to be a shortage of employment in the study area then a balance might be achieved by assuming that migration in search of work reduces the deficiency to half its present level, and that the rest of the deficiency is eliminated by encouraging some industries serving the national market, particularly the faster-growing industries, to move into the area. These industries may be persuaded to move into the area, either because labour is readily available or because of special government inducements, designed to reduce the level of unemployment in certain areas.

An interesting example of the use of separate population and employment projections before obtaining a final balanced estimate is given by the Land Use Transportation Study for East Central Scotland. The need to carry out age-specific population forecasts is particularly apparent from this study.

The study area had in the previous fifteen years suffered from a severe contraction in some of its basic industries, in particular the coalmining and shale oil industries. As a result, there had been substantial migration out of the study area. Average migration over the period 1951–66 was estimated at 4,300 per year, whilst the rate over the last five years had increased to 7,000 per annum. If migration had continued at an average rate of say 7,000 per annum, the population in the study area would have risen over the twenty-year projection period by only 10·9% from 1,201,000 to 1,332,000. By contrast the population growth by natural increase would have been 301,000 giving a total population in 1986 of 1,502,000. This rate of increase was just slightly lower than the UK average, however, because of the peculiar age/sex structure of the present population. While the population went up by 10·9% in the first case and by 25·0% in the second case, the corresponding growth in the study area resident labour force was −5·0% or only 12·4% respectively. By contrast, the employment potential if each industrial category in the study area grew at the same rate locally as nationally was a growth in employment of 4·7%, sufficient to support a population of 1,320,000.

After a reduction in the estimates for the locally dependent industries to allow for the slightly lower growth in the population locally as opposed to nationally, it still appeared that the employment potential in the study area was considerably in excess of the potentially available labour force even assuming an immediate end to all migration from the study area. This, in fact, reflected the fact that most of the 'shake out' from the declining coalmining industry had already taken place by 1966. In this situation it could in normal circumstances be assumed that the greater availability of employment in the study area would lead at the very least to a considerable reduction in net migration from the study area.

However, in the particular area being studied, it was known government policy to induce net inward migration by the construction of a large new town and two smaller new town developments. These schemes were expected to cater for an increase in population of over 125,000, mainly, but not exclusively, overspill from the Glasgow area. It was therefore decided to assume a net migration into the study area of 2,100 per year bringing the total study area population by 1986 up to 1,550,000 giving rise to a corresponding growth in the labour force which in turn meant that if unemployment in the study area was to be kept to the national average that total employment within the study area had to rise to 13·1%. Once all the adjustments to the locally dependent industries had been carried out it was found that notwithstanding the big population influx into the study area the local employment potential was only 7·6% short of the required employment. It was assumed that this would be provided by the diversion into the study area of some employment in industries such as engineering and electrical goods which are growing at a fast rate to serve a national or international market.

APPENDIX C

Vehicle operating costs and the value of time

1. VEHICLE OPERATING COSTS

Vehicle operating costs vary tremendously according to the type of vehicle, speed of travel, nature of the road surface and alignment as well as the country and climate considered. A great deal has been written on this topic, although many of the figures quoted are based on rather inadequate and outdated research. In Great Britain, the standard formulae for road vehicle operating costs have been developed by the Road Research Laboratory and are quoted in Table C1. These costs replace the earlier figures given in Road Research Laboratory

TABLE C1   Vehicle operating costs.

| | | Vehicle operating costs, 1968 prices (new pence) | |
		costs excluding indirect taxation	including indirect taxation
Cars	per vehicle mile	1·00	1·33
	per vehicle hour	8·25	16·14
Light loads	per vehicle mile	2·00	2·54
	per vehicle hour	13·25	21·06
Heavy loads	per vehicle mile	3·88	5·15
	per vehicle hour	24·25	36·07
Bus	per vehicle mile	4·75	6·48
	per vehicle hour	35·75	53·82

Source: Road Research Laboratory.

Technical Paper No. 75 and are based on more recent analysis carried out in 1967.

The costs for private cars include fuel, oil, tyres and maintenance. They also include depreciation due to use but not depreciation which is merely due to the passing of time. Depreciation due to use is estimated at 40% of total depreciation.

The costs for commercial vehicles and buses include fuel, oil, tyres and maintenance. In this case, however, the mileage component of the costs include full depreciation on a replacement cost basis on the grounds that the useful life of a commercial vehicle is directly related to the mileage run. The time dependent element, however, includes an allowance for the interest costs of the vehicle on the grounds that the number of vehicles required by an operator is dependent on the speed at which they can travel.

The costs quoted in Table C1 represent resource costs to the whole community, that is, costs excluding indirect taxation. However, costs to the user include indirect taxation and these costs are quoted in column 2. Indirect taxation has been excluded from the RRL figures on the grounds that it is merely a transfer payment, and does not represent the use of any real resources, so that any reduction in taxation paid, although a benefit to the road user, would involve an equal and opposite loss to the state. This approach is perfectly justified if one is considering a fixed travel matrix, but breaks down as soon as one tries to allow for any generated or redistributed traffic. This point is discussed more fully in Chapter V.

It may also at times be necessary to add a cost for parking. This could include both the price actually paid for parking and an allowance for the inconvenience and delay involved in finding a parking place and in getting from the parking place to the final destination.

2. VALUE OF TIME

In addition to the direct costs of transport, an allowance must be made for the time spent in travel, and possibly for any other discomfort or inconvenience involved.

Three distinct types of time need to be considered, namely business time, commuting time and time spent on all other kinds of trips.

It is normally accepted that business time, that is, time spent as part of one's employment, should be valued at the wage rate of the person in question, although it is not immediately obvious why this should be the case. It is certainly true that in the conditions postulated by nineteenth-century classical economic theory leading to a 'perfectly competitive' world, each employee would receive remuneration equal to the value of his marginal work effort and also such that at the margin his wage rate was just sufficient to compensate him for working the last hour of the day, rather than having one hour's extra leisure. However, in the real world, conditions are usually very different. In particular working hours are to a large extent fixed so that there is no direct relationship between the wage rate, the value of the individual's marginal physical product and the individual's desire for leisure. It can be argued that in certain cases, with fixed working hours, small savings in working time may not benefit anyone. While this may sometimes be true, it does not necessarily mean that it is invalid to estimate such savings at the wage rate, because in other cases small savings in time may be just sufficient to permit large increases in daily productivity, so these two types of discrepancy tend to balance each other out.

It is much more dubious whether the wage rate is a sufficient measure of the benefit received by the employer due to savings in his employee's working time. Most firms have to cover overheads, some of which are not independent of the number of staff employed, and also succeed in making a profit. Thus, it can be argued that there is a case for factoring up the wage rate to allow for overheads and the profit element. Against this, it may at times be the case that the individual employee prefers time spent travelling on his employer's business to more productive time spent within the factory or office. In this case the wage rate may overstate the real benefit from any time saving.

Nevertheless, it is certainly customary to relate the value of working time to the wage rate of the traveller. Working time is currently valued in the United Kingdom at the wage rate of the traveller plus selective employment taxes and other employee related contributions with a further 10% to cover overheads.

In the last few years, several studies have been undertaken either directly to measure the value of commuting time or with such a value as a by-product. Usually the method adopted is to consider what percentage of people choose one of two modes, one of which is quicker but more expensive than the other mode. A range of values between 15 and 50% of the average wage or salary of the particular people travelling have been found from such studies. There is no reason why this fraction should be expected to be the same for all income groups. However, the assumption that commuting time can be taken as some fraction of hourly earnings is not unreasonable. (What little evidence there is on this point appears to be contradictory, one study suggesting an increasing fraction with income and another study suggesting the reverse.) Different values of time could also be expected for different modes and conditions of travel, reflecting the inherently greater discomfort of travel by one mode rather than by another mode. There is some evidence to suggest that car travel may have a lower time valuation (implying less discomfort) than bus travel.

The value of time spent on journeys other than business or commuting trips is extremely difficult to value, although it should not be ignored. There are various types of journey, including shopping trips by housewives, social trips for the whole family, trips by schoolchildren, retired people and other non-wage-earners. As far as the authors know, no satisfactory attempt has yet been made to determine scientifically a value for such trips. In the absence of any such information an arbitrary value has to be placed on such leisure-time savings.

The present suggestion of the Department of the Environment (1971) is that both commuting and leisure travel should be valued at 25% of the wage rate of the head of the household. This value is applied separately to all other adults in the household, and children's time savings are valued at one-third of the adult rate. This means that if a man, wife and one child make a leisure trip together, their time savings will be valued at 58% of the father's wage rate. Because most transportation studies obtain and use information about households rather than individual earners it is often more convenient to express the value of non-working time as a percentage of household income, and the figure suggested by the Department of the Environment is 19% of average household income.

3. Comfort differentials

It has been found by London Transport and other major transport undertakings that people prefer not to change buses or trains even if they could save some journey time. It has therefore become customary on public transport trips to value time spent outside the vehicle, whether walking, waiting or transferring from one service to another at double the standard rate. This implies that time spent outside the vehicle is considered on average to be twice as uncomfortable as time spent in the vehicle.

Some general attempts have been made to estimate the value people place on comfort by a similar analysis to that used to measure time savings. Thus, in the Victoria Line Study it was suggested that the value people placed upon getting a seat could be determined by comparing the number of people who chose a slower journey with a high probability of a seat, in preference to a faster journey with a low probability of a seat. If the value of time is already known, it is possible to estimate the value placed on travelling on the underground in less crowded conditions.

However, one must be particularly careful in a trade-off analysis of this nature to ensure that there is only the one single identifiable difference between the two alternatives being considered, otherwise one cannot decide which of two possible features (e.g. higher speed or higher comfort as in the case of taxis as compared with bus travel) is really the cause of the decision to follow one mode. It is also necessary to make sure that choices are based on a true appreciation of the alternatives, otherwise the measured value of time or comfort may be influenced as much by ignorance of the characteristics of the options as by a true valuation of time or comfort.

4. CHANGE IN VALUES OVER TIME

When assessing the potential benefit from road improvement schemes, it is often necessary to consider developments several years ahead. This means assessing costs and benefits in future years. In order to avoid the difficulties and distortions due to predicting future rates of inflation, it is customary to measure all operating costs and benefits at constant present-day prices. However, this means that any costs which have and will continue to have a heavy proportion of labour costs (direct or indirect) will be underestimated while the costs of resources containing a low element of labour cost will be overestimated. But even when all other costs are measured at constant prices, the value of time can be expected to rise relatively to all other goods and commodities over time (since we will not be able to increase our production of time). It is thus reasonable to assume that the value of time will increase at the same rate as average real income (i.e. monetary income less inflation) per head of the population. The Department of the Environment assume that the value of time should increase at about 3% per annum. In many studies it is customary to consider car-owning and non-car-owning households separately. However, one of the main effects of rising income is to increase car-ownership, and in a situation where the average income of all households increases at 3% per annum, the mean income of both car-owning and non-car-owning groups treated separately will both grow at less than 3% per annum because new entrants to the car-owning subgroup when they transfer, reduce the average income of both the new group which they enter and the old group they are leaving. The Department of the Environment have calculated that if the value of time is assured to rise at 3% per annum, then this is equivalent to an average rise of 2·1% per annum when applied separately to car-owning and non-car-owning households, although this may vary from study to study depending upon the income and car-ownership structure in the study area.

APPENDIX D

The calculation of user benefit using the results from transportation studies

In many studies a fixed matrix of traffic is assigned to two different networks, and it is tacitly assumed that the scale of transport investments considered will not alter the pattern of movement in the study area. In these circumstances, the total user benefit from a new plan can be simply calculated as the reduction in the costs (both operating and time costs) compared with the base plan associated with carrying a fixed matrix of traffic. However, when a full transportation model is applied the trip distribution process usually means that the trip matrix will be different for all the plans that are being compared. When a new plan is introduced, certain trips become cheaper and so potentially more attractive, others become absolutely or relatively more expensive and have less traffic than before. It is therefore no longer possible to use the change in overall journey costs as the measure of user benefit. A low cost of travel can either be associated with a particularly poor network which only generates a low demand for movement or it can be associated with a very good network, which enables an increased number of trips to be made more cheaply.

In those circumstances, it is necessary when estimating the user benefit to consider the journey costs for each possible movement both if the new plan were and if it were not introduced. Journey costs are discussed in more detail in Appendix

C. For analysis purposes, three main types of trip have to be considered.

I. TRIPS BETWEEN THE SAME ORIGIN AND DESTINATION AS PREVIOUSLY

Some trips will be made between the same two points whether or not a new plan is completed. There will, however, be a positive benefit (or loss) associated with the new ease (or increased hardship) with which these trips can be made. This benefit per trip is equal to the cost differential before and after the new facility is introduced.

$$\text{Cost before} = C_1$$
$$\text{Cost after} = C_2$$
$$\text{Flow} = Q_{xy} \text{ trips}$$
$$\text{Benefit} = Q_{xy}(C_1 - C_2)$$

(X) ⸺⸺⸺⸺⸺⸺⸺ (Y)

2. NEWLY GENERATED TRIPS

Certain trips are made with the new plan that would not be made with the old plan. This generated traffic, which should not be confused with any general growth in traffic, only comes into existence because of a reduction in transport costs. Consequently, the journeys represented by this traffic are of less importance (to the persons or organisations making them) than existing journeys that were worth making even at the original higher level of transport costs. It would need only a very small reduction from the original cost to make some trips worth while. Other trips will only just become worth while even after the full reduction in costs between the two plans. Unless the cost before a new plan is introduced is very much greater than the cost after the plan is implemented it is reasonable to assume that trip generation is linearly dependent on cost, over the range of cost variation between the two plans. In this case the benefit to such generated traffic between X and Y is $\frac{1}{2}S(C_1 - C_2)$ where S is the number of such generated trips between X and Y, and C_1 and C_2 are defined as in the previous illustration.

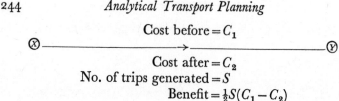

$$\text{Cost before} = C_1$$
$$\text{Cost after} = C_2$$
$$\text{No. of trips generated} = S$$
$$\text{Benefit} = \tfrac{1}{2}S(C_1 - C_2)$$

3. REDISTRIBUTED TRIPS

Some trips used to go from X to Y, but because of a greater reduction (or smaller increase) in the cost of travel from X to Z than from X to Y, they would go from X to Z after the new plan was introduced. Such trips are known as redistributed trips. Since the traffic now prefers to switch from Y to Z, the diverted trip-makers must have received a benefit greater than that which they would have received if they had continued to go to Y. But equally their benefit will be less than that received by trips which were already going to Z.

If we assume, using the same argument put forward for generated trips, that the diversion from Y to Z is linear over the cost differential concerned, then the benefit to such traffic is equal to

$$R(C_1 - C_2) + \tfrac{1}{2}R[(D_1 - D_2) - (C_1 - C_2)] = \tfrac{1}{2}R(C_1 - C_2 + D_1 - D_2)$$

where R = number of trips from X redistributed to Z instead of Y; C_1 and D_1 are the respective costs of travel from X to Y and X to Z with the old plan; C_2 and D_2 are the costs of travel from X to Y and X to Z with the new plan.

Before: R trips at cost C_1
After: No. trips at cost C_2

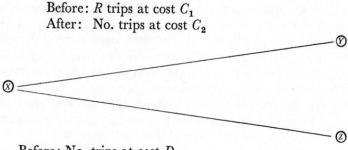

Before: No. trips at cost D_1
After: R trips at cost D_2

All types of trip combined

It is easiest to show how a general formula can be applied to all of the three types of trips considered above by looking at a simple example. Imagine a three-point world X, Y and Z, in which trips are only made from X to Y and X to Z, and all trips between any two points are made at the same user cost to every member of the public. A new facility is introduced which generates some new trips and causes some existing trips to be diverted from Y to Z. Using the notation of the previous paragraphs, the user benefit derived from the new facility is given by:

$$\text{Benefit} = Q_{xy}(C_1 - C_2) + Q_{xz}(D_1 - D_2) + \tfrac{1}{2}S_{xy}(C_1 - C_2) + \tfrac{1}{2}S_{xz}(D_1 - D_2) + \tfrac{1}{2}R(C_1 - C_2 + D_1 - D_2)$$

If q_{xy} is the total flow between X and Y without the new facility, q'_{xy} is the total flow between X and Y with the new facility

$$\text{then} \quad q_{xy} = Q_{xy} + R \qquad q'_{xy} = Q_{xy} + S_{xy}$$
$$q_{xz} = Q_{xz} \qquad\qquad q'_{xz} = Q_{xz} + S_{xz} + R$$
$$\therefore \text{Benefit} = \tfrac{1}{2}(q_{xy} + q'_{xy})(C_1 - C_2) + \tfrac{1}{2}(q_{xz} + q'_{xz})(D_1 - D_2)$$

This is a simple form of a more general formula which can be applied to any proposed new transport facility, namely that the total user benefit from such a facility during the time interval T_1 to T_2 is equal to:

$$\tfrac{1}{2} \sum_i \sum_j (q_{ij} + q'_{ij})(c_{ij} - c'_{ij})$$

where q_{ij} = quantity of traffic flowing from i to j in time T_1 to T_2 without proposed facility, at cost to the user of c_{ij}

q'_{ij} = quantity of traffic flowing from i to j in time T_1 to T_2 with proposed facility, at a cost to the user of c'_{ij}

Thus to measure the direct benefit (or loss) to individual travellers as a result of the provision of a new transport facility, it is necessary to calculate the quantity of traffic that would

flow between any pair of points at any given time both if the
new facility were and were not introduced. The mean of these
two figures is then multiplied by the resultant cost differential
(cost without – cost with), and this total is summed over all
possible movements to give the total direct user benefit during
the given time interval.

This formula is very simple. Its importance is that while it
allows for the effects of both generated and redistributed traffic,
it is not necessary to distinguish how much of each such traffic
there is. The major difficulty lies in estimating the information
required. This is essentially the problem that is considered in
the traffic forecasting model. Theoretically new calculations
including new assignments should be made for every different
time of the day or year that the cost of travel changes. Indeed
separate calculations should be made for all groups of potential
travellers who have different sets of preferences and different
incomes. Moreover the analysis assumes perfect knowledge on
the part of all travellers, so that they can estimate in advance
the likely cost of any alternative actions they may contemplate.
In practice this is of course not the case. Nevertheless for
practical purposes some degree of averaging is necessary both
in the process of traffic forecasting and at the plan evaluation
stage.

There are certain other problems which have to be faced
before the above formula can be applied. Usually the trip
distribution and the economic evaluation models are not based
on strictly comparable formulae. The trip distribution and
assignment process is often based on the assumption that the
individual's choice of destination is determined by the relative
journey times to alternative destinations, while the evaluation
model is based on the assumption that the trip-making pattern
is determined by the relative cost of journeys to alternative
destinations. The two hypotheses would only be compatible if
changes in journey time and journey cost were always directly
related to each other. This is not always the case. In particular
there are cases where, as the result of a new facility, the minimum journey time between two points fall, but the journey
distance by the minimum time route is so much greater that the
journey cost actually rises, giving the apparently illogical conclusion that improved facilities lead to a user disbenefit. It is

undoubtedly true that on certain occasions especially where a small time-saving is achieved at the expense of considerable extra vehicle mileage the 'minimum time' assignment and distribution model is not a good representation of the real position. For this reason it is being replaced more and more by some form of minimum cost model which is based on some combination of both time and distance.

It is, however, equally probable that any apparently illogical result could be due to a poor estimate of the user costs. As mentioned above, the analysis assumes perfect knowledge on the part of all travellers, so that they can estimate in advance the actual cost of any action they contemplate. This is, of course, a most unreasonable assumption. Many people will not accurately forecast trip conditions and consequently costs.

There is also evidence which suggests that the perceived costs on which the user bases his decision whether, when and where to travel are lower than his actual costs. In particular, it has been suggested that motorists tend to consider only petrol costs and ignore other use-related costs such as oil, tyres, maintenance and depreciation through mileage. It is thus possible for extra trips to be generated as the result of some change in conditions in which the perceived costs of travel fall while the real costs actually rise.

In these circumstances, the best approach is to use perceived costs for traffic forecasting and both perceived and actual costs for evaluation. In this case the user benefit is calculated in two stages. First, the change in perceived user benefit, and then subsequently the change in the unforeseen or unperceived user benefit. Thus, if q_{ij} = the flow from i to j, C_{ij} = the actual cost from i to j and, p_{ij} = the perceived cost from i to j for the base plan and q'_{ij}, C'_{ij} and p'_{ij} are similarly defined for the new plan, then the user benefit is equal to

$$\tfrac{1}{2}(q_{ij} + q'_{ij})\,(p_{ij} - p'_{ij}) + q_{ij}(C_{ij} - p_{ij}) - q'_{ij}(C'_{ij} - p'_{ij})$$

where the first term represents the perceived user benefit and the second and third terms the change in the unperceived user costs.

The reason for treating perceived and unperceived costs and benefits separately is to allow for the possibility that newly generated traffic or redistributed traffic may, if actual costs are higher than perceived costs, obtain less benefit than expected if the actual cost of making the trip has been underestimated. The benefit to existing trips common to both plans will not be affected, by the separate consideration of perceived and unperceived benefits as any reduction in the perceived user benefit will be counterbalanced by an unperceived user gain. This can easily be seen by setting $q'_{ij} = q_{ij}$ in the formula for perceived and unperceived user benefit which then reduces to $q_{ij}(C_{ij} - C'_{ij})$, the result that would be obtained by considering only actual user costs. It may therefore be possible in studies where the assumed traffic does not vary appreciably between plans to calculate the user benefit direct from the change in actual costs between plans without the need to include the added complication of distinguishing between perceived and unperceived costs and benefits.

Costs and benefits of trips that switch mode

The analysis so far in this appendix has been based on a simple example where there was a common cost of travel between any two points to all members of the population. It was suggested that while this may not always be true, it was nevertheless reasonable for evaluation purposes to assume certain average costs which would be the same for all travellers. There is, however, one special case that requires consideration in more detail and this is the case when there is more than one possible mode between two zones.

In this case application of the average costs per mile and per minute of travel would normally lead to different total costs of travel between the two points by the two modes. If the average cost functions accurately measured the cost to each individual user of the cost of travel by the respective modes, in other words, if everyone had similar valuations of the marginal direct and indirect transportation costs by these two competing modes, there would be no effective modal split. Every individual would use the least cost alternative and no one would use the more costly alternative. In practice of course this does not normally happen. Some people will prefer to use one mode of travel (i.e. this mode is less costly to them), others will prefer to use the alternative mode. This spread of preference is often reflected by the use of diversion curves to assess the modal split between any two districts.

If a new plan were now introduced there would be consequent changes in the relative costs of travel by private and public transport, and as a result some travellers might decide to switch from one mode to another. It is a difficult question to decide how the economic analysis should deal with this problem. One possible approach that has to be rejected is the use of a weighted average cost. It is easiest to show why such an approach is inadequate by means of a simple example. Suppose initially fifty people travel from A to B by car at a calculated cost of 20p per person. In addition 100 people travel from A to B by train at a calculated cost of 10p. As the result of a road improvement the cost of travel by car from A to B falls to 18p and in consequence fifty train passengers decide to use the road instead. The weighted average cost initially was $50 \times 20 + 100 \times 10$

$$= \frac{50 \times 20 + 100 \times 10}{150} = 13\frac{1}{3}\text{p}$$

but the final weighted average cost

$$= \frac{100 \times 18 + 50 \times 10}{150} = 15\frac{1}{3}\text{p}$$

Applying the user benefit formula total user benefit

$$= \tfrac{1}{2}(150 + 150)\,(13\tfrac{1}{3} - 15\tfrac{1}{3})$$
$$£3 \cdot 00$$

But this is plainly an absurd answer since an apparent disbenefit has arisen from a situation in which the cost of one mode has fallen while the cost of the other mode has remained the same.

The reason why the formula gives an absurd answer is that the travellers who decide to switch from train to road obviously value the relative cost of train as opposed to car at more than the average value. This is perfectly liable to happen in practice especially if the people in question have above average incomes. As long as only one mode is considered, any discrepancy between average costs and actual costs only leads to a distortion if there is a difference between the change in actual costs and the change in average costs. Moreover any deviation above the average by 'above average' people is likely to be counter-balanced by a corresponding deviation below the average by 'below average' people, so that any resultant distortion is unlikely to be important.

Such a conclusion is not, however, justified in the situation in which people change mode. The people changing mode are unlikely to be a representative selection of average people but are much more likely to be people with a particular non-average preference for one mode rather than another. As a new mode is introduced, the first people to divert to the mode will be people with a particular preference for that mode, for whom the cost of such a mode is abnormally low relative to the cost of the old mode. As the two systems become more and more competitive, people with progressively nearer to average relative costs of travel will switch from one mode to the other. But after any given change in circumstances which alters the relative attraction of one mode rather than another the people switching modes will fall within one particular class of people with a given relative cost preference for one mode rather than the other and so will not be representative of the average.

The best way to deal with this problem is to apply the user benefit formula separately by mode, treating traffic that switches from say, rail to road, as degenerated rail traffic and generated road traffic. Thus if, as the result of a change between two plans, conditions on the roads grow better but the service provided on the railway remains unaltered, a certain number of trips will switch from rail to road. Some of these trips would require only a small improvement in road conditions to switch to road, but for other trips the switch will only just prove worth while even with the full reduction in the cost of travel by road. It is therefore reasonable to assume that substitution is linear over the change in costs considered and that the benefit to traffic that changes mode is equal to:

$$\tfrac{1}{2}M(D_1 - D_2)$$

where M = the number of trips switching from rail to road
$\quad\quad\; D_1$ = the cost of travel by road before improvement
$\quad\quad\; D_2$ = the cost of travel by road after improvement

Equally when there is a reduction in the cost of travel by both modes, but a greater reduction in one than the other, we can assume that the benefit to traffic diverting from, say, road to rail as the result of a greater reduction in rail than road costs is equal to the benefit that would have been obtained if such trips had continued to be made by road plus, on average, half the difference between the saving in rail costs and the saving in road costs. This is equal to:

$$M(C_1 - C_2) + \tfrac{1}{2}M[(D_1 - D_2) - (C_1 - C_2)] \text{ or}$$
$$\tfrac{1}{2}M(C_1 - C_2) + \tfrac{1}{2}M(D_1 - D_2)$$

where M = the number of trips switching from road to rail
C_1 = the cost of travel by road before improvement
C_2 = cost of travel by road after improvement
D_1 = cost of travel by rail before improvement
D_2 = cost of travel by rail after improvement

i.e. the result would have been obtained by applying the user benefit separately to each mode. In fact, the treatment of trips switching modes in a two-point (one journey) world is exactly equivalent to the treatment of redistributed trips that switch destinations in a two-journey (one mode) world.

By combining these two relationships the total user benefit from a new, as opposed to an old plan, during the time interval T_1 to T_2 is equal to:

$$B = \tfrac{1}{2} \sum_{ijm} (q_{ijm} + q'_{ijm})(C_{ijm} - C'_{ijm})$$

where q_{ijm} = quantity of traffic flowing from i to j by mode m in the time T_1 to T_2 with the old plan and at cost to the user of C_{ijm}, q'_{ijm} and C'_{ijm} are similarly defined for the new plan.

ESTUARY-CROSSING PROBLEM

There is, however, one possible set of circumstances in which this formula would be invalid. The formula is of course dependent on the assumption that traffic switching either modes or destination receives a benefit equal to the cost saving if it had not switched mode or destination, plus a half the difference between the cost savings on the mode or to the destination finally chosen and the cost saving on the mode, or to the destination preferred with the original plan. This assumption is usually reasonable; however, in certain circumstances it may not always be justified. For example, suppose that two districts on different sides of an estuary were connected by rail but not by road, the nearest road bridge being some long distance upstream. A road bridge is then constructed as a result of which the road cost of travel between the two districts falls from say £1 to 20p: the rail fare remains unaltered at 10p. As soon as the road bridge is completed a substantial percentage of those travellers who formerly used rail would divert to road. However, it is unlikely that the average valuation they would place on the benefit they receive from the road bridge is as high as 40p, [$\frac{1}{2}$(£1 − 20p)]. In a situation like this where the cost of travel between two points is radically different after an improvement is introduced trips may no longer be generated linearly over the whole of the range of cost differential considered. This is especially the case with trips that switch mode where the benefit from such a switch may depend upon the previous cost by the other mode (not included in the user benefit formula) more than the original cost of a mode (included in the user benefit formula) which previously was too costly to be considered as a competitor for travel between the two points.

This is a rather extreme example, which is only likely to be important when completely new estuary crossings or a set of entirely new public transport routes are included in the networks to be evaluated. If such problems are expected it is, however, possible to adjust the sensitivity of the user benefit to large changes in journey costs by using a relationship of the form

$$B = q_{ijm}(C_{ijm} - C'_{ijm}) + F(q'_{ijm} - q_{ijm})(C_{ijm} - C'_{ijm})$$

where q_{ijm}, q'_{ijm}, C_{ijm}, C'_{ijm} are defined as previously and $F = $ a function varying with q'_{ijm}.

APPENDIX E

Examples of economic evaluation

This appendix gives a number of specific examples of how the economic evaluation of various transport investment proposals might be handled.

EXAMPLE 1   RURAL ROAD INVESTMENT

It is proposed to build a new two-by-two-lane dual carriageway to bypass an existing small town at the junction of two main roads. The new bypass is represented diagrammatically in Figure E.1 by the links *LM* and *MN*. The existing roads in the area are represented by the links *LO*, *OP*, *ON*, *PN*, *OM*, and the continuation of the links beyond *L*, *N*, *M* and *P* to *A*, *B*, *C* and *D* respectively. The traffic terminating within the town is represented by the dotted line *OE*, where *E* is taken to be the centroid of the zone containing the town being bypassed. It is forecast that by the time the bypass is completed the two directorial traffic flows in vehicles per day through the area will be as given in Table E.1.

TABLE E.1   **Flows passing through town bypassed.**

	B	C	D	E
A	10,000	1,000	4,000	3,000
B	—	6,000	2,000	9,000
C	—	—	8,000	5,000
D	—	—	—	7,000

Thus the main flow from A to B that would use both links of the bypass LMN is 10,000 vehicles per day, while a further 1,000 vehicles a day will use the link LM as part of a journey from A to C. Traffic from A to D will use the bypass if and only if the cost (or time if one is using a minimum time assignment technique) from A to D is less by the route $LMNP$ or the route $LMOP$ than by the original route $LOPD$. Similarly if the 3,000

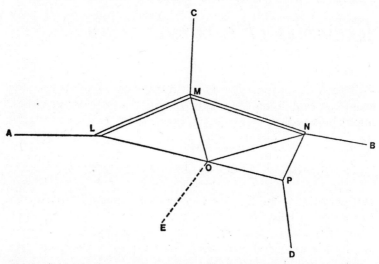

FIGURE E.1   Rural road investment: network example

vehicles a day travelling between A and the town centre would only use the bypass if the route LMO were cheaper (or perhaps shorter) than the direct route LO. Moving to the second row of the table it can similarly be determined whether or not the traffic from B to C, D and E, would use the bypass. Similarly the routing from C to D, C to E and D to E can be determined. The routings between points A, B, C, D and E both with and without the bypass are shown in this example in Figures E.2 and E.3.

The process described above is really a traffic assignment exercise, but such an assignment is an essential preliminary to the evaluation. As usual the evaluation stage can be divided

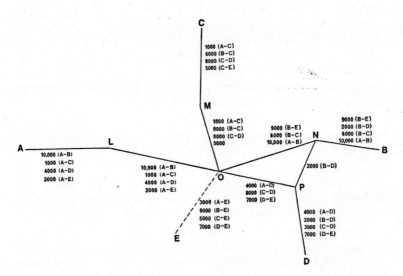

FIGURE E.2   Rural road investment: 'Do Nothing Flows' (example).

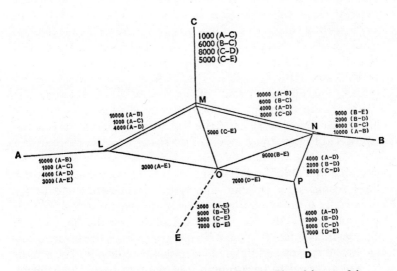

FIGURE E.3   Rural road investment: 'With Bypass Flows' (example).

into three sections: operations evaluation (Will the new bypass adequately cater for the proposed traffic? In particular, will the junctions at L, M and N have sufficient capacity to cater for the forecast traffic?); environmental evaluation (Is the design and location of the bypass acceptable or does it seriously affect important local amenities?); and finally the economic evaluation or quantitative cost-benefit analysis.

The essence of the cost-benefit analysis is to compare the total user cost of moving the given *fixed matrix* of traffic, with and without the bypass, and then equating the benefit to individual travellers to the fall in user travel cost as a result of construction of the bypass. The total cost of travel over the system is simply obtained as the sum of the cost of movement on each individual link. This calculation is shown in Table E.2.

In column (a) of Table E.2 all the links which are affected by the construction of the new route are listed. The length given for each link in column (b) is required to convert costs per mile (based on the average vehicle speed on the link) into total link costs. When the new bypass is opened, it is not only the through traffic that will benefit from increased transit times, but also the more local traffic terminating within the town which benefits from the reduction in traffic congestion. It is thus essential in a calculation of this nature to allow for the effect on road speeds of changes in traffic flows. In general it is assumed that there is a linear relationship between journey speed and traffic flows of the form $dv = -kdq$ where k is a constant representing the 'effective width' of the link being considered. The value of k for each link can be determined from the geometric and other characteristics of the link and is inserted in column (g) of Table E.2. In general the narrower and the more urban the route, the higher the associated factor becomes. In the example in Table E.2 it is supposed that the speed at which the links would flow without the bypass is known. In practice (especially if the evaluation date is some years into the future), this speed may also have to be calculated on the basis of the change in assumed flows and hence speeds from the present-day measured speeds and flows. The costs per mile given in column (i) are assumed to be a function of the link speed. In general the faster the average speed on a link the lower the costs associated with travel on that link. The annual cost given in columns (k) and (l) are simply obtained by multiplying the costs per mile by the journey length and the number of days in the year. The final stage of the quantitative economic analysis is then to calculate the annual rate of return as the difference in user costs expressed as a percentage of the initial capital cost of the investment. In the example given in Table E.2 the annual cost saving is £1,699,000 and if the capital cost of the four miles of new motorway was £4 million this would give a first-year rate of return of 42·5%.

Comment

The method of evaluation described briefly above is the standard method used by the Ministry of Transport to evaluate all inter-urban road schemes. The method has been fully written up by R. F. F. Dawson in Road Research Laboratory Technical Paper No. 75, The Economic Assessment of Road Improvement Schemes, and any reader who actually wishes to apply this technique to a specific problem is strongly advised to read this paper.

Two points of principle of this type of evaluation procedure must, however, be stressed. Both of them may seem obvious but are in fact worth repetition because the authors have noted several instances where failure to appreciate these principles has often led to a fundamental error in the evaluation procedure.

The first point that must be mentioned is that the cost comparison should take place over *all the links* affected by the construction of the new route, that is, every link on which the flow would be different if the link were introduced. If this is not done the cost comparison may be biased either for or against the proposed investment. This is illustrated in Figures E.2 and E.3. As a result of the new road trips from C to D are diverted via the new road. If, however, the cost comparison were restricted to the roads LMN, LON and the connecting route MO, the trips from C to D would be unfairly penalised. With the bypass, $2\frac{1}{4}$ miles of a $3\frac{3}{4}$ mile trip from M to P are costed, whereas in the do-nothing case only the part MO, $1\frac{1}{2}$ miles out of a total journey length between M and P of 4 miles is costed. Obviously such a situation heavily and unfairly biases the results against the new road.

TABLE E₂ Calculation of total user costs.

(a) Link	(b) Length	(c) Flow without bypass	(d) Flow with bypass	(e) Difference	(f) Speed without bypass	(g) Speed flow adjustment factor	(h) Speed with bypass	(i) Cost per mile without bypass	(j) Cost per mile with bypass	(k)* Annual cost without bypass (£'s 000's)	(l) Annual cost with bypass (£'s 000's)
LO	2·00	18,000	3,000	15,000	22·00	0·0010	37·00	6·14	4·40	774	92
OM	1·50	20,000	5,000	15,000	18·00	0·0010	33·00	7·15	4·66	751	122
OJN	2·00	25,000	9,000	16,000	15·00	0·0012	34·20	8·18	4·58	1,431	288
OP	2·50	19,000	7,000	12,000	20·00	0·0007	28·40	6·58	5·09	1,092	312
PN	1·50	2,000	14,000	+12,000	35·00	0·0008	25·40	4·53	5·55	49	408
LM	1·75	—	15,000	—	—	—	50·00	—	3·74	—	343
MN	2·25	—	28,000	—	—	—	50·00	—	3·74	—	833
									Total	4,097	2,398

* Assuming that the annual traffic flow is equal to 350 times the average daily flow.

The other point is that like traffic must be compared with like. In other words there must be a constant trip matrix for both plans being compared. It would obviously unfairly bias the cost comparison against the bypass if the cost of carrying any extra traffic generated solely by the existence of the bypass were computed against the bypass, without such traffic also being costed in the without the bypass case.

In fact generated traffic can be very simply treated by assum-

---

TABLE E3   Calculation of user benefit allowing for generated traffic.

Effect of generated traffic on speed

Speed PN (without generated traffic) $= 25 \cdot 4$

Speed PN (with generated traffic) $= 25 \cdot 4 - 0 \cdot 0008 \times 1,000 = 24 \cdot 6$

Benefit to generated traffic

Cost with bypass $(MNP) = 2 \cdot 25 \times 3 \cdot 74 + 1 \cdot 5 \times 5 \cdot 55 = 16 \cdot 75 \text{p}$

Cost without bypass $= 1 \cdot 5 \times 7 \cdot 15 + 2 \cdot 5 \times 6 \cdot 58 = 27 \cdot 18 \text{p}$

Net saving from bypass $= 10 \cdot 43 \text{p}$

$\therefore$ Annual benefit to generated traffic $= \frac{1}{2} \times 1,000 \times 10 \cdot 43 \times 350 \text{p} = £18,270$

Reduced benefit to existing traffic

Speed on PN falls from $25 \cdot 4$ to $24 \cdot 6$

$\therefore$ Cost per vehicle increases from $5 \cdot 55$ to $5 \cdot 66$ pence per mile

$\therefore$ Annual loss to existing traffic because of the generated traffic

$\qquad\qquad\qquad = 14,000 \times 1 \cdot 5(5 \cdot 66 - 5 \cdot 55) \times 350 \text{ p} = £8,080$

$\therefore$ Net increase in benefit after allowing for generated traffic $= £18,270 - £8,080$

$\qquad\qquad\qquad\qquad\qquad\qquad\qquad\qquad\qquad = £10,190 \text{ per year}$

---

ing that any generated traffic receives a benefit equal to half the cost differential between the old and the new systems being compared. Thus if it were known in the above example that as a result of the new bypass a further 1,000 trips would be generated from *C* to *D*, the extra benefit resultant from the generated traffic could be calculated as shown in Table E.3. It will be seen that the effect of including the generated traffic is made up of two opposite components. First, there is the net benefit to the generated traffic because of the cheaper travel that would result from the existence of a bypass. But against this some allowance also has to be made for the increased congestion caused to other road users by the extra generated traffic. In urban areas this second effect can at times be of great importance.

EXAMPLE 2 SMALL-SCALE URBAN ROAD IMPROVEMENT SCHEMES

The operational and economic evaluation of urban road improvement schemes is usually more difficult than the evaluation of rural road improvements. This is because of the difficulty of predicting accurately the effects of road improvement schemes in congested areas. The interrelationship between traffic demand, road capacity, parking availability and other planning and regulatory controls is at times difficult to forecast. In many ways, it is easier to allow for all these factors at a wide level in the study area as in the more advanced forms of transportation study discussed in Chapter III than at the more detailed level required for the evaluation of individual junction improvements or minor road widening proposals. At the local level, the traffic flows that would use a junction before and after an improvement is completed have to be carefully assessed.

In an urban area it is quite likely that a road improvement scheme will lead to a considerable re-assignment of traffic and also possibly some fresh generation of traffic that was previously restrained by lack of junction capacity. Whether this happens or not will depend upon conditions in the surrounding area. At worst, a junction improvement will have no real effect on traffic flows if the capacity of other adjacent junctions is not also improved. In other cases, the full benefits may not be obtained from an urban traffic improvement scheme, because of insufficient parking available to serve all the demand for movement in the area.

In principle the economic evaluation of an urban road improvement scheme is no different from the evaluation discussed in Example 1. However, each specific improvement will have to be considered on its own merits as no one set traffic forecasting and evaluation method is likely to be appropriate in all circumstances. In certain cases, it may be particularly important to consider the distribution of trips throughout the day. Many junction improvements and traffic management schemes, as well as road-widening schemes are designed to speed up peak-hour traffic flows, and it is quite common for such schemes to give benefits in the peak hours which may be partially or completely offset in the off-peak hours. Junction capacities and delays are so sensitive to the level of traffic that an evaluation based on twenty-four-hour average flows could give a false impression of the benefits to be derived from any investment.

EXAMPLE 3 RAIL INVESTMENT

The evaluation of rail investment (or disinvestment) proposals can also follow the basic principles discussed in Chapter V. The major differences between the evaluation of road and rail schemes are:

1. *The general need to determine a pricing structure for the new investment*
Fares policy can be a key determinant of the use of any rail investment proposal. The lower the fares charged, the greater the use, and, if the system is not loaded beyond its maximum capacity, the higher the benefit derived from the new system. In this case of course the requirements for economic and financial viability may prove contradictory. The Victoria Line Study, the first urban rail investment to be evaluated on the basis of cost-benefit principles, was an interesting example of a scheme which with high fares could be financially viable, or with low fares could give a worth while economic return, but for which it was not possible to devise a fare structure which would prove simultaneously both economically and financially viable. This problem of determining a pricing structure is not solely confined to rail investment proposals, it also applies to toll bridges and perhaps even congested urban road space. The price structure chosen can have a marked effect on the economic rate of return, very high fares will severely curtail the use and hence, except in congested conditions, the benefit derived from any transport investment proposal.

2. *The need to determine railway operating costs*
This should prove relatively straightforward when estimating the operating costs of a proposed rapid transit system or an extension to an existing rapid transit system. In the case of a

I*

mixed all-purpose system, such as the main British Rail system, it is much more difficult to isolate the marginal cost of operating services over individual parts of that system, and such costs can only be determined by very detailed and accurate cost accounting procedures.

3. *The need to estimate benefits (or disbenefits) to travellers changing from one mode to another mode*

This is not by any means an easy exercise. Obviously the benefit or disbenefit is dependent upon changes in direct costs (whether operating costs by private transport or fares by public transport) and changes in journey time, and it also depends upon other factors such as comfort and convenience which cannot be easily measured but can have a profound effect upon preference for private or public transport. This point has been discussed in Appendix D where it was suggested how this point might be covered in the context of a full-scale transportation study. For the evaluation of individual rail improvement schemes no hard-and-fast rules can be laid down but in general traffic diverting from road to rail as a result of a rail improvement should be credited with a benefit equal to half the fall in cost by public transport which causes this diversion.

4. *The need to evaluate the benefit to road transport as a result of some road traffic switching to rail*

In the case of urban rapid transit systems one of the major benefits to be derived from a rail investment scheme may be the reduction in the street congestion as a result of a percentage of the road traffic diverting to rail. Thus in the case of the Victoria Line Study nearly 60% of the total benefit accrued to undiverted road users as a result of the associated reduction in street congestion.

5. *The need to consider the effects of increased comfort and convenience*

In the case of very large cities with a fairly extensive rapid transit system, one of the major objectives of further rail investment may be to reduce the degree of overcrowding and increase the comfort and convenience of travel. Although the Victoria Line Study included an allowance for increased comfort as a result of a reduction in the overcrowding on the underground system, no very satisfactory method has yet been devised to determine a realistic monetary value for such an increase in comfort. At present, the best approach would appear to be a statistical summary of the effect of the new investment on the number of passenger miles, spent seated, standing in reasonable comfort and standing in 'crushed' conditions. The effect of placing a notional value per passenger mile on the value of obtaining a seat, or on the relief of crushed conditions, could then be tested to see how significantly this would affect the rate of return on the investment being considered.

It is difficult in a restricted space to give a complete worked example of the evaluation of an urban rail investment proposal. However, Table E.4 below shows the factors that might be included in such an evaluation.

In the case of rapid transit systems there are several advantages in carrying out a time discounted calculation, both because the construction period is relatively long before the full benefits are received and also because of the possibility of acquiring land which can be sold either on completion of 'cut and cover construction' or in the form of air rights over a surface transit system. In the case of the Victoria Line Study, a time discontinued calculation proved very useful in showing that it was worth while to spend an extra £2 million at the Oxford Circus Station on a quicker form of construction that would enable the whole line to be opened one year earlier.

EXAMPLE 4 THE EVALUATION OF LARGE NETWORKS

The basic theory behind the quantitative economic evaluation of the results of transportation studies has already been discussed earlier in this appendix. The major difference between the cost-benefit analysis required for transportation studies and that required to evaluate the other schemes considered in this section is that the standard output from a transportation study takes the form of a variable trip matrix. If two different transportation plans are tested using the standard transportation study approach, each plan tested has a different trip matrix associated with it. It is thus impossible to evaluate two alternative

TABLE E.4 Evaluation of urban rapid transit proposal.

Initial costs	Actual (at constant prices)
Construction costs	a
Land costs	b
Less sale of air rights	c
Total direct construction costs	$a+b-c$
Plus delays to traffic during construction	d
Total initial costs	$a+b-c+d$

Annual benefits and costs	Actual (at constant prices)
Operators' benefit	
Change in total fares collected	e
Saving in bus operating costs (due to reduction in service after completion of rapid transit system f	f
Less operating and maintenance costs	g
Total operator benefit	$e+f-g$
User benefit	
Benefit to rapid transit passengers	h
Benefit to road users	k
Less disbenefit to bus users from reduced bus service provided after introduction of rapid transit service	l
Total user benefit	$h+k-l$
Government benefit	
Taxation received from operating company	m
Less reduced taxation from road users	n
Total government benefit	$m-n$
Net annual benefit	$e+f-g+h+k-l+m-n$

plans simply by comparing, as in the first example, the total cost of moving the traffic. In these circumstances an increase in the total cost of moving the traffic could either mean that there is a disbenefit because of worsening traffic conditions or alternatively an increase in the total cost of movement could reflect a real benefit, the increase in costs being due to the fact that a reduction in the cost of movement has induced people to spend a greater percentage of their total income on travel to take advantage of the benefits available from cheaper travel. It is not enough to compare two alternative transportation systems merely on the basis of the resultant user costs of travel without also considering the associated user benefits that are obtained from the movement that takes place. This elementary point has often been forgotten in the past evaluation of transportation studies.

The main problem with the evaluation of the results obtained from transportation studies is that it is not possible to distinguish between existing redistributed and freshly generated trips. This problem is covered by use of the formula

$$\text{user benefit} = \tfrac{1}{2} \sum_{ij} (q_{ij} + q'_{ij}) \, (c_{ij} - c'_{ij})$$

described in Appendix D. This formula has to be applied separately for each interzonal pair, and consequently for all but the smallest of studies the calculation has to be programmed for calculation as part of the main transportation study process. The formula is normally calculated separately for different trip purposes, and in order to enable the sensitivity of the results to differences in the value of journey time to be tested the results are often split into time and distance benefit components. It is also useful to process summaries of the total user benefit for all trips to or from selected zones and also the user benefit for all movements between different sectors of the transportation study area.

In principle the treatment of trips by public transport is similar to that for private trips. The problem of trips which switch from private to public mode has already been discussed in Appendix D.

EVALUATION OF NETWORKS WHICH INCLUDE SOME FORM OF TRIP RESTRAINT

One common problem in many urban transportation studies is the problem of excess demand. At the desired operating speeds for each link of the network the demand for movement exceeds the capacity of the road system. This disparity will be resolved in one of two ways. Either a balance will be obtained by congestion, road speeds will fall until demand and supply are in balance or if the desired operating speeds are to be maintained some form of regulation will have to be introduced to ration the available road space. The process of control by congestion can be synthesised by normal speed/flow capacity assignment programs as discussed in Chapter III. In these circumstances the user benefit formula $\frac{1}{2}\sum_{ij} (q_{ij} + q'_{ij})(C_{ij} - C'_{ij})$ is an adequate measure of the user benefit derived from the second plan. The evaluation process can be more difficult if the return is controlled by some form of regulation.

The regulation may take one of two forms. Either the control can take the form of a direct pricing system in which people bid for the right to make the trips they wish to make. In this case people have to pay for the right to use the road system. This can be considered as a user cost and the formula

$$\frac{1}{2} \sum_i \sum_j (q_{ij} + q'_{ij})(C_{ij} - C'_{ij})$$

can still be used to measure the user benefit. The cost terms C_{ij} and C'_{ij}, however, no longer refer solely to the individual users' direct operating costs and inconvenience (or value of time) costs but also include the price T_{ij} that users have to pay for the right to use the system. The sum so collected $\sum q_{ij}T_{ij}$ represents a benefit to the collecting authority and hence when comparing two plans controlled by such a direct pricing system the difference in benefit to the collecting authority $\sum q'_{ij}T'_{ij} - q_{ij}T_{ij}$ also has to be calculated. In general the sign of this term will be opposite to the sign of the user benefit term. It may also be necessary to allow for any differences in the cost of administering the pricing system between the two plans being considered.

If the system is instead controlled by some form of administrative device such as a limitation of parking spaces, or the restriction of the road space to certain essential or predetermined users it is more difficult to estimate the benefit of moving from one plan to another plan. In fact the benefit will depend upon the exact form of regulation used, the more arbitrary and thus the less sensitive to people's preferences the form of control the greater will be the benefit of moving from a network with insufficient road capacity, to one of greater capacity that requires less control.

The process described above is best illustrated by a simple example taken (to avoid the problem of shifting demand curves) from a two-zone world in which everyone travels by his own car. There is some potential benefit which certain inhabitants of this world could get by travelling from one zone to the other

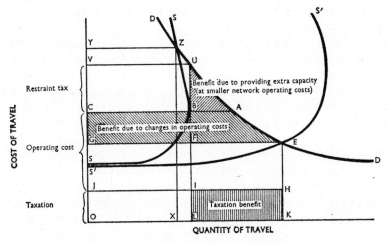

FIGURE E.4 Evaluation of benefits from networks including trip restraint.

zone. This benefit will vary for all individuals and will also vary for each individual, depending upon the number of trips he proposes to make. The cost of travel between these two zones is, however, assumed to be the same for all individuals, being solely a function of the condition of the road links between the two zones. The relationship between the network provided, the demand for travel, the cost of travel, and the quantity of travel between the two zones can then be illustrated as in Figure E.4.

In Figure E.4 the quantity of travel is shown on the x axis; the corresponding cost to the user of travel is shown on the y axis. The user cost consists of three components: first, that element of taxation which varies with the number of journeys made (e.g. fuel tax). This is represented by the height of the line *JIH*, equivalent to a tax of *OJ* per trip (assumed for illustrative simplicity to be independent of conditions on the road links). The second cost component is the direct cost per trip other than taxation (e.g. direct fuel costs, travellers' time costs, etc.). It is shown in Figure E.4 by a varying distance (dependent upon network conditions) above *J* on the *y* axis (e.g. *JG* or *JC*). The third possible cost component is the cost to the individual road user of some form of restraining device, hereafter referred to as a 'restraint tax' that may be imposed to control the flow of traffic on a given network. This 'restraint tax' is assumed to apply to all users who have the option of paying the tax or not travelling.

Also shown in Figure E.4 is the demand curve for travel *DD* which shows the demand for travel between the two zones at any given cost to the user of travel between the two zones. Finally shown are two supply curves *SS* and *S'S'*, which show for road systems with smaller and larger capacities the amount of travel that can take place at given operating plus taxation costs. These supply curves are a function of the size of the system and the quantity of traffic using it. They correspond to known speed/flow relationships.

The quantity of travel that will take place with the larger system is represented by *OK*, given by the intersection at *E* of the demand and supply curve. Similarly, in the absence of any form of restraint tax, the flow on the smaller system would be *OX* (given by the intersection of supply and demand curves at *Z*). In this case the system would be working at a very high cost in an obviously inefficient manner. It is clearly preferable to operate this system at a point at least at, if not below, *B* on the supply curve. To bring this about, it is necessary to impose some 'tax' *CV* which dissuades those people who derive least benefit from the system from using it. With the smaller system users suffer all three costs, namely: the operating tax *OJ*, the operating cost *JC* and the restraint tax *CV*. The government, however, receives operating taxes equal to the area *OJIL* and a restraint tax equal to the area *CVUB* is also collected.

If we now consider moving from the smaller to the larger system, the quantity of travel goes up from *OL* to *OK* and the total user cost of travel falls to *OG*. The benefit to users common to both systems if the larger replaced the smaller is thus equal to *GV* per trip, giving a total benefit equal to the area *GVUF*. However, the loss to the restraint tax authority is equal to their previous receipts of *CVUB*. Hence the total overall community benefit is equal to the area *GCBF*.

The traffic able to use the larger system, but not prepared to pay the costs of using the smaller system, receives a benefit of between *FU* and zero per trip, and the total user benefit to such traffic is equal to the area *EFU*. Here there is no compensating loss to the restraint tax authority, but there is a gain to the operating tax authority equal to the area *LIHK*.*

Thus the total overall benefit of moving from the smaller to the larger system is equal to the area *GCBUE* plus the area *LIHK*. This can be considered as three components: the extra operating tax collected *LIHK*, the user benefit of allowing extra trips to take place at given operating cost conditions shown by the area *ABU*, and the benefit due to changes in system operating costs equal to the area *GCAE*.

In practice it is not always easy to deduce the benefit of allowing some previously restrained trips to take place. In Figure E.4 this benefit is equal to the area *UBA*. In many transportation studies the excess demand at the cost *OC* will be known (i.e. *AB* is known) and the problem is to estimate the shape of the demand curve *AU*. However all forms of traffic forecasting model inherently assume a demand curve for travel (as part of the trip generation and distribution stages). The relationship between travel costs and trip demand incorporated into the trip generation and distribution models is not usually stated as an explicit demand curve, although the underlying elasticity of demand can usually be deduced. Often as in the case of the London Transportation Study this can be approximated to a curve with a unit elasticity of demand for travel with respect to time, that is to say a 1% increase in travel time leads to a 1% decrease in travel demand. This is an elasticity of demand with respect to cost of between 1·4 and 1·75 depending upon the trip purpose being considered.

---

* This is a slight over-simplification. Allowance should also be made for any indirect taxation not collected elsewhere as a result of a transfer of purchasing power from other goods to road travel.

EXAMPLE 5　EVALUATION OF PARTS OF NETWORKS

The discussion in Example 4 was concerned with the differences in costs and benefits between two complete networks. It is, however, worth considering how far the results of complete transportation studies can be used to evaluate the benefits derived from individual routes which form part of that network. This is a difficult question to answer. It is only very recently that much attention has been paid to the economic evaluation of transportation studies and even less work has been done on the evaluation of parts of networks. In general, it is probably fair to say that the evaluation of parts of networks is only really possible with any degree of confidence if the parts evaluated are not too interrelated with the rest of the system. In this case it is a fairly simple matter to evaluate the results of any one link of the network by a constant matrix approach, such as that suggested in the first example in this appendix. Suppose the link in question is part of a maximum network, but not part of the minimum network with which the maximum network is compared. It is a simple matter to modify and rebuild the networks so as to include or exclude the link.

The link can then either be evaluated as an addition to the minimum network which is compared with the minimum network without the addition (probably using the minimum network matrix), or it can be considered as a subtraction from the maximum network compared with maximum network including the link (probably using the maximum network matrix). Alternatively, if a slightly more refined evaluation is required (e.g. for a completely new bridge across a river estuary) the link can be evaluated both using the minimum and the maximum network matrix, the difference in benefit between the two cases being attributed to generated traffic and valued at half its initial apparent value. A process of this nature has proved very valuable in the East Central Scotland Study where the returns on twelve separate road investment proposals were evaluated by this method. If, however, the return on certain elements of say the main London Motorway System were required it might be very dangerous to use such an approach since virtually every link of the system is dependent on the construction of the rest of the system. It might still, however, be possible to use such an approach to help determine the staging of any proposed scheme.

References

Chapter I

1. London County Council, *London Traffic Survey*, Vol. I, 1964.
2. London Borough of Camden, *Traffic in Camden—Study Methods and Techniques*, 1971.
3. General Register Office, *Census of Population*, 1961, HMSO.
4. Dorfman, R., *Measuring the Benefits of Government Investments*, The Brookings Institution, Washington, DC, 1966.

Chapter II

1. Road Research Laboratory, *Research on Road Traffic*, Chapter 3, HMSO, 1965.
2. Road Research Laboratory, *Research on Road Traffic*, Chapter 2, HMSO, 1965.
3. Coburn, T. M., Origin–Destination Surveys, *Chart. Munic. Engr.*, 1962, 85 (5).
4. *Detroit Metropolitan Area Traffic Study*, Volume I, 1956
5. Taylor, M. A., *Studies of Travel in Gloucester, Northampton and Reading*, Road Research Laboratory Report, L.R. 141, 1968.
6. London County Council, *London Traffic Survey*, Volume I, 1964.
7. General Register Office, *Census of Population*, 1961, HMSO.
8. Bureau of Public Roads, *Procedure Manual: Conducting a Home Interview, Origin–Destination Survey*, Volume 2B, 1956.
9. Ministry of Transport, *Land Use/Transport Studies for Medium Sized Towns*, Memorandum to Divisional Road Engineers, 1966.
10. Register of Electors are produced for electoral register districts for each Parliamentary Constituency in the United Kingdom.
11. *Home Interview Survey and Data Collection Procedures*, HRB Record No. 41, 1963.
12. Taylor, M. A., Travel Surveys by Home Questionnaire, *Traff. Engng. and Contr.*, 1965, 7 (3).

13. Traffic Research Corporation, *Merseyside Area Land Use Transportation Study, Technical Report No. 2.*

14. Road Research Laboratory, *Research on Road Traffic*, Chapter 4, HMSO, 1965.

15. Caxton, P. A., Improved Techniques for Registration Number Traffic Surveys, *Traff. Engng. and Contr.*, June 1967.

16. Howe, J. J., *Mass Transit External Survey, Chicago Area Transportation Survey*, 1957.

17. Bureau of Public Roads, *Traffic Assignment Manual*, 1964.

18. Hobbs, F. D., and Richardson, B. D., Volume Measurement, *Traff. Engng and Contr.*, June 1967.

19. Wardrop, J. G., and Charlesworth, G., A Method of Estimating Speed and Flow of Traffic from a Moving Vehicle, *Proc. Inst. Civ. Eng.*, Part II, 1954.

20. Bureau of Public Roads, op. cit.

21. Whiting, P. D., *Computer Programs for Allocating Traffic by the Quickest Route Method*, Road Research Laboratory, RN/3829/PDW, 1960.

22. Freeman, Fox, Wilbur Smith and Associates, *London Transportation Study, Phase III*, London, 1968.

23. Department of Employment and Productivity, Employment records available by individual Employment Exchange, also Employment Register, HMSO.

24. Department of Economic Affairs, *Family Expenditure Survey, 1968*, HMSO, 1969.

25. Board of Trade, *Report of the Census of Production 1962*, HMSO.

26. Board of Trade, *Report of the Census of Distribution and other Services, 1961*, HMSO, 1963.

27. General Register Office, *Sample Census 1966*, HMSO, 1968.

28. Computer Research and Development, Transport Analysis Programs, 1970.

29. Survey Analysis Programs, ICL, 1968.

Chapter III

1. For example, see Wingo, L., *Transportation and Urban Land*, Resources for the Future Inc., 1961.

2. For example, see Greater London Council, *London Traffic Survey*, Volume II, 1966.

3. Oi, W. Y., and Shuldiner, P. W., *An Analysis of Urban Travel Demands*, Northwestern University Press, 1962.

4. Wootton, H. J., and Pick, G. W., A Model for Trips, Generated by Households, *Journ. Tran. Econ. and Pol.*, May 1967.

5. Shuldiner, P. W., *Trip Generation and the Home*, HRB Bulletin 347, 1962.

6. Shuldiner, P. W., *Land Use, Activity and Non-residential Trip Generation*, HRB Record No. 141, 1966.

7. Starkie, D. N. M., Intensity of Commercial Traffic Generation by Industry, *Traff. Engng. and Contr.*

8. Ministry of Transport, *Roads in Rural Areas, Memorandum 780*, HMSO, 1960.

9. Johnston, J., *Econometric Methods*, McGraw Hill, 1963.

10. Wonnacott, T. H., and Wonnacott, R. J., *Introductory Statistics*, Wiley, 1969.

11. Johnston, J., op. cit.

12. Theil, H., *Economic Forecasts and Public Policy*, North Holland Publishing Company, Amsterdam, 1958.

13. Wootton, H. J., and Pick, G. W., op. cit.

14. Oi, W. Y., and Shuldiner, P. W., op. cit.

15. Wootton, H. J., and Pick, G. W., Travel Estimates from Census Data, *Traff. Engng. and Contr.*, July 1967.

16. Greater London Council, op. cit.

17. Reilly, W. J., *Methods for the Study of Retail Relationships*, University Texas Bulletin No. 2944, 1949.

18. Losch, A., *The Economics of Location*, Wiley, 1967.

19. Carrothers, G. A. P., *A Historical Review of the Gravity and Potential Concepts of Human Interaction*.

20. Fratar, T. J., *Forecasting Distribution of Interzonal Vehicular Trips by Successive Approximations*, HRB Proceedings, Vol. 33, 1954.

21. Carroll, J. D., *Future Traffic Predictions for the Detroit Area*, HRB Proceedings, Vol. 36, 1957.

22. Ridley, T. M., *Traffic Distribution*, Interdepartmental Working Paper No. 7, Institute of Transport & Traffic Engineering, University of California, 1963.

23. Martin, B. V., Memmott, F. W., and Bone, A., *Principles and Techniques of Predicting Future Demand for Urban Area Transportation*, MIT Report No. 3, MIT, 1961.

24. Hansen, W. G., *Evaluation of Gravity Model Trip Distribution Procedures*, HRB Bulletin 347, 1962.

25. Bureau of Public Roads, *Calibrating and Testing a Gravity Model for Any Size Urban Area*, Washington, 1965.

26. Wynn, G. H., and Linder, C. E., *Tests of Interactance Formulae Derived from O–D Data*, HRB Bulletin 253, 1960.

27. Greater London Council, *London Traffic Survey*, Volume II, 1966.

28. *Chicago Area Transportation Study*, Final Report, Volume II, 1960.

29. Tomazinis, A. R., *A New Method of Trip Distribution in an Urban Area*, HRB Bulletin 347, 1962.

30. Witheford, D. K., *Comparison of Trip Distribution by Opportunity Model and Gravity Model*, Pittsburgh Area Transportation Study, 1961.

31. Heame, K. E., and Pyers, K. E., *A Comparative Evaluation of Trip Distribution Procedures*, Highway Research Board, Record No. 114, 1966.

32. Wilson, A. G., The Use of Entropy Maximising Models in the Theory of Trip Distribution, Mode Split and Route Split, *Journ. Tran. Econ. and Pol.*, Volume III, No. 1.

33. Moore, E. F., The Shortest Path Through a Maze, *International Symposium on the Theory of Switching*, Harvard University, 1957.

34. Planning and Transport Research and Computation Ltd, *Computer Program Review, Part 1, Transportation Planning*, 1970.

35. Road Research Laboratory, *The London–Birmingham Motorway—Traffic and Economics*, Road Research Technical Paper, No. 46, HMSO, 1961.

36. Moskowitz, K., *California Method of Assigning Diverted Traffic to Proposed Freeways*, HRB Bulletin 130, 1956.

37. Burrell, J., Multiple Route Assignment and its Application to Capacity Restraint, *4th International Symposium on the Theory of Traffic Flow*, Karlsruhe, 1968.

38. Holroyd, E. M., and Scraggs, D. A., Waiting Times for Buses in Central London, *Traff. Engng. and Contr.*, July 1966.

39. Freeman, Fox, Wilbur Smith and Associates, *London Transportation Study, Phase III*, Vol. 1, 1968 (unpublished).

40. City of Oxford, *Oxford Traffic Survey 1957*, Oxford University Press, 1959.

41. Wilson, F. R., *Journey to Work—Modal Split*, Maclaren, 1967.

42. Greater London Council, op. cit.

43. Hill, D. N., and Von Cube, H. G., *Development of a Model for Forecasting Travel Mode Choice in Urban Areas*, HRB Bulletin.

44. Tressider, J. O., Meyers, D. E., Burrell, J. E., and Powell, T. J., The London Transportation Study; Methods and Techniques, *Proc. Inst. Civ. Engrs.*, March 1968.

45. Warner, S. L., *Stochastic Choice of Mode in Urban Travel: A Study in Binary Choice*, Northwestern University Press, 1962.

46. Quarmby, D. A., Choice of Travel Mode for Journey to Work: Some Findings, *Journ. Tran. Econ. and Pol.*, Vol. 1, No. 3.

47. Wilson, A. G., Wagon, D. J., Singer, E. H. E., Plant, J. S., and Hawkins, A. F., The SELNEC Transport Model. Urban Studies Conference 1968.

48. Wardrop, J. G., The Traffic Capacity of Weaving Sections of Roundabouts, *Proc. of the First International Conference on Operational Research*, English Universities Press, 1957.

49. Webster, F. V., and Cobb, *Traffic Signals*, Road Research Technical Paper No. 196, HMSO.

50. Tanner, J. C., A Theoretical Analysis of Delays at an Uncontrolled Intersection, *Biometrika*, 1962, 49 (1/2).

51. Road Research Laboratory, *Research on Road Traffic*, HMSO, 1965.

52. Wardrop, J. G., Journey Speed and Flow in Central Urban Areas, *Traff. Engng. and Contr.*, March 1968.

53. Thomson, J. M., Speeds and Flows of Traffic in Central London, *Traff. Engng. and Contr.*, March and April 1967.

54. Almond, J., Traffic Assignment to a Road Network, *Traff. Engng. and Contr.*, February 1965.

55. Greater London Council, *Movement in London*, 1969.

56. Ministry of Transport, *Road Pricing: the Economic and Technical Possibilities* (Smeed Report), HMSO, 1964.

57. Ministry of Transport, *Better Use of Town Roads*, HMSO, 1967.

58. Powell, T. J. and Roberts, B. W. G. An examination of alternative patterns of development in a rapidly growing city, Institution of Civil Engineers, Civil Engineering Problems Overseas, June 1971.

Chapter IV

1. Willis, J., *Population Growth and Movement*, WP 12, Centre for Environmental Studies, 1968.

2. Willis, J., op. cit.

3. Massey, D., *Some Simple Models for Distributing Changes in Employment within Regions*, WP 24, Centre for Environmental Studies, 1968.

4. Schlager, K. J., *Simulation Models in Urban and Regional Planning*, South East Wisconsin, RPC, Technical Record, Vol II, No. 1, 1964.

5. Employment statistics of the Department of Employment are available from local employment exchanges.

6. *Estimating House Occupancy Rates*, Local Government Operational Research Unit, Report C34, 1970.

7. Keeble, L., *Principles and Practice of Town and Country Planning*, Estates Gazette, 1969.

8. Alonso, W., *Location and Land Use*, Harvard University Press, 1968.

9. Jameson, G. B., Mackay, W. K., and Latchford, J. C. R., Transportation and Land Use Structures, *Urban Studies*, 4, 1967.

10. *The British Economy, Key Statistics 1900–1964*, London and Cambridge Economic Service.

11. Mogridge, M. J. H., *An Analysis of Household Income in Great Britain and its Relationship with Employment Income*, WP 48, Centre for Environmental Studies.

12. Greater London Council, *London Traffic Survey*, Vol II, 1966.

13. Tanner, J. C., Forecasts of Future Numbers of Vehicles in Great Britain, *Roads and Road Construction*, Nov. and Dec. 1965.

14. Mogridge, M. J. H., The Prediction of Car-ownership, *Journ. Tran. Econ. and Pol.*, Vol. I, No. 1, Jan. 1967.

15. Wootton, H. J., and Pick, G. W., A Model for Trips Generated by Households, *Journ. Tran. Econ. and Pol.*, May 1967.

16. Tulpule, A. H., *Forecasts of Vehicles and Traffic in Great Britain 1969*, Road Research Laboratory Report, LR 288.
17. Smeed, R. J., The Road Space Required for Traffic in Towns, *Town Plan. Rev.*, 1963, 34(4).
18. *The Composite Report, Bay Area Rapid Transit*, Parsons, Brinckerhoff, Tudor and Bechtel, 1962.
19. *Traffic in Towns* (Buchanan Report), HMSO, 1963.
20. Leicester City Planning Department, *Leicester Traffic Plan*, 1964.
21. Meyer, J. R., Kain, J. F., Wohl, M., *The Urban Transportation Problem*, Harvard University Press.
22. Ministry of Transport, *Manchester Rapid Transit Study*, Volume 1, Report of the Working Party, 1967; Volume 2, Study of Rapid Transit Systems and Concepts, 1967; Volume 3, The First Priority, 1968; Manchester City Transport.
23. Davies, E. (ed.), *Traffic Engineering Practice*, Spon, 1968.
24. *Working Group on Bus Demonstration Projects*, Report to the Minister of Transport, April 1970.
25. Webster, F. V., *A Theoretical Estimate of the Effect of London Car Commuters Transferring to Bus Travel*, Road Research Laboratory Report LR 165.
26. Ministry of Transport, *Road Pricing: the Economic and Technical Possibilities*, HMSO, 1964 (contains a good bibliography on road pricing).
27. Thomson, J. M., Case for Road Pricing, *Traff. Engng and Control*, March 1968.
28. Freeman, Fox, Wilbur Smith and Associates, op. cit.

Chapter V

1. Greater London Council, *Traffic Noise*, 1966.
2. Prest, A. R., and Turvey, R., Cost-benefit Analysis: A Survey, *The Economic Journal*, 1965. See also Kendall, M. G. (ed.), *Cost-benefit Analysis*, English Universities Press, 1971. (Proceedings of a NATO symposium on cost-benefit analysis.)
3. Kaldor, N., Welfare Propositions in Economics, and Hicks, J. R., The Foundations of Welfare Economics, *Economic Journal*, 1939.
4. Freeman, Fox, Wilbur Smith and Associates, *London Transportation Study*, Phase III, 1968.
5. Dawson, R. F. F., Current Costs of Road Accidents in Great Britain, *Road Research Laboratory Report*, LR396, 1971.
6. Beasley, M. E., and Foster, C. D., Victoria line: Social Benefit and Finances, *Journ. Royal Stat. Soc. I*, 1965.
7. Ministry of Transport (now Department of the Environment), *The Economic Appraisal of Inter-urban Road Improvement Schemes*, Technical Memorandum No. T5/67, 1967. See also, Dawson, R. F. F. *The Economic Assessment of Road Improvement Schemes*, Road Research Technical Paper, No. 75, HMSO, 1968.

Index